The Making of Home

THE MAKING
of HOME

The 500-Year Story of How Our Houses
Became Our Homes

———

JUDITH
FLANDERS

THOMAS DUNNE BOOKS
ST. MARTIN'S PRESS
NEW YORK

THOMAS DUNNE BOOKS.
An imprint of St. Martin's Press.

www.thomasdunnebooks.com
www.stmartins.com

Library of Congress Cataloging-in-Publication Data

Flanders, Judith.
The making of home : the 500-year story of how our houses became our homes /
Judith Flanders. — First U.S. edition.
    p. cm.
Includes bibliographical references and index.
ISBN 978-1-250-06735-7 (hardcover)
ISBN 978-1-4668-7548-7 (e-book)
1. Dwellings—History. 2. Dwellings—Social aspects. I. Title.
GT170.F53 2015
392.3'609—dc23

                                                                2015017946

First published in Great Britain by Atlantic Books, an imprint of Atlantic Books Ltd

First U.S. Edition: September 2015

10 9 8 7 6 5 4 3 2 1

For Naomi and Evangelia Antonakos
and in memory of Stephen Antonakos (1926–2013)

Contents

Acknowledgements

I am grateful to those who have helped me navigate the idioms of home in various European languages: Ana-Maria Astier, Ilona Chavasse, Martijn David, Béla Dekany, Marta Frankowska-Stelmach, Tobias Hoheisel, Alice James, Donna Leon, Zoltán Matyas, Ravi Mirchandani, Jussi Mononen, Jan Morris, Ekin Oklap, Sofi Oksanen, Jasper Rees, Lise Sand, Ewa Sipta, George Szirtes, Fergal Tobin, Aksel Tollåli, Jorunn Veiteberg, Hanna Weibye, Michael Wells, Shaun Whiteside and Frank Wynne. Thanks to the wonders of social media, some of these people were unaware of the ultimate destination of their information. For their disinterested good nature, I thank them twice.

Gerard van Vuuren translated several essays from Dutch for me, and I thank him for his scrupulous care.

I would also like to thank Rodney Bolt, Cathy Lennon, Laura Mason, Ninette Perahia and Bee Wilson; Gabrielle Allen, of Guy's and St Thomas' Charitable Foundation; Katie George, of the Salters' Company; Charlotte Louise Murray, of the University of Reading; Emily Watts, house steward at Knole; and Mandy Williams and Hannah Fleming, of the Geffrye Museum. Peter Kristiansen, curator at Rosenborg Slot/De Danske Kongers Kronologiske Samling, not only responded to a stranger's email promptly and courteously, but gave me additional insights into the painting in question. I am most grateful to him.

As always, the members of the Victoria mailbase fielded my seemingly random queries with good temper and, even more usefully, deep expertise. My thanks in particular for specific responses are owed to Helena Brigman, Lisa Cepluch, Amy D'Antonio, David Latané, Mary Millar, Peter Orford, Malcolm Shifrin, Nancy Strickland, Elizabeth Williamson and Guy Woolnough and, as always, Patrick Leary, list-master extraordinaire. Twitter has brought me another range of experts, and I thank all those who assisted.

At Atlantic Books, Ravi Mirchandani edited this book with rigour and enthusiasm, and in so doing improved it beyond measure. I am also grateful to Karen Duffy, Richard Evans, Lauren Finger, Lucy Howkins, Toby Mundy, James Nightingale, Bunmi Oke, James Roxburgh, Chris Shamwana, Tamsin Shelton and Margaret Stead. My agent, Bill Hamilton, is stalwart, and beyond thanks. George Lucas has supplied US support, and to him I am most grateful.

Despite the efforts of all these good people to keep me on the straight and narrow, errors and omissions will inevitably have crept in. For these, as always, I am solely responsible.

Illustrations

The Making of Home

Home Thoughts:
An Introduction

I n 1900, a young girl in a strange land was asked by a resident why she wasn't content to remain in their 'beautiful country', but instead longed to return to 'the dry, grey' place she came from. She was astonished. She wanted to return there, she said simply, because 'There is no place like home.' The girl was, of course, Dorothy in Oz, and only someone like the Scarecrow, famed for his lack of brains, would ask something so self-evident. To Dorothy's creator, L. Frank Baum, writing at the end of the nineteenth century, it was a commonplace that home did not have to be beautiful, or luxurious, to be the place one wanted to be.

Two centuries earlier, in 1719, another novel, now known simply as *Robinson Crusoe*, was first published. The full title of Daniel Defoe's book was not merely the name of his main character; instead it enticed readers with promises of adventure, exotic locales, violent death and more: *The Life and Strange Surprizing Adventures of Robinson Crusoe, of York, Mariner: Who lived Eight and Twenty Years, all alone in an un-inhabited Island on the Coast of America, near the Mouth of the Great River of Oroonoque; Having been cast on Shore by Shipwreck, wherein all the Men perished but himself. With An Account how he was at last as strangely deliver'd by Pyrates.* The book was a staggering success, going through thirty-seven printings in its first eight months. Over the following century it was translated, adapted for the stage and rewritten for children; there were sequels; there was even a puppet show. Altogether, there were over seven hundred retellings of this story, in almost every form of entertainment.

Defoe's novel is more than simply a rollicking tale of shipwrecks and pirates, however. It has a deserved place in the literary pantheon, not merely for the quality of its writing, but also as the first true novel in English, and among the first in any European language. It should have another place, too, among historians, for it is the first book to treat the details of ordinary domestic life as though they were as gripping as a disaster at sea or the discovery of a fabled new land. Even in the title, Crusoe is presented as not just a mariner. He is Robinson Crusoe *of York* – a man with a home, a place where he belongs. Once he is shipwrecked, long passages in the novel dwell on the arrangements he makes to provide himself with the necessities of daily life: clothes, a razor, cutlery, even writing materials. On the island, Crusoe's cave receives similar attention; its cooking, eating, sleeping and storage areas are described, as is his next 'house', which is a move upmarket for him – this one is large enough to contain the sleeping and living areas under one roof. Then, 'to enjoy the Comforts I had in the World', the castaway builds furniture, and as a good householder he puts up shelves to keep his possessions tidy: 'everything in…their Places'. When, after two decades, another ship is wrecked on his island, he is thrilled to find, not weapons (he doesn't bother to take the muskets he comes across), or marine equipment to help him sail away, but a kettle, a pot 'to make chocolate', a fire shovel and tongs, 'which I wanted extremely'. (He also acquires that ultimate accessory for his fireside, a dog, which he finds starving on board.) This novel, ostensibly one of 'Surprizing Adventures', and of a man who for twenty-eight years has no home, is nevertheless awash with notions of domesticity. Time and again Crusoe uses the word 'home'. It is how he refers to his 'little tent', and in the first chapter alone the word is repeated a dozen times; over the course of the novel it appears more than sixty times, recurring like a steady heartbeat.

Home, according to the *Oxford English Dictionary*, is 'A dwelling place; a person's house or abode; the fixed residence of a family or household; the seat of domestic life and interests'. But more than that, while a house is the physical structure, a home is 'The place where one lives or was brought up, with reference to the feelings of belonging, comfort, etc., associated with it'. It is a state of being as well as the place where one lives or one's place of origin. The word itself is ancient, most likely pre-dating modern European languages and originating in an Indo-European root, *kei*, meaning lying down, or a bed or couch, or something dear: even then, both a place and an attitude. The first known written use of the distinction between house and home in English appeared in a poem of 1275, which mentions separately a man's 'lond & his hus & his hom' [land and his house and his home].

To speakers of English, or the Germanic and Scandinavian languages, or the Finno-Ugric group – the languages of north-western Europe, from Hungary to Finland and Scandinavia, the German-speaking lands, and then descending to the Netherlands and across the Channel to the British Isles – to these peoples, the differences between home and house are obvious. They are two related but distinct things, and therefore they have two words. In the languages of what I will call these 'home' countries, home and house are respectively *otthon* and *ház* (Hungarian), *koti* and *talo* (Finnish), *kodu* and *maja* (Estonian), *Heim* and *Haus* (German), *heem* and *huis* (Dutch), *hem* and *hus* (Swedish), *hjem* and *hus* (Danish), *heim* and *huset* (Norwegian).* Speakers of Romance and Slavic languages,

---

* German *das Heim* and Dutch *heem* had become obsolete by the late eighteenth century, but then revived, partly as back-formations from English.

living in 'house' countries, have by contrast just one word for both meanings. When an Italian goes home he *sta andando a casa*, goes to the house, while the Frenchman *rentre à son foyer*, returns to his hearth, or *rentre chez lui*, returns to his, with where he is returning to only gestured at by the word *chez*, which derives from the Latin *casa*. The French *maison* is also from Latin, *mansio*, staying or a stopping-place, and it follows the Latin in referring to both a building and those who occupy it: someone from *une grande maison* is from an important family. (English has this usage, but confines it to the very grandest of families – the House of Windsor, or of Atreus.) Slavic languages are similar in folding house and home together: Russians and Poles live in a *dom*, and return 'housewards', *domoi* and *do domu*, when they go home. In Russian, the nineteenth-century word for house, *dvor*, encompassed not merely the house and the people who lived in it, but any stables, workshops or other farm buildings, and even the measurement of human labour. Linguistically, the house was inseparable from those who lived in it, united by kinship and economic ties, and from the labour and land it took to maintain them.

The existence of what I will call home and house languages suggests something about the societies in which they developed. There are societies where the community space, the town, village or hamlet, is the canvas on which life is painted, and where an individual house is only a more private area within that primary space. Then there are societies where the house is the focal point, while the town, village or hamlet functions mainly as the route through which one passes in order to reach the essential privacies of the houses. The reason for such differences is frequently put down to climate, and it is certainly more pleasant to spend an autumn afternoon in a market square on the Mediterranean than it is in Oslo. But while the weather is an element in the distinction between home and house countries, it is, as we shall see, only one element among many.

Ask a western European or North American child to draw a house, and the odds are good that the result will be a picture of a detached building with some or all of the following: a pitched roof, a chimney belching out a friendly plume of smoke, a front door at the centre or at the house's gable end, from which a path runs through a garden that is surrounded by a fence. I did not grow up in a house that looked like this, yet as a child I drew plenty that fit this description. Most western European or North American children did not and do not grow up in houses that looked like this. Yet for at least a century and more this was, and for many still is, the platonic ideal of what home looks like to many – the archetype of 'homeness'.

As adults, we have more elaborate notions of what that archetypal home looks like than the children's drawings, but these notions are no less works of imagination. It is just that, for the most part, we are unaware of their equivalent disconnection from reality. We believe instinctively that 'home' is a concrete thing, unchanging through time in its essentials. Our ideas are, in part, based on books and images, which, even if we haven't read or seen them ourselves, have been used by designers as the basis to create later domestic spaces, which we have seen; or they have formed the basis for re-creations in film and television, which in turn have been used by others, filtering through to popular consciousness at large. A primary component of this source material is what we consider to be the very epitome of homeness, Dutch seventeenth-century paintings. These works, by Vermeer and de Hooch, or Metsu, or Maes, or ter Borch or de Witte, show the typical bourgeois interiors of the Netherlands of the time, and say 'home' like no others. Emanuel de Witte's *Interior with a Woman at a Clavichord* (1665; see plate section, no. 2) is, to modern eyes, obviously and primarily designed to show off the beauty of a middle-class Dutch house. Contemporary reports from travellers to the Netherlands seem to back this up: the houses of even people of 'indifferent quality' – that is, what today would be called the ordinary middle classes – were, one English visitor wrote, filled with 'Costly and Curious' furniture, porcelain, paintings and other items to adorn and display. But today we fail to realize that, while the travellers for the most part reported faithfully on what they saw, faithful reportage was not the aim of the painters of the same date. There is little in de Witte's painting that any seventeenth-century Dutch citizens would have thought of as typical of their own houses, or of any house they knew.

Modern scholars have analysed thousands of seventeenth-century inventories of personal possessions and household goods, and have examined the sale details of properties that changed hands in the period.* From this evidence it has been possible to build up a very detailed picture of what the Dutch middle and upper classes actually owned. And what these documents show is that these painted rooms, these rooms we know so well from art, never existed. It is easier to say what was realistic in the de Witte *Interior*, than what was not. A Dutch householder would have recognized the curtained bed in the reception room, the mirror and the map on the walls, as well as the dumpiness of the woman's figure, which suggests she is wearing many layers of clothes as protection against the cold. And

---

* Much of what is known about ownership of possessions in earlier centuries, not only in the Netherlands, comes from inventories that were compiled on the deaths of their owners. Depending on the country and date, inventories might be taken for the poor as well as the rich, although they were more common among the prosperous and wealthy. While they tell us what was owned, they do not always indicate how many items were owned, or where in the house they were found, which would guide us to their usage. Still, these records are frequently all we have, and they are very useful in comparing actuality to what books and journals – or paintings – present as the norm.

that's all. Almost everything else in the picture, and in the hundreds of other surviving pictures from the same period, were constructions of painters' studios.

The beams on the ceiling are typical of Dutch domestic architecture, but they appear to run the wrong way – not parallel to the façade of the house, but placed decoratively, to frame the painting's space for the viewer. The house's floorplan – three rooms leading out of each other, rather than along a corridor, and with windows on both sides (visible on the right, inferred from the shadows on the left) – was an architectural implausibility in this country of terraced housing. These deviations from what would typically have been seen in Dutch cities may be attributed to the requirements of art, the desire for a harmonious composition.

But many other elements in the painting also bear no resemblance to Dutch housing of this time, without any obvious pictorial dictates. The black-and-white marble floors so familiar to us from these paintings were well known in the Netherlands, being found in many public spaces, including government buildings and courthouses. They were, however, vanishingly rare in private houses. Just nine of 5,000 houses sold between 1750 and 1811, almost all large, luxurious properties, had marble floors in their reception rooms. Even the rich generally had wooden floors. Where marble did, exceptionally, appear, it was almost always laid in the *voorhuis*, the public room on the ground floor, and it was customary to see small wooden platforms, called *zoldertjes*, under the chairs (one can be seen in Metsu's *Woman Reading a Letter*; see plate section, no. 3). There are no *zoldertjes* in de Witte's painting, nor are there any of the mats that were to be found laid in crisscross strips in many of the houses of the period. It was not that de Witte alone ignored these domestic commonplaces. Jan Steen sometimes included the mats; otherwise they were rarely painted.

Instead, as in de Witte's painting, artists concentrated their painterly skills on Turkish carpets, even though the inventories of the time make almost no mention of them. Oriental rugs were rare and costly items, and, from Renaissance Italy on, had been used as display pieces, placed over tables rather than left to be scuffed underfoot. But it was another twenty years after de Witte casually placed a Turkish rug on the floor of this middling household before an inventory listed one, and then it was in the house of one of Amsterdam's richest men. In Leiden, no householders on one of the city's most prestigious canals owned carpets of any kind, floor or table, until thirty years after de Witte's picture; the first floor carpet in Leiden is recorded nearly another decade after that. Carpets for tables were also relatively unusual: only a quarter of the better houses inventoried in The Hague included any; a few did in Delft; and about half the houses in Leiden. The lack of carpets in inventories, together with the evidence of Vermeer, who reproduced the same carpet in three of his works, strongly suggests that most of the carpets in these paintings were artists' props.

As marble floors tended to be confined to public spaces, so too were the brass chandeliers that are among the most frequently depicted objects in Dutch genre paintings. This form of lighting was used in courts, in civic buildings and, especially, in churches, but not in private houses. The inventories list just five such chandeliers in Leiden throughout the entire seventeenth century, one in The Hague and none in Amsterdam. Nor did most households possess a clavichord, as painted by de Witte, nor the virginals or spinets that also regularly appear: the Delft inventories list just one from this time.

And even as the paintings suggest these scarce objects were routine, numerous other items that were common in Dutch houses, like the mats, are as regularly missing in art. The paintings rarely depict candlesticks or lamps, and very few fireplaces or stoves, the standard forms of lighting and heating. There are also fewer display items and luxury goods in the paintings than the inventories reveal was the case in the houses of the day. Many householders owned porcelain, especially Chinese, and delftware, and patterned fabrics covered their tables as well as walls, and were also used to cover chairs, and for bed-hangings and (more rarely) for windows. Also missing are the multitudes of paintings that every traveller reported: 'All in generall striving to adorne their houses, especially the outer or street roome, with costly peeces, Butchers and bakers not much inferiour in their shoppes...yea many tymes blacksmithes, Coblers, etts., will have some picture or other by their Forge and in their stalle...' There were thousands of painters in the Netherlands between 1580 and 1800, who may between them have produced over 10 million paintings.* Given a population that numbered just under 2 million in 1700, and even allowing for a large export market, most walls must have been covered almost frame-to-frame to house this quantity of paintings. It may be that seventeenth-century Dutch dollshouses (see plate section, no. 4) are more realistic than paintings of the same date (although just three of these dollshouses have survived: how typical they were, therefore, is unknowable).

Also missing is a vast quantity of furniture. Visitors reported that cupboards were the pride and joy of prosperous Dutch housewives, both as repositories of wealth, measured in quantities of bedding, clothes and linen, and as display spaces for china and silver, which were placed on top (see plate section, no. 4). The inventories bear this out, with cupboards in all ranges of price and style being matched by great quantities of other furniture. De Witte's room is by contrast

---

* It is thought that less than 1 per cent of these paintings have survived, so our knowledge of the genre is, by any definition, a very partial one.

sparely furnished – a bed, a clavichord, three chairs and a small table. If the painting included the furnishings that the inventories suggest was the norm, we would see at least two tables, half-a-dozen chairs and several chests. The man's working tools would also be in the room, as well as his wife's spinning wheel, and basic household items such as pewter dishes and tankards, pots and pans.

The painters and their customers in the seventeenth century naturally knew that these images did not reflect reality. The assumption that they do is a misapprehension that arose only later, when the genre was rediscovered in the nineteenth century.* Some of the objects were probably included for aspirational reasons: the marble floors and brass chandeliers, being found in grand public spaces, made private houses appear richer than they were. Others, such as the many paintings or pieces of furniture, were likely to have been excluded to create a visually lucid composition. But most of the pictorial deviations from typical households were for an entirely different reason. Central to our misreading of these paintings is the fact that the symbolic references with which these pictures abound are no longer immediately apparent. Images of children feeding cats or dogs were not intended as depictions of charming household scenes, but as warnings against profligacy and waste; cats also represent ignorance, or, when painted together with girls or women, love or sensuality. Women making lace are undertaking a good housewifely task, but *naaien*, to sew, was (and is) also Dutch slang for sexual intercourse, which turns the lace into an emblematic web that ensnares unwary men. Vermeer's *The Concert* (1658–60) shows a man between two women, one playing

---

* Throughout the twentieth century, and even today, many Dutch people cover their tables with carpets, assuming it is a tradition handed down from the seventeenth century. In fact, the custom emerged when the paintings were rediscovered in the nineteenth century, at which time it was thought to be a return to a seventeenth-century custom.

the harpsichord, the other singing: to modern eyes a gracious social occasion. But the man holds a lute, a symbol of erotic love, as were most musical instruments. Pictures and maps on the walls routinely reinforce the meanings of scenes in front of them. Here Vermeer chose *The Procuress*, a then-famous work by Dirck van Baburen, a Utrecht artist of an older generation, which indicates that the relationship being played out in front of it is one that has a financial basis. In other pictures, biblical scenes on the walls of the rooms provide a moral counterpoint to the episodes in front of them: shipwrecks and other disasters are warnings; mirrors symbolize vanity; maps, worldly temptations. The characters in the rooms, too, can be symbolic: women sweeping represent the overthrow of Spanish rule, as the hated oppressor was seen to have been swept out by the Dutch Revolt of 1568–1648. Children sometimes embody the birth of the new republic, although more generally they represent the follies of mankind. Jan Steen's rowdy tavern scenes, filled with drunks, lechers, loose women and broken crockery, were not intended only as faithful representations of tavern life, but also as symbols of the vanity of human existence. Still-lifes of tables loaded with expensive foodstuffs, porcelain, pewter and silver were, in part, pictorial reimaginings of the wealth that their owners either had or aspired to. But even when the representation was so faithful that the precise place of origin of the porcelain can be identified, or its factory pattern named, the essential message of the paintings was the same as in the Steen tavern scenes: food rots, porcelain breaks, but God's truth is eternal.

Maids sweeping, as in the de Witte painting (at the very rear, in the back room), are as much a product of aspiration and imagination as the black-and-white marble floors. Less than 20 per cent of Dutch households employed maids, and it is unlikely that this middling house in the painting was one of them. While English travellers marvelled at how 'wonderful Nett and cleane…within doors, as in their streetes' the Dutch were, this cleanliness was comparative. Dutch houses had no running water, and there were no public bath-houses: however clean the rooms may have been, the people who lived in them were less so. Some Dutch almanacs included reminders that if the annual bath were taken in springtime, the larvae in their readers' hair would be killed off before they were due to hatch. And, just as plague beset England in 1665, the year of de Witte's paint-ing, in the previous twelve months it had killed one in every eight Amsterdammers.

With all this information, de Witte's painting becomes a tale not of domestic tranquillity, but of erotic upheaval. The daylight indicates that the man glimpsed behind the bed-curtains is not the husband of the woman playing the clavichord, while her musical pastime confirms it, as do his clothes, evidently hastily removed, for they are on a chair, not put away in a cupboard. The maid in the background is thus the moral counterpoint, as with her broom she sweeps away sin, the bucket of clean water waiting in the symbolically bright sunlight.

For the last century and a half, however, the symbolism of these paintings has been overlooked, and instead we have read the works as a tracing-paper reproduction of a lived reality, a pre-photography photograph. The people who painted these pictures, the people who bought them, who displayed them on their walls, knew that this was not the case – did not expect it to be the case. They were untroubled, therefore, by the presence of goods they did not possess, and the absence of yet others, of pots and pans or crisscrossed mats, in their art. Today, those missing mats, or household implements, are examples of what I term 'invisible furniture'.

Invisible furniture can be found in all countries, in all times. In the seventeenth century, the English naval administrator Samuel

Pepys frequently ended his daily diary entries, 'And so to bed': he wrote a version of the phrase almost once a week over the nine and a half years that he kept his diary. In the twentieth century, it became a punchline, so familiar that in Britain it is even the name of a chain of shops selling beds. What is less familiar is how he continued that sentence on 21 November 1662: 'At night to supper and to bed – this night having first put up a spitting-sheet, which I find very convenient.' Pepys wrote no further of his spitting-sheet, and most editions of the diary pass it by silently, or indicate puzzlement – '??' is all that one editor of the diary has to say about it. My suggestion is that it may have been a piece of fabric pinned to the wall behind a spittoon, so that the wall, which in affluent seventeenth-century households was frequently covered by an expensive hanging, was protected from a spitter's poor aim.

Spitting-sheets are certainly invisible furniture – today we have never heard of them, and don't know what they were. Spittoons, however, are also invisible furniture.* We have heard of them, and we know they existed, but as they were barely ever, or never, depicted in art or mentioned in literature or even in much non-fiction, it has become easy to overlook their ubiquity: they have become invisible.

The knowledge that many people habitually spat is perhaps not hugely important. It didn't change the course of history. But spittoons can be a reminder of how easy it is to imagine that 'then' was just like 'now', that people of one century behaved exactly as people of another, or ours, do. People in the west today do not customarily spit, so we do not notice that spittoons, and spitting, are missing from accounts of daily life in the past, when people in the west did

---

* Spittoons, also called spitting-basins or spit-boxes in the UK, and cuspidors in the USA, were bowl- or vase-shaped metal or earthenware receptacles that sat on the floor, some having an insert with a shaped hole for the spit to run down.

in fact spit. Yet if we look, if we begin with a search for invisible furniture, we can see how behaviour changes over time. And changing behaviour marks changing attitudes. And changing attitudes *did* change the course of history.

Searching for invisible furniture is not straightforward. To continue with spitting as an example, literature is generally silent on the practice, while diaries and letters are more revealing. Pepys, with his endless interest in other people, gives some of the earliest views of spitting as a habit, and its, to us, astonishing ubiquity. Today the common assumption is that whatever spitting occurred was a by-product of chewing tobacco, and the majority of Pepys's references to spitting do also mention tobacco. But one night at the theatre, he reports, 'a lady spat backward upon me by a mistake, not seeing me. But after seeing her to be a very pretty lady, I was not troubled at it at all.' Women did not chew tobacco, so this must have been nothing but phlegm, and was, from Pepys's equanimity, something that women as well as men did both routinely and publicly. A few years later, a Frenchman living in Leiden reported to his compatriots on the curious habits of the Dutch: no one 'would dare to spit in any of the[ir] rooms…those who are phlegmatic must be in great discomfort'. It appears that in France, too, spitting was seen as the obvious, and necessary, way to clear one's throat, indoors as well as out.

In the eighteenth century, spittoons are mentioned in a German magazine as an 'object of ease' among wine-coolers, clocks, foot-warmers, adjustable writing tables and shaving tables with integrated mirrors, all items to make the elegant consumer's life more comfortable. In the nineteenth century, they can still occasionally be spotted, clearly common but rarely mentioned. An American mother writes in 1851 of her toddler's precocious doings as he imitated the adults around him, '*halk[ing]* and *spit[ting]* in the spitbox, and…a good many other funny things.' Yet at the same date, contemporaneous images reinforce the earlier lesson of Dutch art and reality. There are many thousands of nineteenth-century drawings and paintings of parlours, drawing rooms and sitting rooms, by professionals and amateurs alike, of households across Europe and North America of just the type this toddler lived in. Not a single one I have ever seen shows a spittoon, although inventories from the same period list them as a matter of routine.

By the twentieth century, a new understanding of disease transmission had made spitting seem downright dangerous, and references to spittoons tended to be used as indicators of more primitive times, even as other, less literary, documents tell the continuing story of this piece of invisible furniture. The US government's *Railway Sanitary Code* of the 1920s has whole pages devoted to regulating the places where people could or could not spit, not only in trains, but in their offices, waiting rooms and on station platforms. Mail-order catalogues too continued to advertise spittoons in the 1940s, three or four decades after spitting had, according to literature and memoir, been eradicated from daily life. Spittoons were sold, but had become unmentionable.

Invisible furniture is not confined to history. Houses photographed for lifestyle magazines today ostensibly record the houses we live in. Even ignoring the lack of wear and tear, the absence of the stains and scuffs and marks of daily life in those photographs, their resemblance to real houses is merely superficial. Where are the toothbrushes? The power sockets bristling with hedgehogs of electric flexes? Where are the children's plastic toys, or the drain-sieves to catch hair in the bath? The brush to clean the lavatory? If magazine images were all that were to survive of our houses, future generations might not know that most people in the twenty-first century brushed their teeth, just as few today are aware that spitting was, until quite recently, routine.

The ability of the amateur, the non-professional, to take photographs in the twentieth century altered our views on what things looked like; in the twenty-first century the invisible is routinely made visible on Facebook and in images captured with a phone, while websites such as TripAdvisor make a sport out of comparing the reality of hotel rooms against the idealized publicity images of professional photographers. Those professional images are like the novels of the past, or Dutch Golden Age art: their purpose is not fidelity to life as it is lived by most people. Television or film, seemingly more 'real', is also an unreliable marker of daily life. In 200 years' time, a historian who relied on the television programmes of 2014 to understand our daily lives would never know how much time is spent watching television. No matter how grittily realistic a programme sets out to be, it is impossible to imagine a police-procedural where the characters come in after a hard day's investigation and slump down in front of the television, to sit without speaking for the rest of the evening. They don't because it doesn't fit the genre, just as photographs showing celebrities' lovely homes never show overflowing rubbish bins. It is not what the images are for. That is obvious when discussing contemporary source material. The past is, however, a different country, both because the absences and the omissions are less easily identified, and because these sources are, frequently, all that we have.

As with the spittoons, and spitting, invisible furniture can highlight aspects of behaviour that have altered. But we need prompts to remember that how we use our dining tables is not necessarily how everyone always did, even if we are sitting at the very same table. In 1853, a cartoon by John Leech for *Punch* magazine imagined a gender-reversed world, one where the men retire to the drawing room after dinner, leaving the women to drink and smoke and discuss pheasant-shoots. The dining room is in disarray. The tablecloth is rumpled, the chairs pushed back. The women, instead of sitting sedately, behave like men after a meal: they turn their chairs away from the table to chat in comfort; one woman has pulled up an empty seat so she can put her feet up. Many nineteenth-century novels contain scenes of men-only after-dinner drinking, but most concentrate on the conversation, with few descriptions of the participants' physical comportment, and not even a handful of illustrations exist where men use furniture in a similar way. By default, strangely enough, Leech's upside-down cartoon world is what we have to confirm that men did indeed behave in the manner suggested by those other few images. His assumption that the magazine-readers of the day would recognize stereotypical male behaviour, even when applied to women, tells us that such behaviour commonly existed.

THE DINING ROOM.

Lady of the House. "Now then, Girls! Fill your Glasses! Bumpers! Here's just one Toast which I am sure you will all drink with pleasure. The Gentlemen!!"

While reconstructing the physical surroundings in which people lived is not easy, establishing how they inhabited those physical surroundings, how they used them in daily life, is even more complex and multi-layered. There is what was; there are the perceptions of those who lived at the time, which may or may not reflect what was; there is the information that those who lived then chose to record, or failed to record; and there is how that information has been interpreted over time. None of these elements are stable, or have only one simple reading. The standard story of domestic life tells us, for example, that from the eighteenth century sleeping quarters in more prosperous houses in Britain became increasingly segregated, with divisions being made by gender and age (separation of parents from children, girls from boys), and by class (servants no longer slept in the same rooms, much less the same beds, as their employers, but were moved to separate quarters in attics or basements). Yet two court cases in London illustrate the more complex reality. In 1710, in one house the physical separation between servants and their masters was rigidly enforced, right down to who used which set of stairs; in the same decade, the niece of another householder shared an attic bedroom with their female servant, while their titled lodger and his footman slept in the lodger's room. These were two houses at the same date, with residents of much the same social background and financial status. In one, servants and masters were entirely intermixed, in the other, almost entirely segregated. What was 'done' on the evidence of fiction, or conduct manuals, or architectural treatises, was not necessarily what was actually done from one house to the next. Yet our assumptions, whether it be our belief that the Dutch paintings reflect real houses of the period, or our modern amnesia regarding the ubiquity of spitting, are so taken for granted that we barely know we hold them. They just seem to be eternal truths.

The Making of Home is intended to be like the *Punch* cartoon, making invisible patterns visible. In Part One, I will outline the changes, political, religious, economic and social, that produced the circumstances in which 'home' grew and flourished in the houses of northwest Europe, and spread in time to the USA; in Part Two, I will describe how innovations in technology created the infrastructure that has become part of our commonly held notions of 'home', from comfortable furniture to plumbing. Many of these changes began in the early modern period, and *The Making of Home* touches on how those ideas were first established, before they gathered pace in the eighteenth and nineteenth centuries; it will, for the most part, end in the early decades of the twentieth century, when modernism – the movement that has been dubbed 'not-at-home' – presented a radically altered mindset. It is not the style of chair that is my primary concern, but how people sat on it; not what the magazines said was in fashion, but how many people followed that fashion. Not how houses were decorated *per se*, but how the decoration reflected the behaviour of the people who lived there, and how that behaviour, in turn, was guided by their beliefs and values, and the beliefs and values of the society to which they belonged. Ideas of what makes a home are generally distinct from ideas of what makes a house. Yet the notion of home, and its history, has been relatively under-explored. There are books on architecture, on interior décor, on domestic life, on social and economic history. But how homes came to be seen as special places is frequently overlooked.

And just as descriptions of physical surroundings need to be disentangled from the behaviour that was caused by, or altered, those surroundings, so too do we need to separate the realities of the physical surroundings from how people thought about those surroundings. In 1596, Ireland was, said the poet Edmund Spenser, 'wylde, wast[e] and vast': its people, thought this transplanted Englishman, 'care not for pot, pan, kettyl, nor for matrys, fether bed, nor such implementes of houshold. Wherfore it is presuppose that they lak maners and honesty, and be untaught and rude.' That is, by the end of the sixteenth century, those who didn't have – or had, but didn't attach importance to – kitchen utensils, bedding, or other household goods could be dismissed as uncultivated. Nearly three hundred years after Spenser wrote this, an inquest was held in 1865, to investigate the circumstances of a man who had died of starvation. Despite their financial desperation, said his widow, he had refused to go into the workhouse because he couldn't bear to give up 'the comforts of our little home'. The middle-class inquest jury, seeing nothing but a bare room with a heap of straw in one corner, questioned her explanation. The widow, it was reported, 'began to cry, and said they had a quilt and other little things'. Centuries separate these households bereft of 'pot, pan, kettyl…matrys, [and] fether bed', yet there is no reason to believe that the Irish of the sixteenth century cared any less for their 'little home' than the Victorian widow.

Because the word 'home' has stayed the same, and its residents' love for their homes has also been constant, it is too easy to simplify home until it is like the child's picture, a clear, detail-less outline. Home, as an idea, and as that idea played out in reality, changed and developed over the span of modern history. It is the idea, and the change, that we will look at here.

Part One

1

The Family Way

While the word 'home' for many today conjures up ideas of retreat from the world, at the same time few would argue that what makes homes desirable are the products of the industrial world, whether it is readily accessible consumer goods, or the technologies of hygiene, lighting and heating. It is no coincidence that the physical reality of the modern European house on which rest 'the comforts of our little home' emerged as the Industrial Revolution developed in northwestern Europe.

One of the key questions of economic history is, why did a backward region like northwestern Europe, a region that was politically, geographically and economically peripheral, become the engine of the industrial world? Why did the elements that knitted together to become 'modernity' – the concept of nation-states, the technological innovations that fuelled the Industrial Revolution, capitalism itself – arise in this place? In Europe, the city-states of Renaissance Italy or the great courts of worldly, cosmopolitan France might have been more obvious heartlands for such developments; on the world stage, perhaps the monolithic administrative empire of China. But, instead, it was first the Netherlands, then England, most particularly, two countries of minor political importance, that became the seedbeds of change.*

---

* Given a book with such a long timespan, the choice of names to describe countries is not straightforward. The geographical area of the Netherlands in the sixteenth or

Answers to this question have tended towards the circular: the modern world developed where it did because this is where the Industrial Revolution took place. So why did the Industrial Revolution take place where it did? The Industrial Revolution, runs the generally accepted narrative, was precipitated in northwestern Europe by a series of events. The decline of feudalism (and, in England, where feudalism had been substantially weakened far earlier, the collapse of the manorial system) enabled tenant farmers in agricultural regions to strengthen as a class, as it did the precursors to a professional middle class in urban districts. At the same time the population increased, driving surplus agricultural workers into proto-industrial occupations, and encouraging their migration to what were becoming cities. The expansion of shipping and exploration opened trade routes and access to goods and commodities previously unknown, or available only as luxury goods for the wealthiest. State control and subsidized underpinnings of colonization at the same time reduced the power of the trade guilds, which, as cartels, had kept prices up and stifled enterprise.

As all this took place, in Amsterdam first, new financial structures were being created, and the philosophical concepts of free trade were being established. Meanwhile, another belief-system, Protestantism, the religion of northwestern Europe, in its sanctification of hard work, and, by extension, the idea that worldly success was a sign of

---

seventeenth century is not the same as it is today; references to Italy and Germany before, respectively, 1861 and 1871 fail to reflect political reality. I have done my best to conform to contemporaneous political realities, referring to 'the colonies' for episodes in the USA that pre-date 1776, 'the USA' for those coming after, or using England/Britain before and after the Act of Union. Where necessary, however, I use the names of places before they actually existed, for example to make clear whether it is Plymouth, England or Plymouth, Massachusetts that is being discussed. Where historical reality, clarity and concision are at odds, in general I have chosen concision and clarity over history. Mea culpa.

God's favour, developed in tandem with trade and finance to create a new ethos, named 'the spirit of capitalism' by the sociologist Max Weber. Add into the mix a relatively literate population, a new system of patents that rewarded innovation and, crucially, a good supply of natural resources (in 1700, the nearly 3 million tons of coal mined annually in England was five times more than was mined in all the rest of the world combined).

All these elements together produced the Industrial Revolution, not for any of these factors individually, all, or most, of which also occurred elsewhere, but because in northwestern Europe, by chance and circumstance, they all occurred together or serially. As Dr Johnson said in another context, 'It is not always that there is a strong reason for a great event': lots of milder reasons will have a cumulative great effect.

A return to *Robinson Crusoe* shows how many of these different threads had, by 1719, already become intertwined. One of the reasons for the enduring success of that novel is that it can be interpreted in many ways: as a Puritan autobiography of spiritual growth, or a narrative of colonial exploitation and trade, or of modern individualism, or the transformation of capitalism. Classical economists have used Crusoe to illustrate their theories of production, while Karl Marx borrowed the story to show how production for use differs materially from production for exchange. Robinson Crusoe himself can be seen as a personification of the spirit of the Industrial Revolution, flourishing on his island through a combination of hard work – that Protestant work ethic – and careful utilization of the products of modern western European trade and technology, which he salvages from the wreck of his ship.

Certainly Defoe was interested in what would later become the field of economics: 'Writing upon Trade', he confessed, 'was the Whore

I really doated upon.' Adam Smith's seminal *The Wealth of Nations*, published half a century after Defoe's novel, in 1776, identified the central characteristics of the form of political economy that would soon become known as capitalism – competition, resource allocation and division of labour among them. But Crusoe, or rather Defoe, was here first: he had already used the phrase 'the wealth of nations' a good three dozen times in his writings. And when Smith laid out the classical explanation of supply and demand – that the value of goods will fall when a commodity is plentiful, and rise if it becomes scarce – Crusoe had already lived it: before he was shipwrecked, he was, the novel tells us, a trader who had made a comfortable living by importing English commodities to Brazil where they were rare, and therefore much more valuable.

For the Industrial Revolution to flourish, a second revolution was necessary – the consumer revolution, which gathered pace from the early eighteenth century. Over the last few decades, historians of consumption, of material culture more widely, have modified the phrase 'supply and demand', acknowledging that it is historically more useful when it is reversed. For supply does not drive demand; demand drives supply. A desire for goods, for *things*, was what produced the circumstances from which the Industrial Revolution, and modernity, developed. Without the desire for goods, and the ability to purchase them, the various factors that contributed to the Industrial Revolution might well have remained separate events. Without demand, there must – would? – have been no Revolution.

And just as answers to the question 'Why did the Industrial Revolution take place in northwestern Europe?' have a tendency to become circular, so too do explanations of the origins of the consumer revolution. That some people have sufficient income to satisfy more than subsistence needs is a situation that has occurred in many places at many times, yet there was no equivalent consumer revolution in, say, China. The usual explanation is that social emulation, the desire to keep up not only with the Joneses, but even with those one step higher in social rank, drove the desire for consumer goods, and in the Netherlands and England, the first countries to be affected by the consumer revolution, the differences between the social classes were fairly small, and were permeable to cash, in a way that many societies based on aristocracies of birth were not. (In England, the grandson of an impoverished aristocrat was a worker; in France, or India, he too was an impoverished aristocrat.) These smaller social gaps might appear bridgeable to those just below, particularly as the new technologies of advertising and print culture arrived. Newspapers, magazines and prints now disseminated further than ever before information about the ever-increasing range of new commodities, and more widely available commodities. Yet emulative spending, and a commercial world focused on selling, were also not geographically specific, while the consumer revolution was.

What provoked the demand, then – what created this desire for goods? In part, the consumer revolution might be thought of as the end-product of four revolutions: the ending of the Eighty Years' War and the Dutch revolt against the Spanish in 1648; the American and French Revolutions of 1776 and 1789–99; and the century-plus Industrial Revolution. These revolutions produced more fluid social structures in which the middle classes (as they may begin to be termed) wielded increasing power, at the expense of the landed gentry and nobility. These classes benefitted from what, in the Netherlands in particular, had been from the Middle Ages a cash market economy rather than one based primarily on land. It was there that development of financial instruments that enabled commercial credit and government borrowing, the 'very essence of the capitalist economy', first flourished. And it was there, too, that the first modern cities began to develop. The Dutch Revolt and the Protestant Reformation between them both brought about an alteration in land-ownership on a scale never before seen: over 30 per cent of all property in Utrecht had belonged to the church before the Reformation; after it, that property had been transferred to the city itself, or was in private, secular hands.* Urbanization, both a precipitating factor and a by-product of industrialization, meanwhile also meant that social judgements were formed less on the basis of previous knowledge of lineage or character, and more on the presentation of self, which inextricably intertwined with the possessions one owned. Together these factors created an environment where the consumer revolution was not merely possible, but necessary.

Yet what was perhaps an even more important factor in the creation of the consumer revolution was much closer to home, quite literally. The historian Mary S. Hartman has suggested, it seems to me more than plausibly, that the crucial element, one that has previously been overlooked or considered of only minor importance, was the unique marriage system found in northwestern Europe, and nowhere but northwestern Europe. This was a pattern of nuclear-family living that was essentially in place by 1500, and possibly before.† In outline, men and women married late (late twenties for men, mid-twenties or later for women); the age of the couple was much more equal than in early-marriage societies; and both men and women worked for a considerable period of time before marriage, usually in a cash economy, saving in order to set up in their own

---

* The Tudor Dissolution of the Monasteries, while superficially similar and occurring only a few decades earlier, had by contrast transferred church lands to the sovereign.
† Records are scanty, yet each time older records are discovered, the establishment of this pattern is found to have already existed.

household on marriage.* (Prepubescent girls were married to older men in northwestern Europe only for a time, and only among the ruling elites, for dynastic and property-enhancing purposes.)

It comes as a surprise that even a word as apparently immutable as 'family' has encompassed different meanings at different times. In the Roman world, a *famulus* was a slave, and *familia* indicated not a blood-tie, but a relationship of ownership and possession. By the Middle Ages in northern Europe, a family comprised those living together in a household, plus the serfs attached to the house, but not the head of the household himself: 'family' was still a relationship of subservience, not kinship. In Renaissance Italy, the writer and architect Leon Battista Alberti hoped his children would 'remain happy with our little family', but to indicate the quality of the affectionate relationship he had in mind, he had to use a diminutive, *famigliola*, because *famiglia* still meant the entire household, whether connected by blood or not, and had no emotional weight. In the British Isles, too, 'family' was a formal designation for those living under one roof; blood relatives were 'friends'. (In *Romeo and Juliet*, Friar Lawrence advises Romeo to go into exile until 'we can find a time / To … reconcile your friends'.)

This was the way Samuel Pepys used 'family', although by the seventeenth century the meaning had expanded to take in the head of the household as well. 'My family,' he summed up, 'is myself and wife – Wm. my clerk – Jane, my wife's upper-maid … Susan our cook-maid … and Waynman my boy'. A family was therefore not an absolute grouping, but one that expanded and contracted with time and circumstances. An eighteenth-century diarist referred to servants

---

* Historians and sociologists say that marriages that meet these criteria conform to what they clunkingly call the Northwest European Late-Marriage Pattern. I will abbreviate the term to 'late-marriage pattern'.

as 'my family' when they were in his employ; if they left his service they became 'my former servant'. By the nineteenth century, English speakers used 'family' to mean blood relatives in everyday speech, but the older meaning persisted formally. As late as 1851, the census of Great Britain defined 'members of the family' as 'the wife, children, servants, relatives, visitors, and persons constantly or accidentally in the house'. The head of the household was, notably, still not officially part of the family.

Many types of family, and of living arrangements, that are seen across the world even today reveal the wide range of responses to basic needs. In southern Europe, adolescent girls and men in their twenties were historically often paired, with, for example, in southwestern France, the woman moving into the man's family home, the *ostal* (the word, tellingly, means both house and family), which was inherited by a single son, while the remaining children received, at most, cash or movables. In eastern Europe, serfs lived in multiple-family households, while in the southeast, in Croatia and Serbia, the *zadruga*, where all land was owned jointly by the patrilineal extended family, saw sons bring wives into their birth households, to live in large multi-nuclear arrangements.* Other areas favoured what are called non-family groupings (where two brothers, or two cousins, shared a household); or extended family groups (a married couple plus other kin, but not a second couple); or multiple-family groups (two or more couples, in various permutations). There were also stem-family groupings (a son and daughter-in-law living after marriage with his parents) and frérèche arrangements (horizontal multiple families,

---

* Some scholars have questioned whether the *zadruga* was in fact routine, or was a nostalgic view of how families had lived in the Good Old Days. Be that as it may, complex families were the norm in rural districts, with nuclear families limited to urban centres.

such as two brothers and their families). For simplicity, these are all known as extended families and variants were found in different regions across much of Europe.

The nuclear-family pattern that was found across the home countries was not exclusive to this region: it was also common in parts of Spain, Portugal and Italy. The difference was that in home countries, the nuclear family was rarely encroached on, and only a minority of households had other relatives living with them – as few as 3 per cent of families in Rhode Island, barely more even in densely populated seventeenth-century Dutch cities. Over more than two centuries, barely 10 per cent of English households had non-nuclear kin permanently in residence. In house countries with nuclear-family structures, this was unimaginable: more than half of all households in one region of Italy had non-nuclear kin resident.

Those are the broadest outlines of family living patterns. And just as 'family' meant many different things at different times, so too did the notion of marriage. And while the changes have been great, they have been as invisible to subsequent observers as spittoons have become to ours. In *Pride and Prejudice* (1813), Jane Austen's pompous clergyman, Mr Collins, lists his reasons for wanting to marry: first, he says, it is 'a right thing for every clergyman in easy circumstances (like myself) to set the example of matrimony...Secondly...I am convinced it will add very greatly to my happiness; and thirdly – which perhaps I ought to have mentioned earlier...it is the particular advice and recommendation of the very noble lady whom I have the honour of calling patroness.'

The modern reader can still take pleasure in the bathos of dashed expectations, having assumed, together with his appalled would-be fiancée, that what 'perhaps' Mr Collins ought to have mentioned earlier is, if not his love, then at least his admiration and affection for the woman he is proposing to. Instead, his position in the world and relative wealth are first in his thoughts, the pleasure marriage will give him comes next, and then, comically, his hopes for the social and professional advancement it will bring by pleasing his 'patroness'. In addition, early-nineteenth-century readers would have found enjoyment in a further layer of meaning, which today has become obscured. Jane Austen was mocking the pomposity of her fictional character, but, churchman's daughter though she was, she was also parodying the Book of Common Prayer, which enumerates the reasons for marrying much as Mr Collins does: 'First, It was ordained for the procreation of children…Secondly, It was ordained for a remedy against sin, and to avoid fornication…Thirdly, It was ordained for the mutual society, help, and comfort, that the one ought to have of the other, both in prosperity and adversity.' To Austen, writing at the start of the nineteenth century, the fact that the church placed companionship – companionate marriage – last, giving precedence instead to children and the avoidance of sin, was ripe for comedy. To her, and the society around her, the 'Thirdly' should obviously have been first: indeed, all of Austen's novels are, in the most reductionist reading, explorations of the ways to identify those who will make good life companions.

Her parody makes clear how completely ideas of marriage had altered in northwestern Europe in the previous two centuries. For most people, in most periods of history, survival, or, for the more prosperous, property, was the purpose of marriage. For most, marriage enabled the transmission of work and social skills while creating a basic labour force for the maintenance of the family unit; among the nobility and the merely rich, marriage was a social construct that ensured the safe transmission of property, or even its increase, from one generation to the next. By the time Martin Luther's 95 Theses appeared in 1517, feudalism in most of northwestern Europe was entering its terminal stages, and new structures of authority, and new attitudes to them, were emerging. Images that depicted the Holy Family had, in the previous century, become widespread in churches for the first time, an indication of the increasing importance of secular families in society, at least to those who commissioned the paintings. The Catholic church continued to consider marriage a second-best solution, for those who could not manage the ideal of celibacy, citing Corinthians: 'It is better to marry than to burn'. Protestantism, by contrast, placed the married partnership at the heart of spiritual government, citing Genesis: 'It is not good that man should be alone'. A man's partnership with his wife was beginning to be seen as the primary social unit. This new view, from the new religion, took root in precisely those northwestern European territories where the late-marriage pattern prevailed, where two relatively equal partners chose each other as consenting adults, rather than as subordinate members of a kin-group that made a communal decision.

A modern historian of sexuality has suggested that the pre-modern marriage began 'as a property arrangement, was in its middle mostly about raising children, and ended about love', whereas, he continued, twentieth-century marriage 'begins about love, in its middle is still mostly about raising children...and ends – often – [in being] about property'. In early-marriage societies, the married couple had no need, or opportunity, to plan, or make a place for themselves in the world. They moved into a place both literally and figuratively provided by their elders, following arrangements and traditions that had long existed. By contrast, in late-marriage-pattern countries, women as well as men worked outside the home before they married. Up to 40 per cent of the population worked in domestic service for a time, and by the nineteenth century in many home countries, the number of women who worked as servants at some point in their lives, but usually starting aged thirteen or fourteen, reached 90 per cent. Boys were apprenticed at a similar age; in earlier periods they lived with the master's family; later, they lived on their own, and were required to become self-sufficient. These adolescents were exposed to strangers, to new ways of doing things; they saw how different ranks of society lived, with different technology and household arrangements. They travelled the country, formed contractual obligations with employers and renegotiated them where necessary, or broke them if they decided that that was better, and learned to deal commercially and emotionally with strangers. They were, in short, responsible for their own financial and personal wellbeing.

On marriage the couple established a new household, which necessitated purchases of new goods; because of their years of earning, together they had the cash to emulate, at least in part, the households they had been exposed to. Women came into marriage as earning equals, and expected, before the Industrial Revolution, to be economically productive in their marriages as well. Even after industrialization had become widespread, this remained true for most women, the working classes always forming the majority of the population. Women often acted as their husbands' business equals, the men taking on the heavy labour, the women handling commercial transactions for farms, shops or trades – tasks that, in early-marriage societies, were performed instead by male kin living in the parental home. Or male labourers travelled the country following seasonal work, while their wives looked after the family and perhaps a small plot of land, or kept poultry, or ran a dairying business. Or they took in work – doing laundry for other households, or sewing, or carding and spinning wool. Others, especially in rural areas, bartered, trading wool, or dairy produce, or eggs, or honey, for commercial commodities: sugar, or ironmongery, or other items they could not make themselves.

Late-marriage-pattern relationships were ventured into by equals, who went on to function as contributing partners. A religion that endowed individuals with great personal agency, as Protestantism did, was therefore one that meshed well with this family arrangement. As with the causes of the Industrial Revolution, the generally accepted explanation for the origins of the Reform religions is that they grew out of a combination of factors: disgust at church corruption; the decline of the Holy Roman Empire and the rise of new nation-states; the drastic Europe-wide fall in population following the Black Death in the fourteenth century, when 35 million people – half the population – may have died; and the development of new technology, most significantly the printing press. All of these were essential. But as important was the way in which the new religion dovetailed with the changing shape of the family. Martin Luther's Reformation took hold almost precisely in the geographical areas where the late-marriage pattern was operational: the northwestern crescent of Europe – the countries that have separate words for 'house' and 'home'.* The economic historian R. H. Tawney showed persuasively how Protestantism grew with, and in consequence of, the rise of capitalism, not vice versa. Since he wrote, however, the concept of the consumer revolution has gained attention, as has domestic life as an area worthy of study. And they, together, suggest a possible

---

* This is, of course, a matter of a broad correlation over an extended period of time, rather than one of complete identity, and there were many anomalies. Northern France is geographically part of northwestern Europe, but its long-surviving feudal institutions saw its marriage patterns match those of its Mediterranean south; France, Ireland and some German-speaking regions remained predominantly Catholic, and yet Ireland and the German lands culturally fit comfortably into home patterns, while France for the most part did not. I am suggesting a strong overlap over centuries, rather than precise adherence to every detail.

extension to his theory: not only that Protestantism grew with, and in consequence of, the rise of capitalism, but that Protestantism may well have grown with, and in consequence of, the practice of the late-marriage pattern, and of the idea of home, which can be suggested as one of the engines of capitalism, creating a demand that drove capitalism's supply.

How the 'little commonwealth' – the metaphor for the nuclear family that was first used by the English divine William Gouge in 1622 – emerged, and how it was perceived, had a different weight for the adherents of the new religion than it did for the old. Theoretically, the Catholic church's view of marriage was absolute, and absolutely simple: a marriage was contracted when two people exchanged spoken vows. From the eleventh century, if a girl over the age of twelve and a boy over fourteen said aloud the *verba de praesenti*, 'I take you as my wife/husband', or the *verba de futuro*, 'I will take you as my wife/husband', then they were married. Indissolubly. In Protestant Europe, by contrast, secular elements were integral. Banns had to be read before a congregation for a number of weeks prior to the exchange of vows, in effect notifying the community, and the vows were only valid if they were spoken in public, indicating that parental consent had been obtained. Without either the involvement of the community, in the reading of the banns, or the public commitment, a marriage could be annulled.*

Nonetheless, for both Catholics and Protestants, marriage was not, as it is today, a single event, before which a person was single, after which he or she was married. It was, into the eighteenth century

---

* In the sixteenth century, the Catholic church adopted a similar procedure, with some modifications: there needed to be a notice period, the intent had to be announced in church for a number of weeks, the ceremony had to be performed by a priest, and a set number of witnesses needed to be present.

in most places, a process, and a person could be a little bit, or not entirely, married. There were most commonly four stages, all of them binding, so while a couple might not proceed to the next stage, they could not undo previous stages. In the broadest outlines, a couple who agreed to marry made a formal commitment, whether in public or private. After this came the consent, when both agreed publicly – sometimes outside the church, sometimes at home with a notary present – that they planned to marry, and a ring or other token might be given. Then came the wedding itself, frequently but not necessarily in the presence of a minister of religion, after which the couple moved in together. The final stage, consummation, sometimes took place after the first stage, sometimes after the third, sometimes – usually among the upper classes if the girl was very young – not for several years. But the sexual act did not make the marriage any more indissoluble than did the other elements.

Different sects, or countries, or cities, or even families, had their own requirements: the minimum age at which marriage could take place without parental consent varied with time and place, as did the type and exchange of vows, or even whether or not a ring was obligatory. In some sixteenth-century Swiss cities, despite the legal requirement for public, community involvement – banns, parental consent and a church ceremony – many accepted that any couple who had exchanged vows were legally married. In England the consent of the couple was all that was necessary, and a marriage that dispensed with the remaining formalities was 'valid but not legitimate'. Those who exchanged vows without parental consent but had not consummated their marriage were not quite married, but neither were they free to marry anyone else. Ever. One historian has estimated that only half of the 'married' population in the seventeenth century was properly married according to cannon law. In

Britain in 1753, reforms swept away the old three-stage system and these not-quite marriages. Now a marriage had to be performed by a church minister, be registered in church (or synagogue, or Friends' meeting-house) and for those under twenty-one take place with the consent of their parents; if any one of these elements was omitted, the marriage was void.*

Even so, the state of being married was not, in northwestern Europe, standard for most adults well into the seventeenth century. Low life expectancies meant that couples who married in their mid- to late twenties had an average of less than two decades together before death dissolved their partnership. In home countries, men did not substantially outnumber women, unlike early-marriage societies as a rule. In societies where women are wage earners, they survive into adulthood in larger numbers; where they are seen as a financial drain, useful for a short period as the owner of a womb, fewer reach maturity. In some villages in southwestern France in the fourteenth century, records mention twice as many boys as girls. A sympathetic reading is that, as boys mattered more than girls, their lives were recorded in official documents more frequently, or more regularly; the less attractive reading is that, as the early-marriage pattern made girls a burden, infanticide, or at best passive neglect, was routine. Because of the equal numbers of men and women in late-marriage societies, there were always a large number of people who never married at all – between 20 and 30 per cent was common. In general, married people made up only about a third of the population. (The figure in western Europe today hovers around 50 per cent.)

* The Act was not implemented in Scotland, and hence Gretna Green, just over the border, became the place where runaways went to marry without parental consent. Marriages that took place legally but without consent in Scotland could not be annulled in England or Wales.

It might be assumed, therefore, that a side-effect would be a high rate of illegitimate births, and yet, counterintuitively, such high rates were instead found in the house countries of Europe. In Florence in the sixteenth and seventeenth centuries, one in ten babies was abandoned; in Toulouse, the rate of abandonment, previously comparable, had risen to nearly two in ten by the end of the century, and sometimes, in particularly harsh economic periods, to a quarter of all babies. In the 1670s in Paris, over three hundred children were abandoned every year, compared to Amsterdam in 1700, where just twenty illegitimate children were recorded in a population half the size of the French capital. Meanwhile, in the sixteenth century in England, the recorded rates were at the lowest level ever seen: a parish in Suffolk recorded no illegitimate births at all in the dozen years leading to 1600, and only one for every 144 recorded births in the next half-century. By the eighteenth century, when urbanization and industrialization had drastically reordered social practices, that figure rose locally to one for every thirty-three registered births, but these figures were still remarkably low when compared to Austria's one for every five births at the same period. The countries with high rates of abandoned children were France, Belgium, Portugal, Spain, Ireland, Italy, Poland, what is now the Czech Republic (40 per cent of all babies in Prague in the early nineteenth century), and Austria (half the babies in Vienna were abandoned at the same date).*

The low levels of illegitimacy in home countries might in part be attributable to the more equal number of men and women in the

---

* That the countries of abandoned babies are for the most part predominantly Catholic is clear. The explanation for this is not immediately apparent to me, and anyway thankfully falls outside the scope of this book. It must be stressed that abandonment does not necessarily equate with illegitimacy: poverty is always the most immediate reason for child-abandonment, and in both home and house countries there is a strong correlation between years of economic hardship and rising numbers of abandoned babies.

population. (Societies where men outnumber women see far more incidents of sexual assault.) It might also be in part attributable to the relative equality of men and women, with both sexes working from early adolescence.* At some periods, in some areas, safety-valves were built into the system. One was the custom of bundling, where courting couples were permitted ritualized all-night visits, without full sexual relationships, a practice virtually unknown outside home countries. It may also be the case that illegitimate births in home countries were disguised – sudden, or forced, marriages, babies raised by their 'aunts', and so on. But in England and in the USA, as in several other home countries, illegitimate births were recorded at local parish level, and therefore such stratagems would be revealed by wild fluctuations from district to district, and these do not appear.

More generally, late marriages ensured that women in northwestern Europe, simply by postponing marriage, significantly reduced the years they spent in childbearing, both by being married for fewer years, and by being single in their most fertile years. This in turn meant that they were not as resolutely tied to child-rearing as is often retrospectively assumed, even before the nineteenth century, when women in companionate marriages were also able actively to reduce the number of children they bore, by abstinence or other forms of birth control. At the other end of life, it was the unmarried children who took on the care of their parents as they aged. From the earliest

---

* This must be read, as always, in a historic framework. I am discussing gender equality relative to other places at the same time. An interesting sidelight on companionate marriage and the relative equality it presupposed is one historian's suggestion that the witch-hunts of northwestern Europe and colonial America, which peaked in the late sixteenth and early seventeenth centuries, were the expression of male resentment at this new equality. She notes that the accused tended to be women in non-traditional roles, running businesses or owning land, and suggests that the witch-hunts were a power-struggle in a world where male and female spheres were overlapping for the first time. Certainly the witch-hunts lasted for far longer, and were more ferocious, and more organized, in home countries in Europe and America; house countries in Europe saw far fewer.

censuses that have survived in England, the majority of elderly couples have unmarried children living with them. The twelfth-century legend on which Shakespeare based *King Lear* stressed the catastrophic results if elderly parents lived instead with married children. This unnatural situation was clearly a preoccupation of the sixteenth century, as Shakespeare was pre-empted in his use of this story both by the same Edmund Spenser who had dismissed the Irish sense of domesticity, and by John Higgins in his collection of Tudor verse, *The Mirror for Magistrates*.

These changes to marriage meant that by the time Jane Austen was creating Mr Collins, the state was no longer considered to be primarily for the procreation of children. Marriage now created a household, a home, much as Robinson Crusoe had created one despite his adverse circumstances. Crusoe was, of course, wife-less on his island. But as the central character of England's first novel, he initiated a genre – fiction – which would find its main subject in romantic love. As the historian of marriage Lawrence Stone noticed, 'romantic love became a respectable motive for marriage…at the same time [as] there was a rising flood of novels…devoted to the same theme.' And, as this new genre was developing largely in late-marriage Europe, so it seemed natural for fiction to illustrate the fulfilment of these love matches by portraying the couples moving into their own homes, filled with their newly acquired goods, purchased by their years of young-adult earnings. As early as the 1530s, a woman in Hertfordshire justified breaking off her engagement. She had made the promise, she admitted, 'but shall we need to marry so soon? It were better for us to forebear and [get] some household stuff to begin withal.'

If we accept that the creation of new households by couples with cash to spend drove demand, then it is not surprising that many of the early manifestations of home as a private space for a nuclear family appeared first in the centre of both early urban development and trade, the Netherlands. The first of the world's great trading companies, the Dutch East India Company (the Vereenigde Oost-Indische Compagnie, or VOC), was founded in 1602. (Its nearest rival, England's Honourable East India Company, was two years older, but the country's Civil War ensured that it took longer to hit its stride, and throughout the eighteenth century its trade remained a fifth of that of the VOC.) The great strengths of the VOC were that it both brought new goods to the European market and also had a flourishing inter-Asian network of trade, in the early days in spices, and then moving on to trade in metals, textiles and porcelain, as well as that economic underpinning of trade and colonization, slaves.*

The way in which trade operated altered substantially in the early seventeenth century. This new world of capitalist investment took off in the Netherlands, a country chronically short of arable land, and one that therefore had a weak landed aristocracy. The Low Countries had long been a centre of trade – cloth fairs had, from at least the thirteenth century, drawn merchants from across Europe. As the Dutch ports, especially Amsterdam, became Europe's trade centre, trade was no longer a seasonal affair for organized merchant groups or guilds, but was year round and open to individuals as well as what quickly became companies. In a similar fashion, the VOC's Asian trade supplanted Portuguese monopolies: a limited liability company replacing a decaying remnant of an older type of court-sponsored venture. Power as a birthright declined; now a new urban class of professional men, those overseeing the expanding cash economy, took control both economically and politically. (Indeed the *Oxford English*

---

* Slavery was illegal within the Netherlands, but was a major economic component of Dutch trade from the 1630s and 1640s for the next three decades; in those years more slaves were shipped by the Dutch than by any other nation except the Portuguese.

Dictionary locates the first use of the word 'capitalism' in English in a reference to the markets of Holland.) England was not far behind: land, for centuries the prime indicator of wealth, was now being challenged by other forms of capital. A decade after Crusoe returned from his island, Defoe observed: 'The revolution in trade brought a revolution in the very nature of things…now the gentry are richer than the nobility, and the tradesmen are richer than them all.' Financial opportunities were no longer in the agricultural districts, but in what were becoming the world's first great cities. By the late seventeenth century, nearly half the population of the Netherlands lived in towns, compared to a European average of 10 per cent.

Here again, the Reformation, with its emphasis on individual responsibility and the sanctification of work, also played a role. Rich merchants did not make their fortunes and automatically retire to become gentlemen of leisure: work had been redefined, and was now a way of affirming individual value. This produced radical changes both in economic life and in the shape of family life. Dutch notions of marriage and the roles of husband and wife were influenced by the teachings of Martin Luther, and developed by the Rotterdam-born theologian Erasmus, who wrote on matrimony and on the particular responsibilities of family members. In the sixteenth and seventeenth centuries, an outpouring of Dutch conduct manuals simplified and codified these writings, spreading these theological and philosophical views on model households more widely. Many were translated into English and welcomed by an eager audience, especially among Puritans; these books, and the ideas they contained, then travelled with settlers to the colonies, where they flourished.* Calvinism, especially

---

* It is important to remember how Dutch those who landed in the *Mayflower* at Plymouth in 1620 were. The group originated in Scrooby, in England, but in 1607 they had fled to the Netherlands in search of religious toleration. There they lived with their

as practised in a softened form in the Netherlands, was a religion of daily life: God was glorified not through fasting and penitence, but by living a sober, industrious life. From there, it was a short step to believing that the rewards of a sober and industrious life – prosperity – were indications of God's favour. And if that were the case, thought many, it then followed that consumption of the world's goods, the careful and sober acquisition of the plenty given by God, must be a virtue. In this trading nation, as the VOC expanded in Asia, and its counterpart, the Dutch West India Company, explored the Americas, the world's goods were readily available. Swiftly these trade routes spread not only the world's commodities, but also the Dutch view of them as heaven's blessings falling on the righteous.

In the ideal little commonwealth, the husband was the senior partner, the public face of the couple and the primary or entire financial support; the wife, the junior partner, was called on by God to make a home for him, and for their children, by acquiring and caring for the consumables that their partnership had achieved. The value that was given to both roles can be seen by the arrival of a new subject in Dutch genre paintings in the 1630s. Superficially, pictures of women shopping recorded an everyday occupation never before deemed worthy of art. Yet just as scenes of women sewing, or playing musical instruments, were not slice-of-life reflections of reality, so too these images had a symbolic meaning, of wifely virtue and duty, as the women were shown laying out their husband's earnings in

---

pastor for thirteen years, until an advance party of 102 hardy souls sailed on the *Mayflower* to the new world. Of those 102, fifty had either been born in the Netherlands or had been taken there as infants; most probably spoke Dutch and thought of Leiden as their home. Indeed, it was the very fact that they were beginning to sound and think like Dutchmen and -women that pushed their elders to the perilous venture of crossing an ocean. Although the plan had been to head for the British colony of Virginia, in the end, through adverse weather conditions, these Dutchified East Anglians settled geographically much closer to New Amsterdam, in what is today New York and New Jersey.

order to maintain a beautiful and orderly household. Other nations, according to *The Mirror of the State of the United Netherlands* (1706), vaunted their status in costly court ceremonies or spectacular army parades; the Netherlands, in contrast, confined their national pride to displays that were strictly 'in the manner of thrifty and modest households'. Henrick Sorgh's *Portrait of Jacob Bierens and His Family* (1663) depicts husband and son as providers, bringing food, while the wife and daughters cook, that is, they manage these resources, all presided over by another son, a musician, a symbolic enactment of Plutarch's metaphor 'to ensure the tunefulness of marriage and home' through 'discourse, harmony and philosophy'.

This kind of domestic symbolism quickly spread. Even images that today do not appear overtly domestic – images of the greatest in society – quietly partook of, and reinforced, a new veneration of middle-class values, symbolized through elements found in their homes. In 1634, Anthony van Dyck (perhaps significantly originally from the Low Countries) painted a group portrait of the three older children of Charles I (see plate section, no. 6). Rather than setting his subjects in an imaginary architectural space, with the classical imagery that conventionally accompanied royalty, the painter posed the children in front of a window, through which a flower-garden is visible, and then further emphasized the lack of ceremony by setting the Prince of Wales on the same level as his two siblings even though only he, it was assumed, would inherit the throne (as it happened, of course, both James and Mary also ruled). In actuality the royal children each lived in a separate royal household, and this image of them playing together was as fictional as the garden behind them. Yet by now the idea of family trumped the trappings of royal grandeur: it was important that they were presented more as children than royal. The king was reported to be *'fâché'*, angry, that the Prince of

Wales was painted wearing his baby-dress, not the more adult and masculine breeches he would soon assume, but it might be significant that he was not so *fâché* that he had the work repainted.

In eighteenth-century Britain such idealized images of domesticity spread down the social scale. No longer confined to royalty, the new genre of conversation pieces became popular among the prosperous middle classes, who embraced the opportunity they gave to display themselves in their own homes, surrounded by the possessions – porcelain from the Far East, chintzes from India – that stood as a visual shorthand, conveying their social status via their purchases. We now know, from comparing the complete output of the painters in a way that was impossible before widespread reproduction, that the sitters' surroundings were often altered, or entirely invented, to reflect a superior reality, while many of the objects on display, and even the clothes the subjects wore, were the artists' own props. As with Dutch genre paintings, as with van Dyck's royal children, so too eighteenth-century reality was modified towards an ideal. William Atherton and his wife, Lucy, lived in a house that overlooked a butchers' shambles and the narrow lanes of Preston. Yet in Arthur Devis's painting of them in their sitting room in 1742–3 (see plate section, no. 7), the windows open on to a beautiful garden, the plants no less valuable possessions as products of trade and colonial expansion than the elaborate silks and lace the couple wear, or the porcelain vase on display.

This focus on the possessions of the home reflected the new realities of a commodified world. Earlier, as we saw, the betrothal, the vow, not the marriage ceremony, had been the main element of the tripartite wedding. By the nineteenth century, the gap between betrothal and ceremony had grown ever longer, largely to enable the middle-class bride to accumulate her trousseau, the now necessary, now vast array of goods considered essential to furnish her new house, without which a marriage was felt to be incomplete. The house and the wedding had become indissolubly linked, and the purchase or ownership of household goods had in effect become a synonym for marriage. In Anthony Trollope's novel *Can You Forgive Her?* (1864–5), a farmer courts a potential bride by showing her around his house, taking care to display 'every bit of china, delf, glass, and plate', and then encouraging her to check the quality of the household's blankets, adding as a final inducement before he proposes, 'There ain't a bedroom in my house, – not one of the front ones, – that isn't mahogany furnished!' His value as a potential husband is intertwined with the value of the house and furniture his wife would take on with him.

By this time, among the wealthier classes in Britain, it was routinely stated that no man could, as a point of honour, propose to a woman without having the financial wherewithal to offer her a home – that is, a house – that was equal or better than the one she lived in with her parents. For much of the population, even among the middle classes, this could be nothing more than a fantasy. But while few lived the reality, many more believed in the idea. A second fantasy of middle-class marriage that emerged in the same period also measured a man's worldly success through the prism of domestic life. A successful man's wife, it was believed, would not have to work, and indeed many considered the threshold for achieving middle-class status to be not income, nor the financial ability to employ a servant, but whether or not the wife worked outside the house.

This was a significant development, for until then, the house was assumed to be the place of work for almost everyone. Edmund Spenser, who had found Ireland so 'wylde' in the seventeenth century, described Irish houses as 'wretched nasty cabins' not because they were in some way unsuitable for family life, but because they were 'wholly unfit for the making of merchantable butter, cheese, or the manufactures of woollen, linen, or leather'. For him, and his times, houses were assessed not by the wellbeing of the people who lived in them, but by their suitability for work. The household and the economy were one and the same. From the seventeenth to the nineteenth centuries, *Wirtschaft* in German meant household management in the widest sense, anything that sustained the members of the household – *das ganze Haus*, the whole house, 'the unit of production, consumption and socialization'.

As an integral part of *das ganze Haus*, women were not just workers, participants, but were at the centre of a web of reciprocal goods and services that enabled their households to function: helping neighbours with the harvest, dairying, making cheese or other home-produced goods for sale or barter, chopping wood, lending household equipment. In the USA, such goods and services were valuable enough that there existed a well-understood tariff in kind or time, with repayments that were measured and budgeted for.* Where husbands ran businesses from home, certain functions were assumed to be the responsibility of their wives: the women fed, clothed and supervised labourers, looked after the apprentices; or managed the business's paperwork or books. The economic importance of women at home was indicated by the fact that in home countries a swift

---

* This network of obligations was sometimes implicit, sometimes explicit. The British writer Fanny Trollope, on lending something to an Ohio neighbour, was automatically promised 'a turn of work for this; you may send for me when you want me'. This was simply pragmatic. If work could be purchased without cash, so much the better in a country that had long used a variety of currencies. In the nineteenth century, Dutch, Russian, French, Mexican, British and various South American coins were all in circulation, with Spanish and Mexican currencies remaining legal tender until 1857. Many continued to calculate in British pounds, shillings and pence, before converting the sum into whichever currency was available.

remarriage on the death of a husband was routine, in contrast to early-marriage societies, where widows were frequently forbidden remarriage (or even forbidden continued life, as in the Indian practice of *sati*). Up to a third of all widowed women in England remarried, half within a year of losing their husbands. Home-country women were valued, and invaluable.

Yet while the desires of the family may well have spurred on the Industrial Revolution, in turn the Industrial Revolution reconfigured the work, and therefore the life, of the family. Even before full industrialization, the development of proto-industrial economies began to reshape men's and women's roles. Men, who had previously worked at home, whether as craftsmen, tradesmen or professionals, began to move out of the house to work in specialized spaces such as factories, workshops and, later, offices. This happened at different times in different places: agricultural regions were slower to accommodate the change; those living in and around industrial areas saw it happen sooner. The rural nature of the American south, combined with the plantation system, kept production household-based there for longer than it did in the industrial north: farmers did not have the option of moving their workplace, while for others the labour that they owned – the slaves – produced the goods that in urban areas were now products of workplaces, not homes. In urban areas, when the break with the older patterns came, it often came swiftly: in New York City, in 1800, less than 5 per cent of men had a workplace outside the house; by 1820 it was 25 per cent, and by 1840 it was 70 per cent.

The same new working practices saw women leaving the house too, for factories, for workrooms and shops, which were now much less rarely the main room of a private house. Women who did not have paying work outside the house were also affected. From the sixteenth century in the British Isles, the enclosure of common land had brought a consequent diminution of women's work, which had included foraging and gleaning. Later, as their husbands lost their land, or moved to the new urban centres, yet more women found their work vanishing, whether it was poultry-rearing, milking and dairying, or growing vegetables. What work remained – keeping an allotment or a few chickens – continued to contribute to the family's subsistence, but it brought in less, or no, income. And as this was happening, men, working outside the house, whether on the land or in the new towns and cities, were increasingly paid in cash rather than in old-fashioned kind, so their incomes rose as women's declined or disappeared entirely. Cash work became the only sort that was thought of as work, and it was what men did; the work women did, although no different than it had ever been, was without cash payment and so was now redefined as something that was not work. Cleaning, raising children, sewing and cooking were no longer considered work, but were instead an expression of what women were, an innate function of their gender, an instinctive, reflex result of their biology.

This was the final piece in the jigsaw, moving the relationship between women, home and child-rearing into a new phase. Children and their place had always been fluid, subject to alteration as the world around them altered. When men and women had worked at home, children had routinely participated in their household's economic activities, doing small jobs that were within their age-appropriate capacities. As work moved away from the house, children's contributions were in general financially too poorly remunerated for them to be considered worth continuing, and so they went out to work later and later. With the Industrial Revolution this picture changed once more. Working-class children made up a significant part of the work-force of the new factories, while at the other end of the economic scale the railways made the idea of boarding school more palatable to prosperous parents from the 1840s: the new network of trains returned the children of both rich and poor more often and more swiftly than had been possible before. Increasingly, only the children of the middle classes were routinely found at home year round. As the century progressed, improved hygiene and disease control saw child mortality fall. By the end of the century, too, many in the middle and upper classes were limiting their family size. Fewer children, who lived longer, and lived at home longer, meant that each child received more individual attention, and therefore more emotional investment. In the eighteenth century in German-speaking Europe, *das ganze Haus*, the economic as well as the social unit, a hierarchical structure, began to give way to *Familie*, a loan-word from the French *famille*, created to convey the emotional bonding that was changing the nature of home.

Thus children, and childhood, became increasingly central to family life in home countries, its *raison-d'être*, in a way that amazed visitors from house countries. One Italian reported that English parents sang and spoke to their babies, played and even danced with them – almost as though they could understand, he marvelled. In many home societies, the birth of children was treated as a civic event. The Dutch, as with so much to do with the home, led the way. In the seventeenth century, proud Dutch fathers wore special paternity hats to announce the new arrival, and for a period after the birth some civic taxes were rebated. The child's home, too, was marked with a *kraam kloppertje*, or birth favour, a wooden placard covered in lace-edged red silk that was tied to the household's doorknocker to notify the community at large. (Even a stillbirth was announced, by a black silk cover.) This civic publication of private happiness continued for centuries. As late as the nineteenth century in Britain, gloves were tied to the doorknockers to notify an otherwise uncaring, anonymous city that a child had arrived, and later so did newspaper announcements. Whether through pasteboard, gloves or newsprint, songs or dances to amuse the babies, families had been redefined over three centuries: no longer economic units of survival, they had become symbols of human emotional investment.

The late-marriage pattern pre-dated the Industrial Revolution by centuries, but the fact that the geographical areas that saw the rise of capitalism and industrialization are the same as those geographical areas – they are the only geographical areas – where the late-marriage pattern arose does suggest that this marriage pattern may have enabled these later developments. Late marriage produced generations who, by needing to equip new houses, and having the cash to do so, created a demand; in time, capitalism and industrialization produced the means to supply that demand. From there, it is possible to consider that the church and the state might have taken their modern forms, whether Protestantism or democratic government, from the family, and not solely vice versa. To put it in economic terms, the family was the demand, the church, the state, the consumer and Industrial Revolutions the supply. As the attributes of the home family were defined, the state swiftly assimilated its terms for its own use. James I famously presented himself as 'the Husband', with 'the whole Isle' taking the role of his 'lawfull Wife'. In turn, women who killed their husbands in England and Scotland were charged not with murder, but with petty treason, for acting against the 'government' of their husbands. If the little commonwealth was a state, then the husband-killer had attempted a coup d'état. While the idea of the little commonwealth presented the family as modelled on the hierarchy of both church and state, it is possible that the reality was more complex, and more reciprocal: the development of the modern northwest European family may have influenced the development of Protestantism and the new nation-states as much as Protestantism and the shape of the new nation-states influenced the structure of the northwest European family, as traditional readings of history would have it. The places where the earliest lasting modern democratic, or quasi-democratic, political institutions arose – northwestern Europe and colonial America – were also the places where home households, participatory governance at its simplest, were the norm.

When change comes to large numbers of people low down on the social scale, Marxist and sociological interpretations of history every bit as much as the 'great man' school of political history join together in seeing the masses not as actors, but as those who are acted upon, helplessly washed about by the tides of circumstances. For the former, it was the forces of urbanization, or Protestantism, or consumerism that drove the emergence of capitalism and modern nation-states. But, while giving due weight to the difficulty of attributing agency to millions en masse, if we try to see urbanization, or Protestantism, or consumerism as the result of private desires, it becomes possible to read the emergence of the modern world not as a mighty thunderclap where these forces suddenly collided, but as the natural outcome of a series of smaller, private goals of the new middle classes.

The Restoration of Charles II in 1660 put an end, for the moment, to political revolution by the people in England and Scotland. Comparable revolts and uprisings had occurred over the previous half-century across much of Europe, and they, too, mostly drew to a close in the 1660s and 1670s.* That the democratic impulse across the

---

* In his comprehensive analysis of this century of catastrophe, Geoffrey Parker includes, in the years between 1636 and 1660, European rebellions and revolts in what are now

continent was strong can hardly be denied, but its eclipse in England did not necessarily mean it had died. The historian Christopher Hill suggests instead that the democratic impetus which the Restoration ended was merely redirected, emerging, unexpectedly but triumphantly, in the creation of fiction. From *Robinson Crusoe* onwards, the novel was a form that focused intently on ordinary men and women, presenting them as interesting in their own right. No longer did they need to be lords and ladies, or symbols of some attribute or virtue: the middle classes were now felt to be worth reading about in and of themselves; they were 'their own justification'.

One might, perhaps, say the same thing for the family, and for the idea of home: they too precipitated, and then embodied, the democratic revolution. That revolution was slow to develop, and did not arrive fully formed, as *Robinson Crusoe* had done one spring day in 1719. But if men and women on that day thereby became 'their own justification', so too, over the centuries, did the lives these men and women led. It is that slow, ambiguous but determined revolution that this book explores.

France, Austria, Scotland, Portugal, France, Spain, Ireland, Naples, Sicily, Russia, the Ukraine, the Netherlands, Turkey, Switzerland and Denmark.

2

A Room of One's Own

In the summer of 1978, a helicopter carrying a party of geologists across Siberia hovered over the taiga near the Mongolian border, looking for a place to land. There, almost 250 kilometres from the nearest village, in a supposedly entirely uninhabited region, the pilot saw that most domestic of sights, a kitchen garden. The scientists decided it was worth investigation, and landed. After walking 5 kilometres up a narrow path they came to two wooden-planked storage sheds on stilts, stuffed full of potatoes in birch-bark sacks. Continuing, they reached a yard 'piled up on all sides with taiga rubbish – bark, poles, planks'.

At the centre of the yard was a hut, although they thought it barely worthy of the name: weather-stained black, with a single window 'the size of my backpack pocket', it was ramshackle and altogether 'not much more than a burrow' – 'a low, soot-blackened log kennel'. Inside, the hut's single room could be crossed in seven steps in one direction, five in the other. It held just one item of furniture, an axe-hewn table. The floor was earth covered with a layer of tamped-down potato peelings and crushed pine-nut shells for insulation, but even so the room was 'as cold as a cellar', heated by a tiny fire and lit at night by a single rushlight.

This 'kennel' was the home of the five members of the Lykov family. Karp Lykov and his wife Akulina were Old Believers, a seventeenth-century Russian Orthodox sect. After the 1917 Revolution, persecution led many Old Believers to relocate abroad. (Large communities survive in Canada, Australia, New Zealand and the USA, and many smaller ones elsewhere.) The largest group, however, was and still is in Siberia. In the 1930s, during the Stalinist terror, Lykov's brother was murdered, and Lykov fled to the taiga with his wife and two small children. Two more children were born subsequently, and by 1978, when the geologists stumbled across them, the surviving members (Akulina had died of starvation one particularly hard year) had lived in isolation for nearly half a century.

Five people living in one room, with no sanitation, lit and warmed by firelight, 'cramped, musty and indescribably filthy': although the geologists failed to recognize it, what they were seeing were not conditions of unimaginable harshness, but the ordinary living conditions of their own history. And ours. A world where every aspect of life was lived in sight of others, where privacy was not only not desired, but almost unknown. For most of human history, houses have not been private spaces, nor have they had, within them, more private spaces belonging to specific residents, nor spaces used by all the residents in turn for entirely private functions.

The Anglo-Saxons had no word for a house, but used *heorp*, hearth, as a metonym for the entire building. (The word 'hearth' is itself elemental, deriving from the Anglo-Saxon word for earth.) Legally the hearth also stood in for its owners: astriers were tenants with a legal right of inheritance, 'astre' deriving from the Norman French *âtre*, or hearth – the right of inheritance was here linked not to the people, nor even to the house, but to the fireplace. In the houses of the gentry and the prosperous, through the medieval period, the single most important space was the hall, the space where all social, familial, official and professional life transpired, night and day, living and sleeping. And the core of that room was always the open hearth, both a physical and an emotional centre, the focal point of the room. (It is not chance that *focus* is Latin for hearth).

The well-to-do peasantry at the time lived in longhouses with byres that measured from 10 to 20 metres long, and up to 6 metres wide. Poorer inhabitants had cotts (cottages), without any space for animals. Both these types of housing had open hearths in the main room, with possibly a second room at one end; byres, in addition to the space for animals, generally contained another area for sleeping or for storage.

There is always an inherent anachronism in how the great majority of the population experiences housing. For most of history, at the top of the social scale people lived, or wanted to live, in houses that were newly constructed. It was only in the past century that having an old house generally came to be accepted as a status symbol for the rich. Previously, among those who could afford it, each generation frequently razed and rebuilt their houses in the style of the day. Otherwise, living in an older building has always been, and continues to be, the norm. Most people living in London in the first half of the nineteenth century, for example, lived in eighteenth- or even seventeenth-century housing, just as millions of twenty-first-century Britons live in nineteenth- and early-twentieth-century houses, or millions of New Yorkers live in apartment buildings that date from around World War II.

If few people lived in new and fashionable houses, even fewer lived in houses designed by architects. There is an important distinction to be made between architecture, buildings designed by architects, and housing, buildings built by builders, or by their residents. At most, 5 per cent of the world's housing standing today is architect-designed.

(Some think it might be even less, possibly less than 1 per cent.) Those people who do employ an architect for their housing have historically been, almost without exception, the wealthy and privileged, who use buildings to make statements, express power or hierarchy, or reinforce the status quo. Yet these buildings have always been a tiny minority of what was constructed, and lived in. In the early part of the nineteenth century, the aristocracy in Britain, the architect-employing class, consisted of 350 families in a population of 18 million. Only for a few decades in the twentieth century did architects in any number design extensively for the working classes, producing social housing after both world wars. Instead, from the late seventeenth century in the British Isles, from the nineteenth century in the USA, Germany and the Netherlands, most housing was produced by speculative builders, a market-driven approach that meant houses were built for people whose tastes the builder did not know. The results were therefore routinely conservative in style, literally reconstructions of houses that had already proved popular.

Just as we need to be wary about assuming that the people of any one period all lived in houses dating from that time, so too caution is required in assessing the size of houses of the past from what has survived. Most of the population in most areas lived in housing not any larger than the 'kennel' that so shocked the geologists in Siberia. Many of what today are frequently described as old workers' cottages were originally farmhouses of the comfortably-off, or even small manor houses. As well-to-do yeomen farmers built themselves larger houses in newer styles, the older houses were handed down to their workers, inadvertently giving later ages the notion that these houses had been what the working poor had been accustomed to. In England, this was exacerbated by what historians call the Great Rebuilding, a country-wide wave of construction that began in the southeast in the mid-sixteenth century, propelled by, among other things, relative political stability, a thriving economy and new technologies that enabled increased brick-manufacture and fireplaces that were re-sited from the centre of the room to its walls. From the late sixteenth to the seventeenth century, many of the vernacular buildings in England were rebuilt completely, many more were altered to a lesser degree, and more were entirely new. The Great Rebuilding began with upper-class housing, but by the early eighteenth century it had spread to those with less money. This pattern could be seen elsewhere: in Friesland, the standard housing of the sixteenth century, low wattle-and-daub buildings that accommodated animals and people together, was replaced in the seventeenth century by brick houses and separate barns. A second Great Rebuilding took place in the eighteenth century in the USA, but even before this, the original poorly constructed frame houses of the colonies had always been intended to be temporary: as times improved, they were torn down and replaced. As a result, no houses at all survive in the USA from the first half-century of colonial settlement, up to 1667. A 1652 inventory recorded 'one smale house and garden' in Plymouth. The word 'small' is unusual in these inventories, and it may be that this was a house surviving from the 1620s, which already by 1652 seemed unnaturally tiny. From the later part of the century, from 1668 to 1695, only five houses survived, and of these, two were heavily restored in the 1930s, to make them resemble more closely a twentieth-century vision of what colonial America had looked like. Apart from these five, the only surviving seventeenth-century houses in the colonies date from the last four years of the century, and so are, to all intents and purposes, typical of the eighteenth century. It is important to stress this, as most assumptions about early colonial housing are based on five examples, of which just three can be said to be original.

These anachronisms of style and size are essential to keep in mind. We are so habituated to the standard types of housing that emerged with industrialization and urbanization that we have been all but blinded to what went before. We remember the scant number of great halls of the medieval nobility, overlooking the reality that this was less than 1 per cent of what existed at the time; similarly the surviving Tudor great houses or gracious colonial governors' mansions have wiped from our minds the vanished habitations of everyone else; while the terraced townscapes that began to appear in Britain in the eighteenth century created a false history in which 'everyone' lived more or less as we do today. And thus centuries of hugger-mugger, cheek-by-jowl living, which almost everyone experienced, and expected, have vanished from common knowledge. Yet without knowing how people lived, it can be difficult to understand why they acted as they did. It is only when we know what the physical circumstances people lived in were like that we can appreciate how changes to those circumstances reflected changed ideas and expectations.

In general, in sixteenth-century England, labourers who had enough money to have a house at all, or were housed by their employer, lived in a one-room building, which might have a lean-to attached to serve both as a sleeping and a storage space. Among the better-off, most houses averaged two to four rooms. Two-roomed houses consisted of a hall and a chamber; those with more had a hall, a kitchen and chambers. The main function of chambers was storage: most contained anything from two to five chests, and possibly a press to hold more goods; many were also where looms, barrels, tools, churns or other equipment were kept; in larger houses chambers were used for sleeping as well, and most of these therefore had two or three beds.

Colonial America was little different in the size and nature of its housing. The first houses at Plymouth were wattle-and-daub single-room huts, with few, or no, windows and, possibly, thatched roofs. Three years after the *Mayflower* landing, of the twenty or so houses that had been erected, 'four or five' were considered to be 'very fair and pleasant'. These 'fair' houses were mostly single-room, single-storey houses, the hall measuring about 4.5 by 6 metres, and some having an unfinished half-storey above, an open space with unplastered walls and no ceiling, merely the roof's own rafters. There were a few houses with two rooms, the inner room usually containing another bed, and separated from the main living space by a plank wall and the chimney, to maximize the heat in both rooms. These two-roomed houses followed the English hall-and-parlour formula: the front door opened directly into the hall, and the parlour was reached from a door in the main room. A ladder in the hall sometimes led to a loft, sometimes called a chamber, which was, as in England, used for both sleeping and storage. Many of these houses had lean-to additions, also for sleeping and storage, or for the dirtiest types of food preparation, or for all of these things. The service areas tended to be at the back of the house, and later a sloping roof was added to cover these additions, the style being named 'saltbox'.

Such were the houses of the better-off. More common was housing like that of Nehemiah and Submit Tinkham, who emigrated to the colonies in the middle of the seventeenth century and lived a day's journey outside Boston. For the first year, as they cleared the land, their house was a 'half-underground shelter'; in their second year they had time and funds to erect a frame house of four rooms, as well as a barn. Their underground shelter was not at all unusual, and while the Tinkhams' living conditions improved quickly, many others continued to live in similar housing for years. A Dutch immigrant in

New Netherland described people living in cellars that were 2 metres deep, lined with timber and roofed by spars covered with bark or with furze, with, inside, wooden floors and ceilings.

Throughout the nineteenth century on the frontiers, residents often lived in shelters dug into hills or ravines, the sole sign of the structure from aboveground being the tin chimney poking out. They were cheap – in 1872, a minister in Nebraska built a 4.3 square metre dugout for $2.78 – and their interiors were made as homelike as possible: the walls were painted with a mixture of clay and water that was genteelly referred to as 'whitewash' and sheets were hung to divide the space into 'rooms'.* Like the early colonists' cellars, these dugouts were intended to last until time and money were found for better housing. More permanent were sod houses, which were built across the prairies, from southern Minnesota to Texas; by 1890, they numbered more than a million, by then mostly in Kansas and Nebraska. Made from sod bricks, each house again comprised a single room, with one small window and a dirt or, if affordable, plank floor, and clay-and-water whitewashed walls. These houses, however, were not temporary makeshifts the way the Tinkhams' had been, but developed from the traditional building practices of the area's many Russian and eastern European immigrants and represented permanent housing.

In the Middle Colonies and the south, things were little different in the early days: housing was usually poor among all income levels. The colonists arrived in Maryland in 1634, and as late as 1650 a military commander described the local houses as 'wigwams', 'made of nothing but mat and reeds and the bark of trees fix'd to poles'.

---

* The minister's house actually cost $2.78 and half a penny: $1.25 for a window, 54¢ for the lumber for the door, and 50¢ for its latch, 30¢ for a pipe to funnel smoke out through the roof, and 19.5¢ for nails.

(Only a single pre-eighteenth-century house survives there today.) By 1679, thirty houses, 'very mene and Little and Generally after the manner of the meanest farme house in England', had been erected, although by then Thomas Cornwallis, the colony's military captain, had built himself a timber-framed house 'A story and a half high, with A seller and Chimnies of brick toe Encourage others toe follow my Examples'. As in the north, the dominant form in the region soon became the hall-and-parlour house, with, often, two rooms above.

The stereotypical classically proportioned, white, Greek-style plantation mansions of the south did not appear until the middle of the nineteenth century.* Instead small temporary houses, as in the north, were the pattern here too. One Virginia plantation was settled as early as 1619, and in the first two decades it saw as many as ten temporary houses built serially on the site. The 1630s house was just a single room with a cellar, 4.8 by 6 metres in size. Even towards the end of the seventeenth century, when some well-to-do planters began to amass land, their hall-and-parlour houses were frequently unplastered inside, with wood rather than brick chimneys, and few windows, which were generally unglazed. At this stage there was very limited slave housing, in the north or the south. Slaves and indentured servants still worked together, and lived in their owners' houses, until the last quarter of the seventeenth century, when both indentured servants and slaves began to be moved out of the main houses and into purpose-built quarters.

Although the Great Rebuilding arrived later in the colonies than in England, when it did, it came pell-mell. Even so, inadequate

---

* The word 'plantation' originally meant a new settlement, to describe Ireland after England's invasion in the sixteenth century, when the English were 'planted' there. It was also used by the colonists who arrived in Plymouth, and were frequently known as 'planters'. The first use of the word to mean agricultural land tended by slave labour dates from 1706.

working-class housing in the USA was not dissimilar to inadequate working-class housing in England: tiny, two-room, poorly constructed houses, or larger houses split up into single-room or shared lodgings. Average occupation in Philadelphia at the end of the eighteenth century was seven people per room, while even when things improved somewhat, forty years later, 253 people were recorded living in thirty houses, without a single privy.

By this time, among the better-off, many New England houses had begun to resemble what we today think of as traditional colonial style: a timber building with a centred front door, often with a one-storey L-shaped annexe beside the two storeys of the main building. The simplest form, without the extension, became known as the I-house (its popularity spread outwards from Indiana, Illinois and Iowa). In the south, one-and-a-half-storey houses, with a smaller upper floor built into the pitched roof, were more usual. Instead of the front door opening directly into the main living space, these houses now had a central hall. The room on one side of the hall was then divided into two, front and back, forming a dining room and a more private family space. In the eighteenth century, kitchens in bigger houses in the south tended to be moved away from the main house entirely, in part to keep the 'big house' cool, and also as a way of indicating that the races were now to be kept entirely apart whenever possible. In both north and south, the front rooms typically were considered the public side of the house, while the more private areas, for family or family and close friends, were behind.

And also behind the big house, in the south, came the slave quarters. These varied in size and style across the slave-holding regions. Very few eighteenth-century slave houses survive, and the ones that do, as with pre-Great Rebuilding houses, were almost all upgraded in the nineteenth century. Most of the houses were built of logs, with beaten-earth floors, a single window, and sometimes a root-cellar covered by boards.* In the Chesapeake, as late as the start of the nineteenth century, log houses did not necessarily indicate lack of money or status. Many small landowners lived in log houses. But as successful plantation-owners rebuilt their houses in fashionable styles, gradually log houses became the marker of poverty, if not slavery. If the slave housing had more than one room, they were partitioned by boards, and an unfinished loft space reached by ladder might provide an extra sleeping area. The most common arrangement was two rooms, with a fireplace and chimney in between, in what was known as a saddlebag arrangement. Each room housed a family, and had its own front door. A double-pen house had another storey above; sometimes the two downstairs rooms served as a kitchen and sitting room, with two upstairs bedrooms, but more often the kitchen was in an outbuilding and one family lived in each of the four rooms, with numbers per house varying by plantation, but running up to a dozen people per room.

These slave houses were situated at a distance from the big house, or were located among the service buildings – kitchens, dairy, smoke-house, laundry, stabling. When they were out of sight, more freedom was given to layout and construction methods, and then African cultural practices might be observed, as in the Chesapeake, where the west and central African custom of a swept dirt yard around the house flourished, a layout not used elsewhere in eighteenth-century Anglo-American building practices.

Almost everyone in the colonies, from slaves and indentured servants to the wealthy, lived in houses of two rooms, in the northern

---

* For British readers, an American root-cellar is not a cellar in the sense of being an underground room. It is a space that might be less than 1 metre wide and deep, used to keep root vegetables cool in summer and prevent them from freezing in winter.

colonies averaging six or seven people, when lodgers, servants and other unrelated residents were included. This was not the hardship of the new world, but simply a fact of life worldwide that the destruction of most small housing has occluded. In the seventeenth century in Paris, Henri IV's architect, a man at the top of his trade, lived with his wife, his seven children and an unknown number of servants in two rooms. By the early eighteenth century in Britain, records show that four to seven people commonly occupied between three and seven rooms. This figure, however, is based on inventories, which by definition do not include the bulk of the working poor, who had no goods to inventory. The housing of the rural poor especially had become notably poorer. Enclosures swallowed up much of the land of small freeholders, while landowners, following new agricultural practices, increased their arable acres at the expense of their labourers, whose rented cottages and huts on what had previously been wasteland were now demolished. In addition, after 1795 the new Poor Laws compelled local parishes to bear the costs of maintaining the indigent; they therefore often demolished any unoccupied cottages to prevent impoverished incomers from settling. So four to seven people living in houses of just one to three rooms might be more accurate as an estimate for the entire population.

This type of close living continued in the USA, and in the early nineteenth century, free Americans lived in households averaging six people (slaves were not enumerated with the families, so in the south there were more in each house, but how many more is unknown). In Europe, by contrast, household numbers began to decline by the end of the eighteenth century. By 1801 households were already smaller, at about five per household. (As a comparison, in 2012 the European average was 2.4 residents per household.) Many families continued to share houses, and sharing was expected more generally: visitors in taverns or inns expected to share their rooms, and also the beds in them, with strangers.

Houses in the past not only had fewer rooms on average than houses from the twentieth century, but, as importantly, the rooms they had were used differently than ours are today. In the Middle Ages, great families kept open house, with the lord and his family habitually spending their time in the hall together with their servants, their tenants and any other dependants. Gradually, from the fourteenth to the sixteenth centuries, depending on location, the family and particularly valued guests removed themselves from the hubbub of the hall to eat and be entertained in a separate chamber. Privacy was a withdrawal, the privation of the presence of the master of the household. Privacy and the home were entwined. *Der Geheime* in German from the fifteenth century meant an advisor, a confidant, and swiftly came to refer to what in English courts were called privy counsellors. As 'privy' in English indicated the link to privacy, so *der Geheime* in German indicated the link to home, deriving as it did from the root *Heim*: someone who advised privately was a home-advisor.

It took centuries for this idea to unfurl fully. For most of recorded history, even the wealthy performed many actions in public, as a matter of course, that today we regard as private. In the sixteenth and seventeenth centuries, courtesy books, the precursors to the housewives' guides of the nineteenth century, became popular among the elite. These books were written by men for men (or boys) as instruction manuals for elevated living: they described the comportment of the perfect aristocrat, the man whose acquired refinement and social grace – his high birth was a given – made him a leader of society. The rules laid down in previous times are useful for historians, for by telling us what should not be done, they actually reveal what was commonly being done: no one repeats rules for behaviour that never, or rarely, occurs. Although the books were primarily guides to morality, they concerned themselves with physical behaviour as well: a gentleman did not scratch in public, or touch his nose or ears at the table, or gobble his food, or pick his teeth with his knife, or spit. That these prohibitions were printed again and again suggests that many gentlemen did in fact do all of these things. And if we trace the changes to the precepts in these books over the years, we can see how first attitudes changed, and then after a time behaviour followed. The books dating from the sixteenth century openly discuss bodily functions – urinating, defecating, breaking wind. Erasmus, in *On Civility in Children* (1530), for example, tells young gentlemen how to behave when (not if) they come upon a friend urinating. By the early eighteenth century, many books still mention bodily functions, but there is no longer any suggestion that one gentleman might see another performing any of them. They have become private acts. And by the end of that century, they have become so private that the updated editions of the same books don't mention them at all. Physical separation – bodily privacy – had not previously been valued. Now having spaces for these acts which had come to be considered private was not only of value, it was considered strange not to want them.

The idea of privacy came slowly, and to different segments of each population at different times, in both house and home countries. It was in the seventeenth century, in France, that concepts of privacy around lavatories first appear. The French kings had performed their lavatorial functions in public, as they had every other aspect of their daily life, until 1684, when Louis XIV had a curtain put around his close-stool. Yet even now the notion that this was a private act was still incomplete. A few decades later one of the sons of Mme de Montespan, the king's mistress, proposed moving a water-closet into a separate building entirely. The king's response was terse: 'Worthless idea…useless.' Yet even a curtain had created more privacy than the bulk of the population, living five or six in one or two rooms, could ever imagine. The relatively new urban middle-class housing in the Netherlands sometimes had a small area of one room closed off to form a cupboard that contained a bench with a hole in it over a cesspool; more often the Dutch used portable close-stools, which were located throughout the house, or sat next to the bed, as they did in England.

Other areas of the house that are today considered private were historically no less public. In 1665, when Pepys paid a call on the wife of Sir William Batten, his superior at the Navy Board, he 'found a great many women with her in her chamber, merry…where my Lady Pen flung me down upon the bed, and herself and others, one after another, upon me, and very merry we were'. Pepys in his working life was often at odds with Batten, and was a social inferior to these ladies. Yet the bedroom was a perfectly ordinary place for him to be received, and the bed just a place to sit. The upper reaches of merchant society in the Netherlands displayed their expensive four-poster beds, heavily hung with equally expensive fabrics, in their reception rooms, as in Jan van Eyck's *Arnolfini Wedding Portrait* (1434; see plate section, no. 8). The opening up of trade routes and the consequent greater availability of fine textiles for some time further increased the public display of beds, making it possible for the rich too to show off a house's wealth as previously only royalty and the aristocracy had done.

This was not simply a consequence of living in small spaces: it was a state of mind. Royalty had long expected the elite to attend their levees, literally their rising from bed. Less formal moments were still public by modern standards. Mme de Maintenon, the wife of

Louis XIV, undressed and slept in the room where the king and his ministers were meeting. The aristocracy's ceremonial occasions were no less public. In 1710, the Duc de Luynes and his wife as a matter of course received the formal visits paid to congratulate them on their marriage from their bed. The beds of the great were part of the architectural presentation of their houses. Ham House, on the outskirts of London, was one of England's most forward-looking architectural and decorative projects. In the 1650s, the main withdrawing-room, where guests congregated after dinner, held a large bed, and a suite of furniture, two armchairs and ten folding chairs to match the bed's embroidered hangings. The bed was thus decoratively as much a part of the room as the chairs the guests sat on. In aristocratic households in both France and Italy until the middle of the eighteenth century, a parade bedroom was a reception room that had an alcove with a bed separated from the rest of the room by a railing. The area on the reception-room side of the railing was called the *ruelle* or *corsello*, the 'little street', indicating that that was the side where visitors were received.

Over the centuries small gestures towards privacy had been made. In Renaissance Italy, the new urban palazzi still had beds in the great reception rooms, but by the fifteenth century those beds were frequently for show purposes, and a second, more withdrawn room had another bed for actually sleeping in. Yet even here, bedrooms were used by the women of the household for daytime socializing and for meals. It was in the eighteenth century, in the home countries, that ideas began to change, and beds began to be relocated to more private sleeping spaces. And as this move was made, the beds themselves began to alter in appearance. Great beds for reception rooms had had headboards but no footboards, so the occupants could be seen by as many people as possible when they received in public. North of the Alps, cupboard or wall beds, which had long been in use by the less wealthy, blocked draughts by having only one (curtained) side open, the remaining three being inset into the walls. Freestanding beds now had footboards added, and they were turned lengthways against the wall, to give more protection from draughts than curtains on all three sides did, as well as creating an increased sense of privacy. (Thomas Jefferson saw these new beds when he served as the US minister to France between 1785 and 1789, and was so taken with them that he ordered no fewer than nine to go home with him to Virginia.)

In house countries, bedrooms as reception rooms survived. In 1813, a watercolour of the bedroom of the Duchesse de Montebello shows her receiving the Empress Marie-Louise and Bonaparte's doctor – he is carrying his hat and stick, so is apparently paying a formal call, not treating her. In much smaller, more bourgeois spaces, too, this continued. A (probably) Austrian interior of the 1850s shows a bed with curtains, which could be drawn across one end of the room, while the rest of the room is furnished as a boudoir, with a desk, a canterbury for sheet music, a chaise-longue, cabinet, four armchairs and a sofa, plus an easel displaying a painting: a stage-set for the lady of the house to receive her visitors.

In Britain, such an arrangement had already become unimaginable in the previous century. Bedrooms were now both entirely private spaces and also gendered ones, creating a sense of mutual incomprehension across the Channel. A Frenchman reported to his compatriots that in England, 'The lady's bedchamber is a sanctuary which no stranger is permitted to enter. It would be an act of the greatest possible indecorum to go into it, unless the visitor were upon a very familiar footing', while Horace Walpole related how, on his sister's visit to France, when she asked 'for the Lord knows what utensil [possibly a chamber-pot], the footman of the house came and showed it her himself'. The French servants, a scandalized Walpole continued, had even come 'into her bedchamber in person' instead of handing the items to her own servants, as would have been the case in England, to maintain that buffer-zone of privacy.

Walpole's sense that the bedroom was an inviolable private space was now a general expectation among the upper classes to which he and his sister, the children of Robert Walpole, often referred to as Britain's first prime minister, belonged. Eighteenth-century French architects designed houses for their equivalently high-born clients to reinforce perceptions of status and hierarchy: the layout and the decoration were announcements of their owners' importance to the rooms' visitors. While the English and Scottish clients of their contemporaries, Robert Adam and his brother John, also expected to have their position in society reinforced in their architecture, what dominated these architects' discussion was very different from that of their French colleagues. Unlike them, the brothers spoke neither of status nor of society in their writings, concentrating instead on function, on convenience, enjoyment and the habits of daily life. What would a household's residents do in each room, they inquired, and how might the room best be arranged to facilitate those activities? The Adams brothers' clients were at the pinnacle of society, but a handbook written by a Norwich stonemason, to advise the provincial middle classes who were building their own new houses, was little different in attitude, if not in resources: 'Every Man has some favourite Aim in view, be it Study, Business, or Pleasure', and therefore 'the internal Parts [of a house should] be made to suit the Temper, Genius, and Convenience of the Inhabitant'.

The major conceptual leap that had been made was not a matter of the number of rooms in a house. It was rather one of living in a new fashion, one where daily activities were separated by function – eating and sleeping, or cooking and washing – or by gender – boys and girls – or quality – masters and servants – or generation – parents and children – and each separate function, or gender, or quality, or generation, was given its own special space. This idea is now seen as so normal it is hard to remember things were ever organized differently, but it was the fifteenth century before even a small gesture was made towards this idea in some parts of the world. In Renaissance Italy some of the new city-states saw city palazzi built around courtyards, in which rooms were situated together by use: dining and public reception rooms on one side, private reception rooms, a gallery and library facing them, with, in the linking wings, more private family rooms facing a service wing. In the first half of the sixteenth century, further isolated examples among the great appeared sporadically. The Château de Chambord, on the Loire, was designed by an Italian architect with four self-contained apartments of four rooms each – one large room for receiving, two smaller ones for more private times, and a closet for the most private. (This became a common French domestic arrangement until the nineteenth century.)

But even in the largest houses, the architecture made privacy in modern terms impossible. Rooms were laid out *en enfilade*, a series of rooms each opening out of the next, their doors positioned so that they created a grand perspective line of rooms stretching away as far as the awed visitors' eyes could see. Visually these vistas were a physical expression of the extent of their owners' wealth and power. Practicality was another matter, and the *enfilade* forced intimacy every bit as much as a labourer's one-room house. To get to the last room in an *enfilade*, it was necessary to proceed through all the intervening rooms, regardless of who was present in each, or what they might be doing. As the Italian playwright Pier Jacopo Martello asked crossly,

'What, by God, is the purpose of those endless successions of rooms' where one might come across anyone 'bouncing along in front of them' even when on an errand of 'some urgent need'? The order of rooms along an *enfilade* was, generally, antechamber, salon, bedroom, cabinet and finally closet, and so privacy could be achieved only by location. As visitors progressed along the *enfilade* each room became restricted to fewer and fewer visitors, indicating greater privacy, and also an ever-more-privileged status for those allowed access through the sequence and, even more, to the rooms' users – the person who occupied the final room was usually the head of the household. Even when apartments, groups of three or four linked rooms, as in the Château de Chambord, were created for family or personal use, entrances and exits were still via an *enfilade*, providing no way of maintaining privacy for the rooms' inhabitants.

That the desire for privacy had now arrived in many places is indisputable – the desire was there, but it was the ability to achieve it that was, for the moment, lacking. In the seventeenth century, the Dutch created small privacies through changes in behaviour at home, rather than changes to the architecture of their terraced houses. Visitors were expected to remove their shoes, not on entering the downstairs rooms, but on going upstairs. It was a marker that indicated where the private area of the house lay. Civic legislation, too, required that householders wash the pavements directly in front of their houses, that border between public (dirty) and familial (clean). But it was in England that the modern way of shaping domestic privacy in houses great and small appeared. From the early Tudor period builders and designers had worked on the configurations of buildings to produce the desired results. Initially the staircase was thought to be the architectural element that held the key. Staircases were built in some houses to run directly from the ground floor to an upper floor without access to any intervening floors, often as a method of defence, to protect areas of the house from outsiders; or to protect the rooms that contained the house's valuables, where certain rooms could only be reached by certain people. Soon stairs were built to create areas of privacy on the same principle of limiting access, joining one room directly to another, the lord's bedroom to his valet's, or running from one room to an exit – the apartments that Edward Stafford, Duke of Buckingham, created at Thornbury Castle, not far from Bristol, between 1507 and 1521, had stairs leading from his chamber to a privy garden, to which there was no other access. The most successful, and enduring, of these explorations of how stairs might create or enhance privacy was the duplication of staircases, to confine different types of people to different areas of the house: back-stairs for servants were soon a commonplace in large houses. But staircases were inflexible. Once the house was built, the stairs could not be altered without enormous structural upheaval.

The development that did most to enable domestic privacy emerged, paradoxically, from the adaptation of an architectural feature that had appeared in buildings that represented the ultimate in communal living – the medieval monastery. Monastic buildings laid out cloisters with arcades around the four sides of an internal courtyard, giving independent access to individual rooms. Architects in the early Tudor period experimented with the idea, adopting the principle but shaping it for use on the inside of a domestic building, rather than the outside of an ecclesiastical one. The result was the corridor.

The first corridor was designed in 1597 by the architect John Thorpe for a house in Chelsea, and its novelty was made abundantly clear by the elaborate circumlocution needed to describe it to contemporaries:

'a long entrance running through the entire house'.* The sheer origin-
ality of the idea, and the necessity for a total reconstruction of the
house's layout, should have meant its adoption was slow. Instead, a
bare twenty-five years later an English diplomat dismissed European
enfilades as though he had only ever known corridors. The former,
he wrote, put 'an intollerable servitude upon all the *Chambers* save
the *Inmost*', while their *raison-d'être*, the perspective vista, destroyed
the privacy he now automatically expected so that 'a *Stranger* [might
view] all our *Furniture* at one *Sight*'. In his eyes, a desirable house
was no longer designed as a hierarchical series of public spaces, but
as a discrete set of private ones. When the amateur Sir Roger Pratt
designed Coleshill House, in Berkshire, with corridors in the 1650s,
he did so, he said, in order to separate family from servants, as well
as family members from each other.

By the nineteenth century, even those like the designer and socialist writer William Morris, who longed to return to the medieval past,
never questioned the post-Tudor layout of contemporary houses.
Morris and his architect friend Philip Webb planned Morris's first
home, the Red House, as a return to what they knew of the style
of living in the Middle Ages. But their medievalism was entirely
confined to the décor, while the house's layout could have been taken
from a textbook of Victorian domestic segregation. Here was no great
hall for all and sundry. Instead the rooms rarely interconnected, with
most rooms having one entrance only. And when, later in life, Morris
bought the sixteenth-century Kelmscott Manor, he commented on
the 'peculiarity' of living in a house without corridors. Privacy was

---

* The word 'corridor' derives from Italian, where it meant an arcade-like walkway
between two buildings. English initially used the architecturally less precise 'passage',
only in the eighteenth century adapting the Italian word to mean an interior-connecting
route.

now built into the fabric of the building, and into the fabric of their residents' minds.

At least, it was in Britain and the Netherlands. Elsewhere, well into the nineteenth century, many European houses continued to be built *en enfilade*, as were modern Parisian flats. (The English press which reported on these new buildings in the 1840s no longer recognized the architectural form, and were horrified by the number of doors in each room, and how bedrooms were reached via dining rooms.) But despite adhering to the *enfilade* design, the French now also borrowed some elements for increasing privacy, preferring a large number of small rooms over a small number of large rooms, to allow individual family members more private spaces. And other privacies were also valued. French architects for the upper classes advised that houses for their prosperous clients should be designed with two connecting bedrooms, for husband and wife, as well as a private sitting room and a dressing room. Or, they allowed, if space did not permit, a single bedroom might have two beds: even that small amount of physical separation was apparently better than none at all.

This was not, however, a style that all home countries absorbed. Urban Austrian apartments were most commonly designed with inter-connecting rooms rather than with corridors. As late as the 1880s, flats were routinely laid out with kitchens, sitting rooms and bedrooms *en enfilade*. In Vienna, very small apartments, or *Kleinstwohnungen*, comprising a small kitchen annexe, a sitting room and sometimes a bedroom, all opening out of each other, were the standard layout for the comfortable middle classes as well as the working classes. *Gross-wohnungen*, larger apartments for the rich, also continued to follow the older formula, with most of the space given over to the public rooms, and the family rooms compressed into small back areas. Indeed, one Viennese newspaper in the 1860s lamented that 'the *at home* of the

77

English express[es] a comfort unknown to us' ('at home' appeared in English in the original German text, as indeed it did in French texts of the same period: the diarist Edmond de Goncourt wrote that people want '*les quatre murs de son* home *agréables*', 'the four walls of their *home* to be agreeable'). Even at the end of the century, discussions of the housing styles of different countries centred on how rooms were connected, and how those layouts reflected views of what – or whom – homes were for. A German resident in London found the 'most striking' difference between German and English houses was the lack of communicating doors in the latter. The English, he thought, designed their houses for their families, while the Germans designed theirs to entertain visitors.

The USA also had a vernacular architectural tradition of *enfilade* rooms, although there it was a style of the working classes, not of the great. 'Shotgun houses', like French apartments, consisted of two or three rooms aligned in a row, their doors set opposite each other so that the entire house, front to back, was visible at a glance. Folk-etymology explains the word 'shotgun' by suggesting that a single shot could be fired through the house, from street door to the rear. A more plausible explanation places the origins of both the word and the layout in west Africa (from where it spread via the West Indies to New Orleans), with shotgun a corruption of the Yoruba for house, *to-gun*. An associated African domestic borrowing was the veranda, which traditionally ran the length of a house, permitting access to individual rooms from an external corridor, just as medieval cloisters had done. Shotgun houses often had a deep porch at the front at a time when, at most, English houses had nothing more than a small vestibule, a space where inside and outside were separated. Some slave houses with these verandas date from as early as the 1770s, long before verandas appeared in New England. The architectural motif may well have spread north via slave housing in the Chesapeake.

As the actual layout of houses altered to permit new notions of privacy to be integrated, another equally important change was also in process: how rooms were used, and by whom. And because this change did not require the structural upheavals of corridors and other privacy-producing architecture, it affected many more people. When houses of one, or two, or even three or four rooms were inhabited by multiple occupants, the rooms were, of necessity, multi-functional. By the sixteenth century, most people in home countries who lived in houses with more than one room thought of one, or some, rooms as serving public functions, whether it was called the hall or the *voorhuis*. The Dutch word, literally fore-house, spells out the location, for the public room was most commonly the one that linked the house to the outside. But as yet this did not mean that other rooms were considered the domain of specific household members. In all the rooms, many people carried on many occupations, and they were furnished accordingly. In Leiden until the middle of the seventeenth century, three out of every four rooms had beds or at least bedding in them, and their mixed purpose was indicated by the fact that the rooms were almost never designated by function: *slaapkamer*, or bedroom, was barely used. Instead these spaces were given either the generic designation *kamer*, or chamber, or were described by location or feature – the back room, the room with the wall-hangings. At most, activities that made a lot of mess were now confined to a rear space, while clean, or cleaner, activities remained in the main room.

Although wealthy late-seventeenth-century yeomen farmers in England often had houses with three or four rooms, and the names of some of the rooms had become more distinct, distinct functions had yet fully to emerge. The newly named parlours still had beds in them, while almost all domestic life continued to be carried out in the main room. In the smaller houses of the thriving working classes, the room that had previously been called the hall was now often referred to as the house or houseplace, while the chamber became the parlour. At most, a public–private, visitor–family distinction could be made. In the northwest of England, the foreroom was the room where guests were received, the backroom was for services, while in Scotland, two-room houses had a *but* (kitchen) and *ben* (parlour). The *but* was for houseplace activities: eating, sleeping, cooking, laundry; the *ben* served more as a parlour, containing the main bed and expensive possessions, such as linen, as well as being a place for food storage. A watercolour from the 1780s shows a Scottish *but*, where a meal cooks over the fire with its old-fashioned hood with more pans stored above, a bed in the background, and women go about their daily life: reading, brushing their hair, with sewing in a basket beside them (see plate section, no. 9). There are also signs of more rural life: chickens are roosting above, near what are probably hams curing in the smoke. Yet this is by no means an impoverished household, as shown by the luxury goods proudly on display in an impressive dresser.

By the time of this picture, this type of multi-functional room was becoming rarer among the prosperous in Britain. Where possible, separate backstage space was now reserved for food preparation, whether scaling fish and gutting meat, or just washing vegetables. Only the actual cooking took place in the houseplace, following the pattern of the Dutch. And in German-speaking lands, too, the separations became more absolute as the seventeenth century turned into the eighteenth. The *Küche*, which had been the hall, retained its open fireplace and began to be used exclusively for cooking, while the *Stube*, the reception room, heated by a stove, was therefore for guests, being smoke- and cooking-free.

1. Today, seventeenth-century Dutch paintings appear to epitomize 'home', but contemporary viewers would have known that these rooms never existed. Samuel van Hoogstraten's *View Down a Corridor* (1663) was primarily intended to show off his skills as a painter of *trompe l'œil*, but it also had symbolic meaning: the broom, and the caged bird about to fly free, most likely represent the free Dutch Republic after the hated Spanish were swept from the country.

2.& 3. Emanuel de Witte's *Interio* *a Woman at a Clavichord* (1665, *at* and Gabriel Metsu's *Woman Read Letter* (c.1665, *left*) are depictions upheaval rather than domestic ha There is a man in the bed in de W painting, his clothes hastily throw chair, while the cast-off shoe in M a traditional symbol of sexuality, is countered by the presence of th and her cleansing bucket of water.

4.& 5. The crowded rooms in this dollshouse, *top*, from the late seventeenth century, may be closer to domestic reality than the serene minimalism of Pieter de Hooch's *At the Linen Closet* (1663), *above*.

6. By the seventeenth century, pervasive ideas of domesticity led to paintings where depictions of famil[y] harmony took precedence over those of dynastic grandeur, even for children, as in van Dyck's *The Chil[dren of] King Charles I* (c.1634).

7. Portraits of the prosperous at home silently modified reality, depicting an ideal rather than the actuality, one where expensive consumer goods were highlighted, and other less desirable objects omitted, as in Arthur Devis' *Mr and Mrs Atherton*, c.1743.

opening of trade routes and the
ed availability of consumer goods
e of the population encouraged
old display. Frequently, most
ble income was spent on beds,
were given the maximum exposure
nain room of the house, as in Jan
k's *Arnolfini Wedding Portrait*

ns remained multi-
e in most houses for
es. In David Allan's
nd Peggy (1780s),
, eating, reading,
ng and sleeping (the
t the rear, *right*) all
ce in the main room.

10. & 11. The two functions windows serve – light and ventilation – were treated separately for cen[tury]. The top section was glazed, for light, and did n[ot] open, while the unglazed lower section, covered [by] shutters, was for ventilation (*left*, Robert Campi[n's] *Altarpiece*, 1438). Sometimes there was an unglaz[ed] shuttered mid-section, and a lower section with [a] wooden lattice, or wooden shutters, as in Rober[t] Campin's *Merode Altarpiece* (*c.*1427–32, *below*).

, Shutters were for protection,
acy. Until textiles became
y inexpensive, curtains
cy were a luxury, and for
ve purposes were almost
n. Wolfgang Heimbach's
at Rosenborg Castle (1653,
 thought to be the first
; to show a pair of curtains,
an a single one – that is, for
ng rather than utility. Over a
later, Richard Morton Paye's
st in his Studio (1783, *right*)
at many houses still did
 the window here equipped
vith a window-board, which
p out of a slot in the panelling
rivacy.

14. & 15. By the nineteenth century, cheaper textiles meant decorative curtains were available to many more of the population: William Bendz's *A Smoking Party* (1828, *left*) shows a group of young men in a room where the great swag above the window appears to have no functional element; privacy in *Mrs Duffin's Dining-room at York* (*below*) is achieved by both roller-blinds, as in Bendz' painting, and also a green baize screen, while the curtains themselves are for decoration only.

Rooms for specialized activities meant that furnishings, too, were being moved to suit each room's narrowed function. By the early eighteenth century in Leiden, the number of rooms that contained a bed had dropped from three-quarters to fewer than half. In Britain, similarly, in the south it was increasingly the case that goods were now kept quite distinctly in separate spaces in many houses. Even small houses saw this shuffling about to achieve a room's purpose. Where space was too small for each room to become single-function, attempts were made at least to indicate public and private areas. One early-seventeenth-century labourer's house that was typical of many still had beds and storage items in the parlour, but the room also contained a few display elements – a cushion and some pictures – to show that the room was public. Meanwhile, the kitchen, in earlier times used for food preparation and storage, and therefore barely ever furnished, here had two tables, seven chairs and a bench, as well as a cupboard and a shelf, and the eating and cooking implements previously kept in the hall or houseplace: pewter and trenchers, as well as new commodity items such as delftware and a clock. The upper floor was made up of two chambers, which continued to serve as traditional multi-purpose sleeping-plus-storage rooms. The room over the parlour contained a bed, household linens and a lot of storage – two chests, a trunk, a coffer and a cupboard – while the second chamber contained both a bed and cheese-making equipment.

This style of living survived for a surprisingly long time in the most rural regions of the home countries. Many agricultural areas of Germany, for example, maintained a proto-industrial economy into the twentieth century, with the entire family functioning as an economic unit, and living in a style that had become outmoded some two centuries earlier or before in more industrial home regions. In Sweden, too, old patterns remained: until the end of the nineteenth century children slept with the servants, or wherever there was space, just as families had for centuries.

It was the urban centres that were the generators of change. In the eighteenth century, the standardization of terraced housing in many British cities collected the service areas (kitchens, sculleries and, in the larger houses, laundry areas) in the basement, or at worst on the ground floor, while family spaces were on the ground and first floors. Increasingly in theory, even if it wasn't practicable in actual houses, servants slept in basements and attics, with children, segregated by gender and age, in the attics near the servants, or on upper floors, above their parents. It is important always to remember that there is a gap between what architectural plans, journalism and household manuals say is desirable, or fashionable, and what the lived experience of the population was. Today a common view of upper-middle-class family life in Victorian Britain is that couples slept separately, men in a dressing room, women in the master bedroom. However, inventories and sales catalogues show that only 30 per cent of houses large enough to be inventoried had such a separate room for the man, and of those, just 20 per cent contained a bed – that is, less than 6 per cent of larger houses had any accommodation for men sleeping apart from their wives. In the eighteenth and nineteenth centuries, many guides to domestic life wrote as if all middle-class family houses contained a separate nursery for children; in reality, this was aspirational wishful-thinking, and few beyond the very wealthiest had enough space to be able to devote an entire room to the sole use of any one group of inhabitants.

Yet the desire for increased segregation meant that the concept, if not the reality, of single-purpose rooms spread rapidly from the urban, fashionable elite to the rural prosperous. In 1825, a magazine article described the alterations made to a farmer's home in Derbyshire over three generations. The author tells how her grandmother had on her marriage moved into a house with five ground-floor rooms and an unfinished loftspace, 'open to the beams and the thatch', that housed the servants as well as providing storage. She built 'a handsome parlour…with a handsome chamber', with beds in both. She and her husband slept in the parlour while the chamber was reserved for visitors. When their son inherited, his wife redecorated the now old-fashioned 'house', the room the family used as a sitting room, removing the dresser, oak settle and table at which the servants and family ate together, moving the bed into the room next door, covering the bare floor with carpet and building a 'closet' out of screens, to store her new items of conspicuous display: a tea service, a silver jug and earthenware dishes. The next generation in turn replaced her pewter dishes in the houseplace with a display of prints, and turned the bedroom next door into a drawing room: a carpet was laid, the walls were papered and the oak furniture replaced by mahogany.

Some could afford neither the goods, nor did they have the space for these types of improvement. Others, even among those who could afford it, chose to live in old-fashioned multi-purpose style long after. The architect Sir John Soane's family, at least according to a watercolour of 1798, ate breakfast in a room that also contained a desk; his library, meanwhile, as late as 1830, was also the family's reception room, dining and drawing room. Far below both of these examples in terms of income, a 1790s painting shows a shopkeeper and his family at home above the shop (see plate section, no. 24). The family here appears to eat in this space as well as using it for a sitting room – there is a sideboard with a knife-box for cutlery on it, and a drop-leaf table to pull out at mealtimes. While the painting is obviously intended to be a record of the family's prosperity, the modern fashion in room allocation was not part of their self-presentation. As we have seen, pictures may not reflect reality, but these two examples at least imply a wider range of possibility than household manuals suggest.

Among the working classes, the main room continued to be a place of labour. This might include sewing, weaving and other types of piecework, or taking in laundry, but also included many trades that with industrialization would shortly move out of the house to dedicated workspaces. An early-eighteenth-century widow in Birmingham kept a shop in her downstairs room, from which she also carried on her trade as a file-maker, the room therefore also containing an anvil and a bellows. Things were much the same in the USA, where in the late eighteenth century, 90 per cent of the population had beds or tools in the main room of their houses. In 1822, a blacksmith's family of five moved into a house in Barre Four Corners, in Massachusetts, that had been built twenty years earlier. It had a kitchen at the front, a bedroom at the back where the family also ate, and a small sitting room that served as the family's workroom. In the 1840s, however, they became 'parlour people' when the bedroom's rear door was blocked up, a second window was added, and the room became the house's best room.

The nineteenth-century parlour was more important as a symbol than as a physical space, marking the final shift from a multi- to a single-purpose room, for the parlour was a place for receiving company, and only for receiving company. Even then, it was reserved for the most important guests, more routine visitors being accommodated in the houseplace. Some families did not even do this, but kept the parlour for much rarer, ceremonial occasions – weddings, or the laying out of the dead. Others used it once a year, for their Christmas dinner. As late as the 1920s, in a cooper's house in Sweden, the best room was kept for holidays, or for serious ill-health: 'you had to be very sick to get to lie down in there', remembered the cooper's

son. The parlour became such a status symbol that many householders who could otherwise have had one good-sized living area instead
divided that space into two tiny rooms, in order that one could be
kept for use only once or twice a year.

That urbanization and the desire for privacy went hand-in-hand
was not because fashion tends to originate in the prosperous cities.
The urge physically to mark the boundary of one's house, and family,
from the undifferentiated masses living all around occurred first in
densely populated areas. In all the inventories for the city of Leiden
up to 1650, there were only two that listed window-curtains; in the
following decade, half the inventories of the rich in The Hague, Delft
and Leiden, the Netherlands' most populous centres, included them.
No reason for this particular change has been found, and therefore
we must piece together the impetus for their arrival from their usage.
That these early curtains indicated a new desire to regulate light
indoors is unlikely, for they covered just the lower sections of each
window. Furthermore, the curtains were without exception hung
only in the windows of the *voorhuis* or the *zijkamer*, the ground-floor
rooms that faced the street and were the public face of the house.
Thus two possibilities emerge: the desire to display new trade goods
to the world passing outside; or the desire to screen a newly private
home life from the gaze of the same world passing outside.* In reality,
it was probably a combination of the two, with the predominant urge

---

* The Dutch author of 'The Social History of the Curtain' mentions only the former
possibility. The omission of the idea of privacy may link to her passing comment that
it is uncommon in the Netherlands today to draw the curtains at night. It has been
suggested that the Dutch today don't have curtains in the front rooms because 'good
Calvinists have nothing to hide', that the desire for privacy is an indication of the
presence of something shameful. By contrast, residents of the inward-turning homes of
the UK would regard not blocking a lit room from the view of the street as anything
from unusual to unimaginable. One cannot imagine a British historian omitting privacy
from the list of motivating factors.

being privacy, for if it was display, it seems likely that the upstairs rooms that fronted the street would also have had curtains, and they did not. Furthermore, the curtains were generally hung singly, rather than in pairs, without any gesture towards classical symmetry, a preoccupation of the interior décor style of the period.* Nor was this simply a matter of cost. Single curtains were found at the very apex of society, in the Mauritshuis in The Hague, in the 1680s, and the Rijswijk Palace, just outside the city, even after it was redecorated in 1697.

As they were adopted first in urban centres in the Netherlands, so too in England were curtains at first almost entirely a London phenomenon: between the mid-seventeenth and the mid-eighteenth century, 81 per cent of houses in the densely crowded city had at least one set of curtains, while 87 per cent of their provincial counterparts did not. This disparity strongly suggests that privacy, not light-regulation, or fashion, was the motivating factor. This is reinforced by evidence from the sparsely populated colonies, which were slow to adopt curtains. Between 1645 and 1681, only ten inventories in one county in Massachusetts included any curtains at all. Theophilus Eaton, the Governor of New Haven colony, was extraordinarily wealthy – he died in 1658 leaving an estate valued at £1,565 – yet only his wife's chamber was furnished with curtains. A full century after that, another wealthy landowner, this time in Delaware, had none.

For those who didn't live in cities, or among the aristocracy, window-boards in many middle-class eighteenth-century houses gave privacy and protected the room's inhabitants from draughts. These boards slid out from a slot in the panelling below the window, and pulled a third of the way up the window at night (see plate section,

---

* Although the curtains, and often their number, were listed in inventories, the number of windows rarely was, so it is difficult to say when paired curtains became the norm.

no. 13). By the end of the century, however, the price of textiles fell, and curtains became affordable for the majority of the middle classes – so much so that many could even afford more than one set for each window: a roller or venetian blind to control the light; lace, net or muslin curtains for privacy during the day; and a heavier set of curtains over them, often drawn back in swags by ornamental ties or pins, and finished at the top by a pelmet or more fabric. By the 1820s, curtains had become an integral element of many middle-class houses. It was not just their decorative appeal. Now privacy was so valued that further elements continued to be added to protect the inhabitants from prying eyes during daylight hours, as well as when the rooms were lit at night. The dining room of a comfortable widow in York had decorative curtains as well as a green silk shade that pulled across the bottom of the sash, which functioned not unlike the earlier window-boards (see plate section, no. 15).

This mix of form and function was seen in Denmark too. In Wilhelm Bendz's 1827 *A Smoking Party* the students in the room obtain privacy by both a blind and a pair of thin curtains pulled across the lower two-thirds of the window; in contrast to these objects of utility, the great fabric swag above them appears to have no purpose apart from the decorative (see plate section, no. 14).

By the mid-nineteenth century, living without curtains would have seemed as odd to the British as living without corridors. No longer simply a protective barrier to shield those inside from the gaze of strangers outside, curtains had now come to be viewed also as a way to protect the inside of the house, more generally, from everything outside, even light. In the seventeenth century, Enlightenment thinkers had used light as a symbol of the age of reason. Dr Johnson, in his great dictionary, suggested that the 'sash' in sash windows came from the French verb *savoir*, to know, as 'a sash window [is] made

87

particularly for the sake of seeing and being seen', that is, automatically equating light and knowledge. (In reality, the word 'sash' is a corruption of the French *chassis*, a frame; the English was originally 'shashes', or 'shassis', or 'shashis'.) In the nineteenth century, light became more available – new technologies produced cheaper glass in bigger panes; artificial lighting technologies proliferated; improvements to heating meant the size of windows could increase. And as it did so, many began to see light itself as breaching the household's privacy. 'Hard, sharp sunlight', previously in scarce supply and therefore valued, was now seen as a nuisance, 'a glaring mass of light'. The sheer availability of cheap and easy daylight had increased the value of darkness across the home countries.

Darkness had become aesthetically valued for its ability to create mood, or at least moodiness. The Anglo-German taste for Gothic fiction, fed by books like Horace Walpole's *The Castle of Otranto* (1764) and Friedrich Schiller's *Schauerroman* (shudder novel) *Die Räuber* (1817), spread the fashion for gloomy medieval castles and moonlight meetings. The Romantic movement built on these ideas of the tenebrous, linking them to the emotional responses its adherents valued above reason, and identified in the irregular picturesque rather than the classically balanced. Gothic Revival architects such as Viollet-le-Duc in France and Augustus Pugin in Britain attempted to express these feelings in their work. They reconfigured ecclesiastical features to accommodate them to secular buildings, creating interiors that, Pugin claimed, were stone versions of spiritual truths. They were, according to one influential contemporary American landscape designer and writer on architecture, found desirable by 'those who love shadow, and the sentiment of antiquity and repose'. As a consequence, home-makers, and those who wrote on home-making, were united in rejecting clear, unfiltered light indoors. 'No one could possibly detect properties of beauty in large sheets of glass,' wrote one guide to interior decoration. Instead, light must be 'educated' – that is, filtered, softened and dulled – 'to accord with indoor life'.

Germany adopted these darkened interiors wholesale (so much so that some sarcastically dubbed this the *braune Soße* – gravy – school of interior decoration). Curtains, by keeping light out, became not just useful, but acted as an indicator of the morality of the household, a way of showing that, through the 'educating' of the light, the residents too were educated. *How to Furnish a House and Make it a Home* (*c*.1853) was clear that curtains were there to 'show order to the outside', to indicate to passers-by that decent people lived inside. This survived into the twentieth century. German colonists in Africa felt they transported both their style of home and its values. One woman wrote of her pleasure in hanging clean white muslin curtains at the windows of her African dwelling, which gave it 'the stamp of a German home'. It was clear from her letter that all three words – clean, white, muslin – were to her redolent of Germany, and expressions of household virtue.

As darkness became more desirable, curtains alone were no longer enough, and stained-glass was recommended for domestic settings – Jakob von Falke, the author of the influential *Die Kunst im Hause* (*Art in the House*, 1871), thought clear glass indicated 'banality'. Windows and lamps began to be obscured. Cathedral glass, a textured, usually green, opaque coloured glass, became popular, as did the even denser *Butzenscheiben*, bottle-glass, through which only vague suggestions of shapes could be seen. In 1890, a furnishing company used engravings to show the modern style. One view of a room had large-paned plain-glass windows, the second small-paned bottle-glass. Underneath, the caption marvelled, 'How unfinished and cold a room can be without coloured glass lowering the light.' In the USA Louis Comfort Tiffany and John La Farge were the foremost artist-designer-manufacturers of coloured glass, making an art out of an emotional response to new technologies.

Two hundred years earlier, as the new sash windows arrived in England, they had been valued for making it possible to admire the outdoors from inside the home: 'what can be more pleasant and Beautiful…than to look out of the Parlour and Chamber windows into the Gardens,' enthused even a writer who specialized in gardening and agriculture. Now this viewpoint was turned upside down across the home countries. Jakob van Falke spoke for them: 'There is no need for a good view of the outside from the dwelling'. Instead, the 'attraction must be directed inside', while the German art-historian Cornelius Gurlitt added that a 'dusky, hidden' light indoors was even better, as it allowed one to feel that 'What is happening outside is far away'.* This was widespread. In Britain Oscar Wilde pronounced that looking through windows, whether from inside or out, was simply an 'extremely' bad habit. Coloured glass was commended precisely for the degree it demarcated the separation of inside and outside. William Morris added that small panes of glass rather than large were preferable, as 'we shall then at all events feel we are indoors'.

The question of indoors vs outdoors was one that exercised, in particular, the British, who increasingly felt that for a house to be a home, it had to be separate from the world. As a consequence, the British looked at the development of the European apartment

---

* Gurlitt's book, *Im Bürgerhaus,* was published in 1888, and the author should not be confused with his grandson, also Cornelius. Cornelius Sr's son Hildebrand was deeply implicated in looting art treasures for the Nazi government in the 1930s; his hoard of more than a thousand works of art was kept secretly by Cornelius Jr until it was discovered in 2013.

block with horror.* In Paris, new buildings were up to eight storeys high, with shops, restaurants and cafés on the ground floor, and a concierge, or porter, posted just inside the front door. The boundaries between street and home were, to the eyes of those from home countries, constantly being breached: the ground-floor shops were commercial premises in residential buildings; the concierge was neither a family member nor a family employee and often did not live on the premises; the restaurants' shellfish stands were open to the street; and the cafés had outdoor seating. From 1833, too, benches were placed at intervals on the main *grands boulevards*, making the indoor act of sitting an outdoor activity.

In home countries, therefore, alternatives to apartment buildings were found where possible. In both Britain and the USA, lodgings could be pleasant, desirable even, for those with some money, with a woman or a family – not a single man – living in the basement to look after all the residents. (Sherlock Holmes and Watson, for example, do very nicely as lodgers.) Up to half of all Americans in the nineteenth and early twentieth centuries had at some point either been a lodger or lived in a boarding house. In the late eighteenth and early nineteenth century, couples frequently did not set up their own household – did not 'go to housekeeping', it was called – immediately after marriage. Yet, unlike early-marriage societies, they also did not expect to live with their parents. Instead they moved into a boarding house for a period of time.

---

* There is the anomaly of Scotland, which alone in Britain took to apartment buildings for the middle classes before the twentieth century. Elsewhere, no matter how small or inconvenient, or how divided up into multiple occupancy, houses were the basis for most housing. Londoners, with 40 per cent of its families living in some form of shared occupancy, none the less grimly rejected apartment living as long as possible.

However achieved, by the nineteenth century the middle classes routinely expected to be able to create privacy through architecture. Middle-class and urban upper-class houses had public façades, their frontages set proudly to the streets, even as what went on behind them became increasingly hidden. By contrast, a large proportion of working-class housing had long been hidden by being situated in courts set behind the public streets. These tenements and lodging houses bore no resemblance to middle-class lodgings, especially as urbanization and the Industrial Revolution increased overcrowding by a large degree: 2,500 people lived in just 222 houses in one area of Leeds in 1851, with five people for every two beds. Within these courts, however, much of life had been lived in public. The privies and the running water were located in the courtyards, as well as what little fresh air there was, and they were therefore much used by the residents, happy to be out of their tiny, overcrowded, damp and poorly ventilated rooms. In the nineteenth century, slum clearances led to the imposition of middle-class standards, by rehousing workers in suburban developments or in back-to-backs, the first housing specifically planned for the working classes. The back-to-backs, particularly in Britain's industrial heartland, had one downstairs room and one (sometimes two) upstairs.* To middle-class observers, these houses provided their residents with the privacy of a home, and thus seemed to be an improvement on the old courts. Yet the water and privies were still situated outside, and so the residents' lives continued to be lived in public, outdoors. Tucked away behind the main streets, the life of the courts had been partly sheltered; as the back-to-back design meant privies and standpipes had to be located on the streets, the residents' lives, paradoxically, became more exposed.

* Back-to-back houses shared party walls not only with the houses on each side of them, but also with the house directly behind, thus having no rear lighting or access.

The domestic privacy of the middle and upper classes, meanwhile, was being redefined in quite another way. In the early eighteenth century, Robert Walpole redesigned his family home, Houghton Hall in Norfolk, separating it into two areas. The grand state rooms were the 'floor of taste, expense, state and parade', for public display, while the ground floor was given over to the 'noise, dirt and business' of family life. This architectural division between family and working life was of course not possible for most, but as many men's work was being moved out of the family home and into specialized workplaces, the distinction between working life and home life began to appear not as an artificial one created by history and circumstance, but as one that merely reflected a divinely ordained social structure. And, it followed, if that were the case, then men and women should logically inhabit 'separate spheres', men in the public world, women in the privacy of the family home. This idea was to dominate notions of home for the next century and more.

3

Home and the World

In colonial New England, men and women were seated in separate sections in church, with their children sitting together in a group at the rear, rather than with either parent. Within each of the three groups seating was then determined first by age, then social status, then wealth. It was only from the early nineteenth century that families began to sit together, a development that can be seen to typify changing attitudes to families more generally. Families were no longer considered to be one group among many interlocking, and competing, social groups. The family was now given precedence. It was the primary unit in society.

Ostensibly the family was a private group – out in the public sphere, men were considered, at least theoretically, on their individual merits. Politically, its privacy had been confirmed in 1763, when William Pitt rejected a bill in parliament that gave the excise – tax – authorities the right to search private houses for contraband. No contemporaneous record was made of his speech, so his exact words are unknown, but within three decades it was reported that 'He [had] opposed this bill very strongly…Every man's house was his castle he said.' If Pitt did use those precise words, he had chosen them as a reference to the seventeenth-century legal-writer Sir Edward Coke, who had first written 'A man's house is his castle'. But by the mid-nineteenth century, this bare statement was no longer sufficiently forceful, and Pitt's reported speech had been endowed with greater emotional resonance: 'The poorest man may in his cottage bid defiance to all the forces of the crown. It may be frail; its roof may shake; the wind may blow through it; the storms may enter, the rain may enter – but the King of England cannot enter.' The privacy of the home, and the family, had come to be acknowledged to be paramount, overriding the considerations and the needs of the public sphere.

Across the Channel, the home as a shelter, especially for women, was, briefly, retrograde among the ideological ferment of revolution for a brief period after Pitt's speech. In the late 1780s and into the 1790s and the early days of the French Revolution, several Revolutionary clubs, including the Jacobins, had welcomed women as audiences for their debates. After all, women were fellow citizens. But this was not to last. In 1793, at the height of the Revolutionary Terror, the Jacobin Fabre d'Eglantine inveighed against those very same women appearing in such public arenas. These women were not 'mothers of families, daughters of families, sisters occupied with their younger brothers or sisters', but instead could only be 'adventuresses, knights-errant, emancipated women, and amazons', and the clubs that admitted them were guilty of subverting the natural order: women belonged in a family setting.

The Catholic theologians who wrote on the subject of original sin generally treated it as an aspect of sexual desire, an adult concern. In contrast, Martin Luther and, after him, John Calvin, gave much consideration to the idea of original sin, and, treating it as a 'hereditary depravity' passed on at conception, turned it from being an adult wrong to being the inheritance of every child. Baptism was the first step towards its eradication, but that had to be followed by education, and behavioural control, matters of discipline and rigour: sparing the rod spoiled the child. In Calvinism, education had a crucial role in extirpating hereditary sin, while to Enlightenment thinkers in the eighteenth century, it became paramount. John Locke, in *Some Thoughts Concerning Education* (1693), had already moved down this path: 'of all the Men we meet with, Nine parts of Ten are what they are, Good or Evil, useful or not, by their Education. 'Tis that which makes the great difference in Mankind.' The child was a *tabula rasa*, born clean and innocent, an innocence that was all too easily lost by coming into contact with the corrupt world. Educating a child was therefore less a matter of inculcating knowledge than it was of preventing the child from acquiring the wrong sort of knowledge. This was the background on which Rousseau built his theories of child-rearing, which became widespread through his hugely popular *Émile, or, On Education* (1762). Rousseau's book promised that women who raised their boys according to these educational and behavioural precepts, while keeping the world at bay until they were strong enough to confront it, would mould future men of honour and sensibility. And while *Émile's* narrator at points heartily rejected bookish learning for children – 'I hate books!' – he makes an exception for 'the happiest treatise on natural education', *Robinson Crusoe*. Desert islands were not a viable location for most readers, but the concept of a protected, private space became a fundamental of child-rearing, and by the nineteenth century Crusoe's isolation was held up as an example: Coleridge thought the fictional character was what all men might have been had they not been tainted by society.

It became increasingly accepted that a woman's primary duty was no longer to act as her husband's partner, but as her child's mother. This was her fundamental role, to train her children to be their own Crusoes, with the home as their desert island. From the safety of this isolated location, boys would learn the skills that would enable them to leave their desert island homes and enter the outside world, while girls learned to guide more Crusoes when their turn came, 'to educate them when [they are] young, to care for them when [they are] grown…to make their lives agreeable and sweet at all times – these are the duties of women at all times'. While many of Rousseau's suggestions for child-rearing were revolutionary – he supplanted rote-learning with child-initiated discovery through play, for example – his view of girls and women was in step with that of both the church and middle-class society as a whole. In 1797, Thomas Gisborne, a Church of England clergyman, sounded little different from the radical philosopher as he outlined women's subordinate role: women's duty was to 'daily and hourly' think of ways to increase 'the comfort of husbands, of parents, of brothers and sisters…connections and friends, in the intercourse of domestic life'. Rousseau put women at the centre of their children's upbringing; the church confirmed their roles as gatekeepers to Crusoe's island, the family home, as a place where their own weaker natures could be permanently sheltered, and where, finally, men could find solace and renewal, where they could temporarily be protected from the hurly-burly of commercial life, or the sinfulness of male sociability, by those whose job it now was, not to share their burdens, but to 'make their lives agreeable and sweet'.

The fierce rigidity with which these ideas were embraced was unsurprising in a world that was rapidly changing, and therefore felt unstable. Women's withdrawal from the public sphere began to seem natural and right. For centuries the words 'economy' and 'household' had been interchangeable. The household had been a self-sustaining unit designed to keep its family members fed, clothed and sheltered, to rear children and train them to hand on, in turn, the skills needed to keep their own children fed, clothed and sheltered: the entire family worked together to this end. Tasks were gendered – in agricultural areas, men ploughed, women reared chickens; in shops and taverns, men did the purchasing, while women waited on customers; craftsmen kept for themselves the high-skilled, or brute-strength, elements of their trades, while their wives took on the more delicate, or the more routine, elements.

As we saw, with the enclosure of land, and in the early days of industrialization, even before the full development of the Industrial Revolution, men had become cash earners, while women's economic contributions had appeared to diminish. Men began to be perceived as the family's main, even only, providers. Yet barely had this financial change occurred, than industrialization altered men's status once more, whether in the working class as cash earners, the upper class as property-owners, or the middle class as professionals, or the managers of trades or businesses. Now merchants and industrialists became a new caste, a challenge to the landed and professional classes of old. Even the status that all men assumed, as the head of the family, was less secure. By the beginning of the nineteenth century, the new factories employed more women than men; together with the increase in domestic service, women were once more earning cash for their labour as they had in pre-industrial times. Children's roles, too, had altered. In peasant societies children were financial burdens on their families until they were in their mid- to late teens. The economic value of the tasks they were able to perform were always less than the cost of their food, lodging and clothes, as well as whatever education they might receive. With the development of proto-industrial society and the spread of home-based piecework, children had contributed more, and earlier; with the coming of the factory system, however, children were often the first hires, both their small hands and their malleable characters being of value.

As the workforce was reshaped by the Industrial Revolution, therefore, so too was the home. Among the middle ranks, professional life for men was expanding, allowing them to earn sufficient to enable their wives and children to relinquish paid labour, whether outside the house, or from traditional work such as poultry-keeping and dairying. At the same time, men's work migrated from their homes to offices, counting-houses and other specialized locations, and their apprentices naturally followed. Fewer rural workers too were housed by their employers, instead being paid in cash and finding their own lodgings. More and more, homes therefore housed a nuclear family alone, or, at most, a family and a few servants. Houses were becoming places for those related by blood.

Given this instability, this level of change, it was very natural that a belief-system developed to explain why the new living pattern was in fact an old one, and the only one possible. Men, according to this theory of gender roles, were designed by God to perform one set of functions, women another, and each most usefully did so when they operated in their own 'separate sphere'. This notion was disseminated through sermons, educational literature, novels, magazines and journals. Yet it is of course entirely possible to believe one thing absolutely, while living in a fashion that contradicts it entirely. And so it proved. On a day-to-day basis, separate spheres were adhered to only insofar as the variables of geography, circumstances, class, income, status and personal volition permitted.

Because the 'separate spheres' were never more than an idea, and an idea for the prosperous. To believe that they had a full, physical reality, creating borders between home and not-home, between public and private, is comparable to believing that a nation's borders are a painted line on the ground, which has been there since the creation of the world. The spheres were in practice permeated routinely. Many women worked in the public sphere: in shops, inns, and in many trades. The private sphere meanwhile was a worksite where employees – domestic servants – were trained, supervised and paid by an employer – the very women whose house was, ostensibly, sheltering her from the world of work. Some societies have physically cloistered women, but in nineteenth-century home countries, the women who were supposedly comfortable only in the private sphere in reality spent a great deal of their days in public spaces, whether on trains and buses, or in shops and theatres and eating-places. Some places were an ambiguous combination of public and private. Men's clubs, nominally public spaces, were designed to resemble upper-class private houses. Shops and hotels and first-class railway carriages, also all in the public sphere, were customarily furnished to look like private parlours, making them pretend privacies where nominally home-bound women could take part in the public world without openly occupying male space. A journalist in 1854 recommended to his women readers in New York that, 'if slightly fatigued', they should head for the lobby of a hotel on Fifth Avenue. 'Here…we feel at "home".' While many spaces in the public sphere took on the appearance of private spaces, so too did private spaces adopt elements of those that were public. The parlour in particular, with its furniture in matching sets, a room of unused chairs and tables, of display, drew heavily on the appearance of hotel lobbies.

For whatever the theory, in reality the home was never, and could never be, a non-commercial private space. Nineteenth-century houses contained far more people than twentieth-century ones do. They were filled with more children, more servants, with lodgers and boarders. And through them daily passed an endless procession of people who carried work and services directly into this supposed private sphere: delivery boys for butchers, bakers, dairies and greengrocers; sellers of household goods and equipment; menders and repairers; buyers of old clothes, rags and other items of what today is called recycling; even entertainers who performed on the pavement outside. Despite the theory of home being a refuge from commerce, the reality was that the house, daily filled with employees and subcontractors, remained as much a worksite as it had been when the craftsman and his family earned their living there.

Perhaps because of this unacknowledged reality, developments in house layouts for the more prosperous in many home countries increasingly suggested a desire to establish areas that were for family only, a recognition that the 'separate sphere' of the home was routinely breached by outsiders. Robert Walpole's redesign of Houghton Hall was what could be done if money and space were liberally available. Among the wider population architectural alterations on a smaller scale gave houses both public and private faces. In the USA yards now began to be fenced in. No longer just areas where waste was stored, they were being turned into gardens for the use of those who lived inside: private outdoor areas, not public ones. Once past the yard, in both Britain and the USA, the hall-and-parlour house, with its front door opening directly into the main room, mixing residents and visitors together promiscuously, gave way to the I-house, where a porch or veranda filtered visitors before they entered. Inside, the I-house had a central foyer (confusingly also called a hall), which was a second filter, sending incomers to the appropriate area of the house, depending on whether they were guests, family, or servants and tradesmen. Upstairs more generally in many houses, unfinished loft rooms were plastered and partitioned and beds were moved into them, out of the public rooms. The private space for the family had been the main downstairs room. Now that was extended by these even-more-private areas above.

Such were the houses of the prosperous classes in industrialized areas. Most people, however, had no likelihood of ever experiencing these changes, and the stability of building practice reflected the unchanging domestic circumstances of many householders. For those who lived in less urbanized areas, pre-industrial rhythms continued into the eighteenth century in Britain, and later in much of Germany and Scandinavia. This applied as much to the way the household was run as it did to the way it was organized structurally. As it is difficult to remember today how small houses were in earlier times, so too it is hard to comprehend the sheer labour, and time, involved in keeping that small space functioning. It has been estimated that three to four hours were spent daily on food preparation, an hour to fetch water, an hour to feed the children and keep the fire alight, an hour in the kitchen garden, two to three hours to milk cows and goats, feed chickens or perform other animal husbandry, an hour to clean, an hour spinning and an hour spent looking after the children, teaching them to read and write, or knit and sew: a total of sixteen hours a day. Add in the laundry, which occupied approximately eight hours weekly, and by the time meals were eaten, there was little time to do more than fall into bed in order to get up and do it all over again the following day.

In many rural areas of the USA, this lifestyle remained standard throughout the nineteenth, and in some places into the twentieth, century, even as the extremes of the climate and the isolation of a scattered population made these already heavy daily routines more onerous than they were elsewhere. The woman's sphere for those who lived like this was not a matter of creating comfort, as it was perceived by urban writers in technologically advanced London or New York. It was a struggle to ensure survival. In districts just being settled, there were even more tasks. The land had to be cleared before it could provide bare subsistence, and in the meantime the men hunted to feed their families, while the women made butter and cheese and raised chickens for their eggs, as well as sifting ash, used to manufacture soap, and maple sugar, by tapping trees, or spinning or weaving. The goods these activities produced were then bartered for essential items that could not be home-produced: tools, ironmongery, needles.

Even though tasks were divided along gender lines, and denominated 'women's work' and 'men's work', in reality these tasks were component parts of wider activities to which all ages and genders contributed. Housework was truly the work of the household, for the maintenance of the household. A single example of this interwoven labour can stand in for much of daily life. Most rural families cooked over an open fire, and thus, like generations before them, their diet was primarily various forms of stew. To make the stew, the men trapped or shot and butchered the animals. The women and girls plucked birds and cleaned fish, they carried water for the pot from streams or wells, which had been dug by the men, to cook with vegetables grown by the women and grain grown, harvested, threshed and taken to be milled by the men. The stew then cooked in a fireplace built by the men, over wood they had cut, stacked and carried into the house.* The meal was dished up into wooden trenchers and eaten with wooden spoons, both carved by the men and boys on winter evenings. Afterwards, the women and girls wiped the trenchers clean with rags they had woven if there was enough help available, or not too many small children, or bought if there was enough cash, and shops nearby. They scoured the pot with brushes made of twigs the children had gathered, before sweeping the floor

---

* A New England household typically burnt up to 40 cords of wood a year, which theoretically stretched over 90 metres. A full third of a man's working life was spent doing chores linked to keeping warm.

with another twig broom. The men looked after the cows, the women or children milked them, and women made the butter; men grew the grain, women baked the bread; men grew and prepared flax, women spun it. Women and children fetched the water for cooking and daily cleaning, men did it on laundry-day, when up to 400 litres was needed for a week's wash; women made soap, and braided horsehair or grass for clotheslines, men and boys whittled clothes-pegs.

The differences in urban, settled areas of the USA and in Europe were differences in kind, with many of these tasks vanishing, work replaced by consumer purchasing, but the partnership and labour divisions remaining constant. In the 1820s in New York, John Pintard earned more than $1,000 a year, which put him among the elite, and yet his wives and daughters made the family's clothes and cooked; they did carpentry jobs around the house, whitewashed rooms, and even the house's exterior; they cleared the yard and pruned hedges. Half a century later, Esther Burr, the wife of a minister and college president in New Jersey, had a slave who did the cooking, and hired other help when necessary, but her own jobs included childcare, teaching, nursing, cleaning, laundry, spinning, dressmaking, sewing household items, shopping, entertaining, supervising her husband's students, who lodged with them, and 'visiting' – making social calls – a task she disliked, but which she regarded as her job no less than the laundry. The accounts for many small shops were often intermixed with a family's household accounts, reflecting the equal contribution of husband, wife and children to both arenas.

While amalgamated roles remained a constant, the vocabulary used to describe them, and therefore the way people thought about them, had been modified over the centuries. In England in the sixteenth century, men's wills had often referred to their wives as 'fellow labourers'; by the mid-seventeenth century that term had disappeared, and wives were now the source of 'wise Advices', dispensed through 'their holy Examples, their devout prayers, and *Labours of Love*'. By the eighteenth century in Germany, a new term, *Hauswirt*, a household manager, replaced *Hausvater* to describe the head of the household, while *Hausmutter* became *Ehegenossin*, a marriage partner – now defined not as part of the economic system, but as a personal adjunct to the manager. No longer were the household and the economy the same thing. And so by the nineteenth century, housework was being redefined as those tasks confined to the province of women, tasks that were entirely separate from the cash economy. When women earned cash, it was commonly described as 'supplementing' the family's income, not contributing, or supporting the family, despite the fact that at the middle of the nineteenth century 42 per cent of American women were in paid employment, and a quarter of British women were; three decades later, half of all women in the Netherlands worked outside the home. In D. W. Griffith's silent film *The Mothering Heart* (1913), Lillian Gish is 'the good wife' whose job it was, in the words of the caption, to make 'The Path of the Struggling Young Husband...Smooth'. He goes out to his unnamed job while she takes in laundry at home. Yet the captions tell us that while he is 'struggling' to make his way in the world, she is only 'Helping'. At the end of the working day, his exhaustion is a sign of his manly labour. By contrast, Gish's good wife fixes her hair and pretends not to be tired at all: her work has not been work, and must be hidden. She was only doing what good wives were supposed to do: household manuals routinely advised women to hide their labour and consequent fatigue from their husbands.

By this time, women as well as men believed that their tasks were not work. Esther Burr, whose tasks were itemized above, was surprised to find herself tired at the end of the day; it was, she wondered, as though she had been hard at work – her 'as though' conveying clearly that she thought what she had done could not properly be so called. This was common. A housewife in Salem, Massachusetts, whose days were occupied in weaving, tending livestock, boarding lodgers, working in the fields, tanning leather and carting wood, wrote of her regret that she 'in no way [did] any thing towards earning my living'; instead, she lamented, she was entirely 'provided for in the best manner' by her sailor husband.

Women's tasks had become perceived as non-work. Many household manuals implied, and many novels and magazines agreed, that the main female task – or, as it became restated, her mission, through her biology, and ordained by God – was twofold: looking after their husbands at home, and child-rearing. It was not merely that the heavy labour involved in housekeeping became invisible. As women's work was increasingly dismissed as housework, no longer productive, so women themselves, whatever the complex realities of their lives, came to be reduced to their biological function, reproductive.

As early as the sixteenth century, sewing, knitting and embroidery had been called 'work'. It was not paid for, but it had recognizable economic value. By the nineteenth century, the value was no longer apparent, and 'work' meant its diametric opposite, a 'tranquil pastime'. As women's work, whether sewing or more, began to be seen as non-work, so the stereotype of women as a gender entirely devoted to spending their husbands' money also developed. Now, went these new morality tales, women busied themselves with 'work' not to keep households in shirts and sheets, but simply to pass the time: they were producers of fripperies that no one wanted. As early as 1758, the *New York Mercury* had run a comic piece in which a woman, 'an irreconcilable enemy to Idleness', made 'twice as many fire-skreens as chimneys...three flourished quilts for every bed...

futile pictures which imitate tapestry...[and] curtains wrought with gold...which she resolves some time or other to hang up'. A century later, this previously satirical view gained a formal governmental imprimatur. In 1871, the British census gave a token nod towards housework as 'noble and essential' in its introductory remarks, but in the main section, only female labour outside the house was classed as 'productive work', which implicitly rendered all work inside the house as 'un-productive'. The 1881 census made the implicit explicit when it re-categorized housewives as 'unoccupied'. If there was no cash pay, it was no longer work.

While most housewives barely had time to sit down, much less be 'unoccupied', the nineteenth century nevertheless saw a reshaping of the entire nature of housework: what it entailed, how people thought about it and how it was performed. In that itemization of the sixteen hours spent on chores in the eighteenth century (p. 103), it is notable from a twenty-first-century viewpoint that cleaning occupied barely 10 per cent of the housewife's time. Hearths were swept, floors swept and sanded, pots and pans scoured, trenchers, spoons and drinking vessels wiped, and then the housewife was ready to move on to the next task. In the nineteenth century, however, changing attitudes, changing medical knowledge, and especially changing technology, turned cleaning into the core activity of every housewife's day.

Advice books for housewives became popular from the middle of the nineteenth century, their penetration into the middle-class market and beyond a publishing phenomenon. In Germany, a cookbook by Henriette Davidis, a minister's daughter, went through sixty-three editions in the decades following its publication in 1844. Frau Davidis was sometimes described as the 'German Mrs Beeton', whose own *Book of Household Management* (1861) sold two million copies in the first decade after publication. These books were for middle-class urban women who were running their own homes, without much money and, as a consequence of the new world of technology and urbanization, perhaps far away from their mothers, or with food available that their mothers did not recognize, or faced with technology that had been unknown to previous generations. Or they were moving up, or down, in the world, facing social situations their mothers had never encountered. The books had internalized the previous half-century's theories of separate spheres, taking them now entirely for granted. And so, if a woman's mission was found in her home, then the state of that home was the most telling indicator of her own merits or demerits as its housewife.

If a woman was defined by her ability to rear the next generation, and her house was the crucible that shaped those children, then the woman's ability to keep house became central: it reflected her value. It was no longer simply a matter of was the house adequately cleaned, scrubbed, polished? It was how the upkeep had been achieved, which measured not hygiene, but morality. And so physical labour became a measure of assessment, and purchasing ready-made products to replace labour was frowned upon. American advice books warned that while 'some people' thought shop-bought baked goods were as inexpensive as homemade ones, they were 'not half as cheap' really. The vagueness of 'some people' and the lack of price comparisons suggest that the value was perceived rather than actual. German advice books were no different. Starch laboriously made out of potato peel, the housewife was told, was superior to shop-bought starch, omitting to consider that the former worked no better and the latter cost less. Similarly, using oilcloth instead of a fabric tablecloth at mealtimes was condemned: 'nothing leads so easily to uncleanliness and care-lessness at mealtimes as these convenient waxed tablecloths, which can be simply wiped off'. Convenience led to dirt and carelessness, because housekeeping was valued by the physical labour put into it, by the effort it took.

Purchasing labour was every bit as dubious as purchasing goods, as though bringing the cash nexus into the supposedly non-commercial sphere brought contamination with it. German women were quick to praise Dutch houses – they were wonderfully clean, they agreed – but they were much less quick to praise Dutch housewives, who were less admirable than their German counterparts because they employed servants. In the 1860s, one German woman spoke severely to her neighbour for sending her family's socks out to be darned. The younger woman's rationale – she had children to look after and, without a servant, had no time to darn; the woman she sent the work to needed the income – were swept aside, and she was warned that she had taken 'the first step on a [downward] path…no family could get ahead, if a healthy woman paid for things to be done that she could do herself'. She must 'never think of such a thing again'. Abashed, the neighbour accepted the reprimand, and so the older woman's tone softened: if her neighbour gave her the socks, she would darn them herself 'this once'. Hiring someone to do housework was wrong, but having it done for nothing, as a favour, was not. American manuals also focused on commercial labour vs labours of love, but while in Germany it was the monetary payment that polluted, in the USA it was the work migrating out of the house to commercial premises. 'Attend to all mending in the house', advised one manual. But 'If it be impossible to do it in your own family, hire someone into the house'. In Britain, where there was a higher proportion of domestic servants in middle-class households, domestic work came to include a number of daily tasks that were seen as essential, but in reality made no contribution to hygiene. The most common of these was whitening the front doorstep, in which the step was washed and a white paste applied. This whiting was impermanent, scuffed away immediately it was walked on. Had hygiene been the aim, washing the step alone would have sufficed; had it been appearance, whitewash or paint would have produced a more permanent solution. The combination of spotlessness and impermanence instead indicated the householders' belief in the value of labour.

The insistence on this labour was, at least in part, a response to the way nineteenth-century technology was changing the household, just as the belief in separate spheres was, at least in part, a response to the arrival of industrialization. Once a place of production, new technology was now turning the house into a place of consumption. Many basic foodstuffs (bread, jam, butter, cheese, meat, beer and more) and items of clothing had been made at home by many, if not by all; now for many, they had become goods to be purchased. And by the end of the century, most households bought at least some of these goods as a matter of course. They were, as the advertising said, 'labour-saving'.

What, or whose, labour was being saved was not, however, a straightforward question. We saw how many elements of housekeeping had, earlier, been a combined effort of both man and wife. To return to the single example of making a stew: by the eighteenth century in Britain (and in some areas as early as the seventeenth) and in parts of urban Europe, and the nineteenth century in frontier America, it was cheaper for most families to buy grain than it was to grow their own. Growing wheat or corn, and shucking the corn or transporting the wheat to a mill to be ground into flour had been a man's contribution to the stew. His contribution now might be making the purchase, or that task might equally devolve onto his wife. But using store-bought flour didn't decrease *her* work. It increased it. Laura Ingalls Wilder, in her fictionalized 1870s and 1880s frontier childhood, describes her mother baking cornbread: after heating a metal dish in the open fire, 'she mixed cornmeal and salt with water and patted it into little cakes', put them in the dish, covered them, then set the dish on the fire. For those with an indoor hearth and able to purchase baking soda (bicarbonate of soda had been available from the early nineteenth century, baking powder from mid-century), the method was the same, except that the cornmeal mix was left to rise slightly by the fire before baking. But with the arrival of store-bought flour, low-rise breads became food for the poor, or slaves, while yeast-breads were what every family would have if they could. Yeast-breads involve far more time, labour and planning: flour could be bought in bulk and then stored, but a trip to buy it had become necessary; live yeast lasts only days in liquid form, requiring regular replenishment; the dough needed an overnight rise, and so required advance planning.* Suddenly, stew and bread was no longer a meal produced by two people working together, but a meal planned and produced by one.

The new technology of cast-iron stoves, also called closed ranges or kitcheners, similarly increased women's work while eliminating men's. Stoves consumed up to 90 per cent less fuel than open fires, reducing the cutting, hauling and stacking of wood – the men's contribution – almost to vanishing point. And when coal replaced wood as the primary fuel, it was delivered by a coalman, and carrying the buckets – a mere 10 kilograms – to replenish the fire, and now the new kitchener too, became a woman's chore, not a man's. Men's

---

* With care and a temperate climate, yeast can survive for a week or two, but in hot weather it perishes quickly. There were ways of drying it, but these too required time and careful planning (and the leavening power of the yeast declined). Raising agents, their availability and differences in ease of use require an entire book to themselves. In areas where spirits were distilled, yeast that could be used as a raising agent was sometimes, but not always, available as a by-product. Sourdoughs, where natural yeasts can survive for years, were the mainstay of many regions, but they too required more time and planning than low-rise breads.

involvement with the fire had become transactional – paying the fuel bill. It is difficult to use more than one pot when cooking over an open fire, hence the prevalence of stew-like meals, where meat, vegetables and grain were all cooked together. Closed ranges created the possibility of cooking with several pots in action at once, and so meals became more elaborate, with more dishes. The time devoted to food preparation and cooking, both women's tasks, increased, as did the number of pots that had to be cleaned afterwards, another job that was undertaken by the women.

In addition, a hearth had only needed to have the ashes swept out before a new fire was laid; a kitchener too had to have its ashes emptied and sifted daily, but then a number of new cleaning stages had to be undertaken twice a week. The flues had to be cleaned, any spilled grease scraped away, and abrasives used on the metal; then the cast-iron areas were blackleaded: the work of almost six and a half hours.

The kitchen was only one area where men's household work was outsourced. Mass production of shoes meant that men did less leatherwork at home; mass production of household implements, from spoons to plates to clothes-pegs, released men from whittling and carving for the household; commercial butchery, and later refrigeration and railway transport, made home butchery redundant. And while all these items could be purchased, freeing men from hundreds of hours of labour, it was not they who took on the new task of shopping for these goods. Buying was women's work. Other jobs remained in the house but, as they became less physically arduous, they too switched from being men's work to being women's. Men had emptied the waste from privies, carting it to fields to be used as manure, or in towns to be sold to farmers; cleaning their replacements, flush-lavatories, was women's work.

Technology for the most part did not alter men's domestic tasks, it made them disappear. While technology altered some of women's tasks, for the most part their work did not vanish. Candle-making had been a terrible chore – 'sevenfold worse in its way even than the washing day', according to Harriet Beecher Stowe. When oil lamps became both cheap and efficient, making candles was no longer necessary, but the lamps themselves required repetitive and time-consuming maintenance. Other jobs for women increased. The world of trade and industrialization brought cheap textiles, with cottons and muslins becoming the most common fabrics for clothes, replacing the traditional wool. While women no longer had to spin and weave, they had to shop for fabric, and they continued to have to sew it; cottons were less expensive, but they were also less durable, and so everyone had more clothes, which meant more sewing for women. Even 'labour-saving' sewing machines in reality increased the amount of work women did. As clothes could be produced more quickly with a machine, fewer women hired seamstresses or went to dressmakers, instead making their own, at least in part. New clothing styles for men popularized shirts that no longer had detachable collars and cuffs: now the entire garment had to be washed. And finally, wool, being difficult to wash, had most often just been brushed; cottons could be, and therefore were, washed more frequently, increasing the household's laundry, one of the heaviest of all housekeeping chores. Even a blessing such as running water, and stoves with boilers that heated it, led to baths becoming more frequent: more cleaning of baths, more washing of towels.

Household cleaning took longer more generally. Coal fires were dirtier than wood ones, while the new lighting technologies and improved glass for windows meant that the dirt was also more visible. Windows that had previously been small, with tiny panes of glass, or with no glass at all, were glazed and enlarged, and needed to be washed regularly; then, as 'Glass windows must have curtains', so fabric had to be purchased, sewn and then regularly laundered. Meanwhile, brick or earthen floors were being replaced by wooden ones, and then covered with newly affordable carpets, producing two layers that needed to be cleaned. Likewise the new world of commodities brought increased quantities of household objects, both functional and ornamental, all of which also had to be cleaned.

By 1940, middle-class housewives equipped with the latest in labour-saving technologies actually spent more time on housework than their mothers had at the turn of the century: because fewer households had servants; because technology had reduced heavy labour, so more work was undertaken by the housewife, and less by commercial services; and because, finally, the new technologies and advances in science had, when combined with older views of women's roles, produced a change in expectations of living standards. An acceptable standard of living was no longer a matter of what could be achieved within the economic unit of the family. Now it was, said one advice book, 'a set of attitudes towards certain values, toward articles to be bought and used, services to be paid for, and conditions under which we prefer to live'.

Together technological advances and alterations in standards ensured that a woman's work not merely increased in the house itself, but now spread outside, even when she didn't officially 'work'. Public transport, and then cars, removed the need for service-providers to bring goods and services to the house; instead housewives increasingly travelled to places of business, whether shops, or locations where services were offered, such as doctor's surgeries, or workshops, where goods were made or repaired. And in the USA towards the end of the nineteenth century, even where goods continued to be delivered, they were no longer brought by a regular procession of individual traders but, as catalogue shopping spread, came as a once-a-day drop through the letter box. Technology, for women, came accompanied by solitude.

Few, if any, of the steps that produced the isolated 1950s suburban housewife had been intended to have anything to do with domestic life at all. At the start of the nineteenth century, Napoleon had offered prize money for the invention of a method of long-term food preservation, to feed his armies on campaign. Sealed tin casings, it was discovered, could be heated sufficiently to, as later was understood, destroy the bacteria that cause putrefaction. The original food tins weighed over 3 kilograms and could be opened only with a hammer and chisel, hardly a housewife's dream. Production of tinned food in the USA was initially geared to supply Civil War soldiers, but with the end of the war, the new industry merely adapted its products for home consumption. By the 1870s the Chicago meat-packing industry was established, and by 1892 even such exotic items as Hawaiian pineapples were available in tins. The invention of the rotary tin-opener came in 1890, and soon tinned food was an everyday household item. Tinned food, in turn, led both to fewer outings to shops, and to fewer tradesmen making daily or weekly visits to the house. At the same time, while the technology of ice-chests had long been known, by the end of the century mass production brought them within reach of many of the middle classes, which in turn reinforced the shifts in household buying-patterns precipitated by tinned foods, even before the arrival of electric refrigerators just as World War I was ending. That meat, fruit and vegetables could be bought in quantity and kept over a long period of time further decreased women's contact with the outside world.

As with ice-chests, so with oscillating washing machines, which washed clothes at the turn of a crank, and which arrived in the 1880s and 1890s. Weekly laundry for a family of four took a hired washer-woman two days, for which she charged 16s. A machine cost £8, ten weeks' worth of a laundress's wages, and reduced the time spent on laundry by half, enabling the housewife to tackle it herself, or with the help she already had in the house.* It is unsurprising, therefore, that there were nearly a thousand dealers selling these machines in Britain by 1892, and the USA had many more. As electricity reached more households, the market expanded and prices continued to drop. In 1926, nearly 1 million machines were sold, at about $150 each; less than a decade later the price was $60, or, in Britain, £25, and nearly half as many again were being sold annually.

The mechanization of these tasks, decreasing as it did the need for hired help, was the continuation of a long progression whereby technology was harnessed to increase the privacy of householders. In 1663, Pepys had installed a bell outside his bedchamber to summon a servant. The distance the sound carried was not great (and, failing to wake their servant, he resolved to 'get a bigger bell'). Nonetheless, it was further than a human voice travelled, enabling, for the first time, family spaces to be separate from servants' spaces. When bells were connected by wires, in Britain from the 1770s, in Germany from the 1830s, a still greater distance between family and servants could be established. Germany and Scandinavia led the use and technological development of porcelain stoves that heated rooms better than open fires did, and could be re-fuelled from passageways outside the room

---

* At this stage the machines had to be started, stopped and the water filled and emptied manually – the one automated procedure was the rotating and rubbing of the laundry. That even this reduced the work so substantially gives a very clear indication of how arduous the task had been.

they were heating: the family remained warm without their activities being interrupted by servants coming and going. The British, unwilling to give up their fireplaces even for increased privacy, had buckets of coal set by the fire, which enabled several hours of privacy before the bucket had to be replenished by a servant. In dining rooms, too, the installation of dumbwaiters, which delivered food without servants being present, increased separation between servants and the family; for the less well-off, chafing-dishes performed the same function.*

Central heating and lighting technologies increased privacy too. The cost and labour-intensive nature of fires meant that the family, and often their servants, routinely gathered in the one room that had a fire. Gas lighting and oil lamps also promoted the group nature of activities, keeping the family around a central table that was used for sewing, reading and writing. Central heating, when it arrived, however, heated an entire house, or at least an entire floor, and there was no reason now for different, sometimes conflicting, tasks to be performed in the same space. Electricity meant that lamps could either be placed in different areas of one room, or they could be in separate rooms. Now the residents could occupy the entire house comfortably, each of them warm and well lit in their own room, at little extra expense.

Single items of technology followed a similar pattern. When telephones were first installed in private houses, it was generally in the most public space in the house, often the hall. They then migrated from public to private rooms, first to a living room or kitchen, and

---

* An advertisement for an electric chafing-dish in 1904 boasted that it could be used on a train or in a hotel room. It was not male travellers who were expected to cook when away from home, but women who, instead of joining the men in dining-cars or hotel restaurants, could carry their home-like isolation with them. It seems unlikely that this was common, but that advertisers thought it desirable is telling.

then to bedrooms. Radio migrated from being the centre of the living room, the surrogate hearth around which families gathered in newly centrally heated, fireless rooms, to being a transistor that was carried from room to room, then to a Walkman and finally an iPod or an app on a mobile phone, the private possession of a single person. Television initially took over radio's hearth-substitute position, before it too moved to kitchens and bedrooms, and, with iPads and tablets, also became something that was tied to an individual, turning what had been a communal family activity into an entirely private one.

In the twenty-first century, technology has created the possibility of many private entertainments occurring in each family member's private space. But one of the most important pieces of privacy-creating technology was a twentieth-century one, one that returned the house as a whole to a state of isolation from its neighbours: the car. In the American Midwest, as early as the 1920s, residents had already noticed a change. By 1923, two out of every three families in the town of Muncie, in Indiana, had a car, and yet many mourned the vanished summer evenings and Sundays spent sitting on front porches 'visiting' with neighbours in these outdoor rooms as the world walked past. Now people went out for a drive, whizzing past those on porches without stopping to talk. By World War II front porches on existing buildings were often used as little more than covered entranceways, while new houses more commonly had their porches situated at the rear, away from exhaust fumes and noise. Horses and buggies had been noisy, and smelly too, but their relatively low speed and the accessibility of the passengers meant they also fostered sociability. There was no longer any point to front porches, and the house increasingly turned in on itself.

In Britain, likewise, by the end of the nineteenth century, the little street-facing balconies of the Regency period were no longer in fashion, replaced instead by railings that kept house-fronts at a distance from passers-by, which became the default design for middle- and upper-class urban housing, while their raised ground floors lifted the life of the interior above the life of the street and out of sight. Where gardens fronted houses, hedges were planted to add a further barrier between passers-by and home-owners. Hedgerows had originally been planted on the borders of grazing and agricultural land to stop animals from straying; as the familiar suburban privet hedge they were repurposed, now designed to stop neighbours' eyes from straying. (Front gardens continue to be found in many of Britain's residential areas today, but they are barely, if ever, used by adults as an extension to the house, a place to be sociable: if people sat in their front gardens, they would be considered decidedly odd.)

Yet even as the house, and the housewife, became increasingly isolated, housework became increasingly subject to scrutiny from outside. While domestic manuals, the nineteenth-century descendant of the earlier conduct manuals, had been popular for the previous half-century, they had been written by, and for, supposed amateurs. The start of the twentieth century saw housework take on many of the aspects of a profession. In factories, a new type of manager, the efficiency expert, was being employed to advise on layout and design to maximize output and therefore profits. The American efficiency expert and writer Christine Frederick, who was married to another of these experts, extrapolated her husband's experience to what she bluntly referred to as '*my* factory', her house, to enormous success. In *The New Housekeeping: Efficiency Studies in Home Management* (1912–13), she positioned the housewife in the consumer economy, instructing her on how to purchase mass-produced goods efficiently and how to install and utilize new technology for her household's benefit. For Frederick and her many readers, the output that in a factory was measured in profit was at home measured by the comfort and professional advancement of her family.

If housework had come to be written of as a profession, then how was it that the house, and its housewife, continued to be considered part of the private sphere? Mrs Beeton, in 1860, had compared the housewife to the commander of an army, or 'the leader of any enterprise', both openly and publicly male roles, but if anyone at all noticed it, and there is little indication that they did, it was no doubt considered to be nothing more than a rhetorical device. But she, like Christine Frederick after her, was also unusually frank about the commercial and public aspects of women's work. More common were the experts who cloaked the new field of scientific and industrial management in the language of stereotypical femininity. Frederick W. Taylor, one of the founders of the profession of scientific management and industrial efficiency, wrote the introduction to Mary Pattison's *The Principles of Domestic Engineering* (1915). Both title and subtitle – *an attempt to evolve a solution of the domestic 'labor and capital' problem – to standardize and professionalize housework – to reorganize the home upon 'scientific management' principles – and to point out the importance of the public and personal element therein as well as the practical* – stated baldly that this was a book about business. But from then on, while implicitly the text made clear that the author fully understood that the private sphere she was describing was an integrated part of public life, both she and Taylor did their level best to disguise the fact. Taylor assured her readers that applying his business model to the house would not make women neglect the 'aesthetic' element of home-making, and added comfortingly that Pattison was 'always...well and artistically dressed'. And Pattison's frontispiece echoed his aside, being a photograph of the indeed well-dressed author, with a caption reading 'An Attempt'. Not only is the author disguising her labour, but the humility of the caption further downplays her achievement.

While the ambiguous nature of the housewife's job was thus contested – was it a job, or an offshoot of gender? – the language of the home straightforwardly acknowledged the porous nature of both public and private spheres. The Dutch word *gezellig*, most commonly translated as simply 'cosy', means far more to the Dutch, both physically and emotionally. An etiquette book from 1938 outlines the duties that help create feelings of *gezelligheid* entirely in terms of a housewife's role: the housewife must ensure that the room's furniture is comfortable and elegant; further, she must ensure the room is clean and tidy, with pretty flowers well arranged; and then she must provide delicious refreshments. But in daily usage it is clear that *gezelligheid* was, and is, as much something that is experienced in public, communal spaces as in private ones. Eating out can be *gezellig*; some cafés, restaurants, bars or parties can be *gezellig*. This epitome of home words in reality clearly describes something that is felt as much in public as in private.

In the nineteenth century, magazines and newspapers frequently used the words 'family', 'home' and 'household' in their titles, to emphasize that these were publications to be read at home, that although they were the products of commercial enterprise, they were to be consumed as part of the private world. There was *The Family Herald, The Christian Family Advocate, The Illustrated Family Budget of News, The Family Guardian, The Home News, The Christian Tomes and Home Journal, The Bristol Household News* and many more. The British Library catalogue lists sixty-four newspapers published between 1800 and 1900 that incorporate the world 'family' in their titles, but only fifteen dating from 1900 to 2000. This doesn't mean that the notion of family became less enticing. It just migrated. No longer as frequently attached to commercial items that were brought into the home, from the twentieth century the words 'family' and 'home' were repeatedly attached to commercial industries outside the home, to suggest subliminally to customers that these businesses were their intimates: family restaurants, family holidays, leisure parks that are 'fun for all the family', hotels that are 'a home from home', 'homemade' supermarket food and more.

In the twentieth century, the commercial utilization of the idea of home merely made explicit what had long been an unspoken reality: there might be no place like home, but most of its component parts could be purchased.

4

Home Furnishings

In 1785, the poet William Cowper wrote a verse paean to domesticity, the first section of which is entitled 'The Sofa'. Then, to evoke 'The Winter Evening', another section begins with a postman making his rounds before the action swiftly moves from the dark outdoors to draw a picture of the comforts to be found inside:

> Now stir the fire, and close the shutters fast,
> Let fall the curtains, wheel the sofa round,
> And while the bubbling and loud hissing urn
> Throws up a steamy column, and the cups
> That cheer but not inebriate, wait on each,
> So let us welcome the peaceful evening in.

By the late eighteenth century, even a modest household, here represented by its symbolic focus, the fireplace, was deemed worthy of an English poem. So too were the new luxury commodities that these households routinely possessed – curtains, a sofa, china, implicitly tea.*

Previously, the architects of houses of the great had used furniture as part of their overall design schemes, the location of each individual

---

* From Cowper onward, tea was frequently referred to as 'the cup that cheers', and the phrase is generally attributed to him, even though he borrowed it from Bishop Berkeley, who applied it rather less domestically to tar-water, a medicinal drink made from pine resin.

piece carefully chosen to counterpoint an architectural element. The room's aesthetics, rather than the behaviour or needs of the people in the room, were the guiding factor: the space and its fittings were one. So tables were placed between windows, commodes beside doorways, chairs against walls, all to complement the structure's proportions. In the post-Renaissance world, the ornamental furniture of the great was an expression of its owners, and their household, objects of display, not of utility.

But apart from such display pieces, even the very rich otherwise expected their houses to be filled with purely utilitarian, multi-purpose items of furniture, to suit their multi-purpose rooms. The word 'furniture' in English derives, via French, from Old High German, ultimately from the verbs to supply or to provide; most other European languages, however, make clear furniture's mobile history. French *meubles*, Italian *mobili*, Portuguese *mobiliário*, Spanish *meubles*, German *Möbel*, Dutch *meubilair*, Norwegian and Danish *møbler*, Swedish *möbler*, Polish *meble*, Russian мебель: all clearly derive from the same root that gives English the word 'mobile'. And true to this etymology, furniture for use, rather than for display, which included all furniture for everyone but the very wealthiest, was historically almost perpetually on the move.

In part, furniture was mobile because there was very little of it, and what there was necessarily moved around to fulfil many and different needs. Until well into the late seventeenth century the household furnishings of the modestly prosperous were so scanty that it is possible to itemize them almost entirely in a few sentences. In England the main room in such houses had a table, benches, a chair, a cupboard; those with more money or land would have had another chair or table, and perhaps a decorative element, possibly a painted wall-cloth, or cushions or a bench cloth. The fireplace had its own furnishings: a gridiron, a flat rack to stand pans on; cob-irons, or bars for the fire that had hooks to hold meat-spits; the spits themselves; and pothooks, from which a stewpan hung. Less well-equipped houses might not even contain a gridiron or pothooks. Kitchens, where they existed, held the pots and pans, kettles, plates or trenchers that were in most houses more commonly kept in the hall. In wealthy households, kitchens were also the location for equipment for activities such as preserving, dairying, brewing or baking. But these kitchens were for storage and food preparation, not cooking, and they never had any furniture: nothing to sit on, not even a table. Lower down the scale, the entire household goods and furnishings of one late-seventeenth-century labourer consisted of a tabletop without legs (buckets or barrels probably substituted), a cupboard, two chairs, a bench, a tub, two buckets, four pewter dishes, 'a flagon and a tancard', three kettles and a pot; a bed with two blankets and three pairs of sheets; a trunk, two boxes, a barrel and a coffer, a drainer, and assorted 'lumber and trash and things forgot'.

This man was by no means impoverished. His three sets of sheets marked him as a man of some substance, and, even more, so did the bed, for beds were far from common. Until the fifteenth century, most Europeans slept on sacks stuffed with straw or dried grass, which were nightly placed on boards, benches or chests, or directly on the floor, in the main, or only, room. In the colonies, in Maryland and Virginia, up to 80 per cent of lower middle-class households had no beds at this date. Many slaves slept in barracks, or in basements or attics, kitchens or stables, or in more makeshift fashion on stair-landings and in corridors, and while they might have bedding (although they might not), there were rarely any beds. Even in the eighteenth century, when purpose-built slave quarters had begun to be built, the low level of personal possessions – a few stools, tables, chairs or benches

– meant that at most the fortunate had a low-level bedframe topped with, perhaps, a straw-filled mattress and a blanket for sleeping. A person who slept on a bed, or even sat on it in the daytime, was like the person who had the chair – the chair-man – the head of the household, and of a household that had some cash to spare. In the Netherlands in the seventeenth century, a plain bedstead cost up to 25 guilders, or five weeks' income for a labourer; a four-poster was 100 guilders or more, depending on its decorative elements. In some regions of Italy as late as the eighteenth century, it might take six years for a labourer to save enough to buy a bed and bedding.

Altogether, often more than half of a family's wealth was invested in its beds, bedding and clothing. For this reason, beds were given pride of place in the main room, where visitors were able to see them. The grandest beds in the richest households were state beds, perhaps slept in once in a generation by a royal personage on progress, or never slept in at all, simply functioning as a symbol of the family's status, expressed in both materials and craftsmanship: carved wood posts, bed-curtains hanging on three sides, their elaborately embroidered rare fabrics then topped by layers of valances in yet more rich fabrics, all possibly further embellished with braid and fringe.

Until the seventeenth century in both the Netherlands and England, a curtain was sometimes a fabric hanging placed in front of a door, or a fireplace, to protect the room's inhabitants from draughts. But most often a curtain meant a bed-curtain, which surrounded four-posters in much of England, or the open side of cupboard-beds in the Netherlands. And then suddenly a great change arrived. In the seventeenth century, the increasing supply of textiles, both manufactured at home and imported via the new eastern trade routes, and their decreasing cost, created new possibilities for household decoration, and the Low Countries participated enthusiastically, demonstrating a hearty appetite for display. Fabrics were among the most expensive decorative household objects, and by placing them in the windows, home-owners were signalling their wealth publicly.

In 1653, Wolfgang Heimbach, a German painter trained in the Netherlands and working at the royal court in Copenhagen, painted what is believed to be the earliest known representation of a pair of curtains, divided to frame a window (see plate section, no. 12). Although, as we have seen, verisimilitude in paintings, no matter how apparently naturalistic, is not a given, it is possible that this painting does depict something the artist saw, including as it does a small rod for pulling the curtains closed without risk of damage to the fabric. This touch of practicality suggests that the room may really have been furnished in this way. It is known, too, that several aristocratic households also participated in the new fashion at the same date. Ham House was using symmetrical curtains in some of its windows at roughly the same time, and by 1679 they were also seen in Dublin Castle.

In the following century, curtains became fully fledged status displays, some lavish beyond imagining. France led the way in this, as in so much to do with interior decoration for the upper classes. In 1755, the windows in the apartments of Mme de Pompadour, mistress to Louis XV, were framed with 'a blind in Italian taffeta painted with translucent bouquets and garlands...the cord in silk and gold, with a pear-shaped tassel ornamented with spinach seeds, jasmine flowers, and sequins'. Many more who were not quasi-royalty, or even aristocrats, but were just rich, now elaborated their original desire to have their windows covered for privacy into a profusion of layers of different fabrics: first blinds; then, to cover their roller mechanisms, valances; then draping to cover the curtain rods; and, later, sheer fabrics over the glass, while heavy fabrics framed them on each side.

It took far longer for even simple paired curtains to reach the affluent middle classes, and longer still until the additional drapery and swags did. A watercolour by a Danish customs-house inspector, Friderich Lütken, of his study in Elsinore in 1765, shows single curtains at all three windows; only in a drawing of the same room approximately fifteen years later do paired curtains appear.

Many items of household furnishings followed a similar route, beginning as a functional object before becoming a costly item of display. In *Romeo and Juliet*, written in the 1590s, the Capulets' servants are ordered to 'give room', or make space, for the dancing by removing the furniture after the meal: 'Away with the join-stools, remove the court-cubbert' (a movable sideboard used to display plate) and 'turn the tables up', which was done by lifting the tabletop off its trestle legs, and turning it on its side to store it.* It was only from the end of the seventeenth century, as some of the great houses began to allocate a separate room for eating in, that heavy tables that were not routinely moved came into use. Even the rich, who had the income but not necessarily the space, were slow to adopt these pieces; lower down the social scale they were unknown. One-room living – or even two- or three-room living – was not conducive to heavy, single-purpose furniture. Instead small, light tables continued to be moved around the room to serve different purposes: the family ate on a table near the fireplace before pushing it against a wall so they could sit near the fire between meals, or sleep in front of it at night.

Householders moved their table around, that is, if they had one, and sat at it if they had anything to sit on. Most people did not. In the

---

* Traces of the movable history of tables can still be heard in English idiom: tables continue to be turned, if only metaphorically, laying, setting and clearing tables are equally metaphorical, since in none of these cases is a table actually laid or set out or cleared away any more.

Middle Ages chairs were found in courts, and in the homes of the very great, but rarely anywhere else. Their purpose was to convey status and power, and rank was indicated by types of seating: those who sat in the one or two chairs available were clearly privileged. In Louis XIV's reign, the highest-ranking at court sat in chairs with arms, the next level down in chairs without arms, below them, people sat on stools with backs, below them again, on backless stools, and finally there were folding stools. Yet even the stools did not demarcate the lowest level of court society: many at Versailles were not entitled to sit at all, but remained standing at all times in the presence of their betters.

Below this level in the seventeenth century, chairs were found only intermittently in daily life, and were by no means routine items of household furniture, whether in Europe or the colonies. In Plymouth, Massachusetts, in 1633, a household valued at £100 – very wealthy – possessed two chairs. Half the houses in Connecticut before 1670 had no tables, and while 80 per cent had chairs, each household averaged fewer than three, less than half as many as there were residents. As late as the mid-eighteenth century, a third of houses in one county of Delaware still had no tables, and the same number had no chairs. Some adult family members sat on benches or chests at meals, their food resting on their laps, while children rarely had chairs, and were usually expected to stand while they ate. In the Netherlands, Jan Steen's 1665 *A Peasant Family at Meal-time* shows only the man of the household with a seat at the trestle table (see plate section, no. 20). If there was enough seating for the adults, children might be allowed to use a chest while they ate off their laps, or, if there was a more than usual amount of furniture, they might sit on chests with their trenchers on stools beside them.

Well through the seventeenth century, chests, or trunks, or boxes, were the primary objects of use, as storage of course, but also as seating, as a flat surface to eat from and, later in the day, as a base for bedding. As the most multi-functional pieces of furniture, they were therefore the most useful. But as is so often the case with multi-functional items, chests, in doing everything, were never ideal for any of the single purposes they served. Even as storage spaces, their primary function, they have drawbacks. If a chest is carefully packed, things can be kept in separate layers within its single space. Even so, each layer has to be lifted out in order to reach items in the layer beneath. There is also no way of keeping disparate items apart, and indeed it appears that not only was there, initially, no separation of different types of stored items, but apparently there was no thought that this might be practical. In Bologna in 1630, a theft of linen and cheese from the same trunk was recorded without surprise.

While most houses continued to rely on the centuries-old storage–seating combination, a quiet storage revolution was brewing, with the Low Countries once again leading the way. The design of the chest, so simple, began to be modified. Each alteration, at each stage, must have seemed negligible. In the late fourteenth and early fifteenth centuries, short legs were affixed to deeper chests, so that their users no longer had to bend over headfirst in order to reach the bottom. But even this small increase in their height prevented the chest from being used as seating, so at first these leggy chests were found only in rich households, which could afford both chests and stools or benches.

What might have been a drawback, that chests were now confined to a single use, in fact permitted further modifications. That they opened from above had been a constraint on innovation: their height had to be limited, or access to the contents became impossible. In the sixteenth century, however, the hinges were moved from the top to the front panel. Now the legs could raise the chest to any height below eye-level, and the new side-opening had the added benefit that the entire contents could be seen at a glance: no longer did each layer have to be lifted out to reveal the one below. Shelves, which previously had only been affixed to walls, were adapted for use inside the new side-opening chests, to create a more definitive separation of, and support for, the stored items. With that, the chest ceased to be a chest. It had evolved into a cupboard.

As with beds, tables and chairs, cupboards began as luxury items for the wealthy. A chest might already cost a craftsman two weeks' wages, but a cupboard, if carved, was twice the price, while one made from a more elegant wood might cost six times more. By the late seventeenth century, however, prices had dropped, and in the Netherlands middle-class housekeeping had come to revolve around two cupboards. One was usually for storing eating utensils, the other for linens – bedding and personal items such as shirts, collars and caps – coats, silver and gold items, and Bibles and prayer books, particularly if they had decorative metal hinges or mounts. These cupboards, and their contents, were status symbols, and therefore they were almost always placed in the *voorhuis*, the front room. A poem reminded a Dutch bride that 'All the precious beauty in the world…[was] gathered in [her] cupboard', but it was not for her alone; rather, it was a 'treasure to be admired' by 'many guests'. China, delftware, pewter and silver were displayed in sets along the top of the cupboards (see plate section, no. 4). (This style did not travel. As late as the 1720s, Daniel Defoe looked back with little admiration to the habits of the late Queen Mary, English-born but resident in the Netherlands from the age of fifteen until her return as queen aged twenty-seven; she had, he noted, brought with her 'the custom…[of] piling…china upon the tops of cabinets', which he thought led to 'fatal excesses'.)

Another new type of furniture, the chest-of-drawers, arrived in the same century. Drawers had been in use for two centuries, as a method of storing ecclesiastical documents. While tables had occasionally had a drawer under the flat surface, and the German *Stollenschränke*, chests on legs, also sometimes had one or two drawers under the main cupboard area, they were otherwise almost unknown outside the church world. It was at Versailles in 1692 that the first secular furniture in which drawers were the primary component made its debut: the chest-of-drawers, in French a *commode*, or 'convenience'.* The new piece of furniture was wonderfully useful, and it spread swiftly, both geographically and down the economic scale. In the 1730s, walnut chests-of-drawers with an integrated glass-fronted display case above were the fashion among courtiers in Brunswick; by the end of the century more than half of working men in Paris had at least one simple chest-of-drawers. Now, as a Dutch poem instructed, 'Everything has its place and everything in its place.'

Another innovation, also French, brought even greater changes to furniture design. Padded furniture had appeared in the seventeenth century, and the technique spread quickly among the highest in society, and even abroad: we know that by the late seventeenth century Whitehall Palace in London contained at least two upholstered

---

* The meaning of commode, convenience, has seen the word used, although now rarely, in the UK as a synonym for that ultimate convenience, the chamber-pot, and also for its container, the chamber-pot cupboard; in some parts of the USA commode is used this way, but in others it has migrated to mean a lavatory. The various euphemisms for this object, and the room that contains it, also need clarifying. Before the twentieth century, the British lavatory was a place to wash; after that, the word was transferred to the lavatory itself (which is the way I use it here), or to the room in which the lavatory was located. US usage varies with geography, a lavatory being a sink, the room that contains a sink or, as in the UK, a WC. It was not merely furniture that evolved: so too did its vocabulary.

chairs.* By the end of the century, padding was being added to the seats of chairs, and horsehair stuffing to their back-supports. The early method of stuffing, where padding was tacked directly on to the wood, was replaced by a more sophisticated method, where intervening stretchers allowed the padding to be suspended from a frame. The stuffing could now be held in place by stitching across the entire surface, which meant that larger areas could be upholstered. The stretcher also allowed the fabric coverings to be replaced, and now chairs became fashion items.

For centuries, chairs, tables, benches and other furniture had all remained lined up in rows against the walls unless they were in use, the centre of every room remaining empty most of the time. When needed, individual pieces of furniture were pulled into place, and then, after use, were again returned to the wall. Over the course of the eighteenth century, as the decorative element of furniture came to be considered equal to its utilitarian purpose, this arrangement began to seem old-fashioned. The more informal court-style of Louis XV led the way: here furniture was placed not to awe and impress, but to aid socialization. Chairs and tables were arranged in groups throughout a room, whether they were in use or not – it was almost as though now, in empty rooms, the furniture was socializing on its own. And with this change in emphasis, chairs began to be designed not merely for utility (in lesser houses), or for display (in the houses of the great), but foremost for both social interaction and comfort: they were wider, with their seats set lower to the ground, and, most importantly of all, they were upholstered. Ease now appears to have

* These two walnut armchairs are attributed to Thomas Roberts, furniture-maker to the royal palace from 1686 to 1714, and their upholstery is thought to be by the French craftsman Jean Poitevin, who also worked for the English court. (The chairs are now at Knole, in Kent.)

become desirable. And sure enough, the paintings of this period show people lying back in their chairs, or leaning casually on the arms of chaises. Upholstered furniture provoked a change in patterns of use; the changing use provoked further changes in design; the changes in design in turn encouraged new changes in patterns of behaviour. And so furniture that encouraged sociability became as important as furniture designed for display.

The first entirely new piece of seating designed for both sociability and comfort, the sofa, encouraged the shift. By its nature – upholstered, and with seating for two or more – the sofa was no longer about a single person's display of authority. By 1743, Horace Walpole, that man of fashion, casually wrote in a letter, 'I am not quite so much at my ease as on my own sofa'. His correspondent was forced to admit that he didn't know what a sofa looked like, but he could not have remained ignorant for long. In the second half of the eighteenth century, the amount of seating in all households increased sharply, not coincidentally as upholstery techniques and padded furniture became more widespread. By the late eighteenth and nineteenth centuries, instead of the earlier paucity of chairs that surprises us today, houses began to be so full of chairs that it is difficult to imagine where they all went, or what purpose they served. In the seventeenth century, a barber-surgeon in Battersea owned elegant green and gilt hangings, a mirror, several tables, one fabric and two leather carpets, but just one 'couch chair' and one 'great chair'; seating in his fashionable house was still mostly on stools. By 1774, a Hamburg merchant owned eighteen beechwood chairs, upholstered in matching sets of six; a century later, in 1877, the cartoonist Linley Sambourne's London house contained sixty-six chairs, ten of them in the master bedroom. Among the wealthy, not only was there a superfluity of chairs, but they were frequently 'bought together', that is, they matched; they were for fashion, not utility, previously within the reach only of the wealthiest. What had been the prerogative of courts, or the very greatest houses, became increasingly common among the middling classes.

Until the first third of the nineteenth century, and later in many places, for most people below the rank of French kings, furniture, no matter how fashionable, remained pushed back against the walls. It was in Britain that the more informal style of furniture arrangement spread, under the influence of the Romantic movement, with its love of the picturesque, which prized the asymmetrical over classical order. In the drawing rooms, initially, of the middlingly prosperous in Britain it quickly became expected that furniture was permanently situated wherever it was deemed either comfortable or useful – by the fireside, by a window, by a communicating door, or in conversational groupings in the centre of the room. But outside the British prosperous middle-class, the radical overturning of a centuries-old habit took time to be accepted. One foreign visitor dismissed the practice: it made rooms look like furniture shops, he said. While grouped furniture today symbolizes rooms filled with sociability and conversation, the idiom of the time might suggest the opposite. In France and Germany, silence was known as '*une conversation à l'Angloise*' [sic]. It may, perhaps, therefore have been the very awkwardness of English social life that led to furniture being placed in more informal groups. One diarist recorded, 'At first sight, society abroad often appears formal to English taste, because…people do not sit in all parts of the room. But foreigners do not feel under any particular restraint…and never feel the slightest scruple in traversing the empty space if they wish to converse with any one on the other side.' The English, in contrast, he thought, used furniture 'to remedy' their native lack of sociability.

For decades after the new, more informal arrangements became common in all ranks of life, the style of the previous centuries remained a byword for old-fashioned stuffiness. In 1861, a woman complained that her husband's family home was 'exceptionally stiff and proper...you could not but feel if you moved a chair out of its place...it would of its own accord walk statelily [sic] home again... *back to the wall*.'*

As furniture moved permanently from the edges into the centre of rooms, smaller, lighter pieces of furniture became popular, defining individual sections of each room, and functioning as specialist aids to this new, more informal living style. Now small tables were set beside a chair to provide a place to put down a book, or next to a sofa for a cup and saucer, or nestled by the door to hold the household's bedroom candles; sewing tables were moved to whichever seat had the best light. Bedrooms were furnished with dressing tables (although bedside tables had to wait until the nineteenth century in much of Britain and Germany, a chair generally serving this purpose until then), and delicate writing tables for women, smaller than the desks that were the preserve of men's working spaces.

Most people welcomed these pieces for their convenience. Yet a minority dissented, not for practical reasons, but because they were somehow too insubstantial, too French. The aversion was both instinctive, and almost visceral – an upper-class Englishman at the end of the eighteenth century shuddered at the 'little skuttling' things, his objection apparently vested in their very lightness and mobility. Two decades later, at the other end of the political

---

* And it may be that traces of this older style have remained, all but invisible to modern eyes. Pubs in Britain were originally simply the front rooms of private houses, and were decorated as such, the bar counter being a nineteenth-century addition. Today's pub layouts, with tables and benches placed around an empty central space, might suggest a surviving remnant of pre-eighteenth-century furniture arrangement in daily use.

and economic spectrum, the radical journalist and MP William Cobbett was outraged that a simple farmhouse had 'a parlour!', and one furnished with a mahogany table, a sofa and even 'showy chairs', not to mention a carpet, a bell-pull, decanters, glasses, a dinner service and 'some swinging book-shelves'. It is hard to say what upset Cobbett more – the number of objects, their novelty or their quality. All these elements played a part in his outrage, no doubt, for they were all features of the great changes in domestic furnishings that had come with the Industrial Revolution.

Previously, the possessions of the upper classes had been distinguished from those of the less wealthy by their quality. They were made from rare materials, or costly ones, or, preferably, both. In the thirteenth century, a list of the contents of an English gentleman's house included, in its entirety: 'a decent table, a clean cloth, hemmed towels, high tripods [for the fireplace], strong trestles, firebrands, fuel logs, stakes, bars, benches, forms, armchairs, wooden frames and chairs made to fold, quilts, bolsters, and cushions'. While the economic and social distance between peasants and aristocrats was great, nevertheless comfortably-off peasants owned similar items: a table, at least one stool, a chest or two, pots and pans, cooking technology, serving dishes, spoons, drinking vessels, towels and bedding. The difference was almost entirely in the quality of the goods. And for centuries, that was how it remained. In the seventeenth century, one aristocratic Englishwoman wrote to her husband to discuss the acquisition of a number of household items. She grouped 'earthen things' (earthenware) or 'wouden things' merely by material, but when it came to porcelain, she listed each piece by its function as well: 'tee dishes & plates to them', 'a shuger thing' and a 'coufey pot'.

This woman would have recognized the impetus behind the comic parable written by the French philosopher Denis Diderot in 1772, in which he satirized the lust for fashionable novelty. The narrator of 'Regrets for My Old Dressing-Gown' relates his tragi-comic tale: once dressed in a glamorous new scarlet dressing-gown, he begins to feel his old desk looks shabby in comparison; on replacing that, the prints that are hanging above it now show their age, and so on, until his cane chair has been supplanted by a Moroccan-leather one, his pinewood bookshelves by inlaid marquetry cupboards, the old plain list rug by a Savonnerie carpet. He ends, finally, with a lament against the 'fatal longing for luxury', and inveighs against 'Sublime fashion that…empties our father's treasuries', as each new item produces a desire for another novelty.

This rage to buy was the culmination of a series of social upheavals. In the seventeenth century, the English and the Dutch had fought a cycle of wars in the attempt to gain domination of the world's markets. But the great discovery of the age was that trade was infinitely expandable, because desire was infinitely expandable. Unsatisfied desires continued to seek satiation, while satisfied desires only created new demands, which had to be satiated in turn. The expansion of trade made goods that had once been luxury items more widely, and inexpensively, available, which in turn drove down costs even further. These trade goods were not things that made daily life possible; they were things that made it more comfortable, or more enjoyable. And, readily available, these items, once reserved for the rich and aristocratic, became quickly assimilated into the daily life of bourgeois domesticity.

Bedding was one of the earliest consumer goods. Beds had originally been objects of status and display for those fortunate enough to have them, and significant proportions of a family's wealth were frequently invested in its bedding: in the seventeenth century, up to a third of a Dutch household's worth might be tied up in the bedding;

into the eighteenth it might be up to 40 per cent for a working man's family. More generally, a quarter of all expenditure on household goods was typically laid out on bedding upon marriage. Initially, the focus was on an increase in quantity, rather than quality: beds for more members of the household, or more mattresses. Mattresses were still nothing more than stuffed sacks, and increased comfort was achieved only by piling one mattress on top of another. Some engravings show beds with what may be up to five in a heap. This was followed by acquisition in range, with different types of bedding becoming available – bolsters, pillows, sheets, blankets, various types of covers, spreads and quilts. And then came improvement in quality: straw was replaced by hemp or flock stuffing, and then by wool; feathers ranged from down, to goosedown, to eider, while from the eighteenth century, factory-manufactured cotton waste was also available; finer wool blankets replaced felted ones; and flax and linen replaced coarse canvas.

All forms of fabric, particularly linens, an industry in which the Dutch excelled, were valued. While clothing styles remained fairly limited, the desire for quantity seemed ever-increasing, even among middling families. One seventeenth-century Dordrecht housewife owned nearly three hundred shirts, as well as bonnets, handkerchiefs, neckerchiefs and other linens – not just her own and her family's, but pieces inherited from her mother and grandmother as well. These were kept with her almost five hundred tablecloths and napkins, which had been set aside to pass on in turn to her children when they married. She was not unusual. A less well-to-do Amsterdam trades-man of the time owned sixty sheets and more than three hundred napkins.

Linens were just the most extreme example. Amsterdam tradesmen filled their houses with items of local manufacture that would have staggered their English counterparts. The very wealthiest lived in houses containing 'at least' fifty paintings, up to a dozen cupboards, as many as fifty chairs and ten or more tables. Mirrors were found in every home that had even a little disposable income, and so were clocks, maps, pewter, silver, vases, jugs, tea services, tiles, candlesticks, snuffboxes and books, all ranged on mantelpieces, tables and cupboards, or placed in cupboards behind glass doors. Amsterdam, as a great trading city, was also a showcase for the new luxury goods being imported from the east: ebony, silks, chintzes, cottons, or Japanese porcelain wine-pitchers made to order to traditional Dutch designs. For those with less money, local manufacturers copied the imports, often integrating Far Eastern shapes with Dutch motifs – delftware pitchers were one prized example. Even households with much lower incomes commonly contained mats on the floor, curtains, a mirror, one or two prints, or perhaps a painting. Everyone, wrote a visitor to Amsterdam in 1640, 'in generall striv[es] to adorne their houses' with 'Furniture and Ornaments…very Costly and Curious', including 'Ritche Cupboards, Cabinetts, etts., Imagery, porcelaine, Costly Fine cages with birds, etts.', which together make a space 'Full off pleasure and home contentment'. Nor was the urge to acquire confined to urban centres. Householders in rural areas quickly gained both knowledge of and access to the newest goods. Pendulum clocks were invented in 1657. Two decades later, no modestly prosperous Dutch farmer owned such a novelty; but twenty years after that, nearly nine in ten did.

In England, too, the spread of better quality goods occurred first among the wealthy, and by 1727 in Bath, that most fashionable of fashionable towns, the changes in construction materials of new houses, and their contents, were reminiscent of the Dutch gradations to their bedding, with improvements in both quantity and kind. Now floors were made of oak instead of the deal that had previously been considered good enough, and the floorboards were covered with carpets; walls were panelled instead of plaster, and marble chimneypieces replaced stone, while rush-bottomed chairs gave way to leather-upholstered ones, oak chests were replaced by mahogany and walnut chests-of-drawers. Mirrors appeared over mantelpieces, and brass fire-irons adorned hearths, while 'the Linnen for the Table and Bed grew better and better till it became suitable even for People of the highest Rank.' Households of the middling sort had somewhat broadened their number of possessions too. By the late seventeenth century over half owned tables, cooking pots and pewter dishes; nearly half had table linen; one in five owned a mirror, a chest-of-drawers or a cupboard or books; one in four owned some earthenware dishes; one in three a feather-bed. And as with the Dutch, as well as quantity, the reasonably affluent also turned their attention to quality, replacing their wooden trenchers with pewter, their wooden spoons with silver and their iron candlesticks with bronze. And yet at the same time, none of these middling households owned any cups at all, and barely any – under 1 per cent – had knives or forks. Just fifty years later, these houses were transformed: over three-quarters of households had not only tables, cooking pots and pewter, but also upholstered furniture; half had feather-beds, chests-of-drawers, earthenware dishes and mirrors; over a third had table linen; more than one in five owned books, clocks or pictures. The number of households possessing cups had risen from virtually none to one in six. In thriving parts of London, nearly everyone owned what had, half a century before, been rarities – earthenware dishes, books, clocks, pictures, mirrors, table linen, curtains, even cups. The consumer revolution had crossed the Channel. And then it crossed the Atlantic.

As this revolution spread, those who had the means but nevertheless did not choose to acquire or enjoy the fashions of the day were regarded as somehow failing in their obligations to society, just as previously among the landed gentry those who chose not to serve as magistrates, or attend church regularly, had failed in their duty to their class and birth. In 1715, it was reported, shockingly, that a wealthy planter in Virginia had 'nothing in or about his house... He hath good beds...but no curtains; and instead of cane chairs, he hath stools made of wood.'* For the successful, furniture had become a way of expressing gentility. A chair no longer conferred status only on the person who sat in it, but on the entire household in which it was found. Even those with very little could participate. Militiamen on the American frontier in 1744 owned brass snuffboxes, imported drinking glasses and earthenware, and they wore metal buckles on their shoes and knee-breeches. By the 1760s in Virginia, the wealthy began to wear imported silks, disdaining the imported cottons that, a generation before, they had been proud to purchase. These cottons were, in this new world of commodity, now fit only for their slaves. In the north, earthenware was within the reach of the working poor, and they could even afford to buy it in sets that matched, and in quantity, so that no one had to eat from shared dishes. These purchases were partly a matter of comfort, partly a matter of status, but none of them were a matter of necessity. And there was always something new to acquire. In 1758, a New York merchant was instructed by his British supplier that his order

* It must be stressed that this was life as lived among the elite in colonial Virginia, where otherwise 80 per cent of the population continued to inhabit, at most, two-roomed houses. In general, North America lagged behind Europe: as late as the 1750s, in parts of the mid-Atlantic states, only 65 per cent of households owned a table. A full century after that, many pioneer families continued to live in a style Europeans had left behind nearly two centuries previously.

for 'dishes' was meaningless, and he had to be far more specific. Did he want 'round or long common Dishes for Meat, Soup Dishes, or deep Sallad or Pudding Dishes'?

There were, of course, many who disapproved. Philosophers, educationalists and clergymen warned of the damage that was done to the moral fabric of the country by this new, and insatiable, appetite for things. In 1714, a magazine with a readership in the urban English upper classes claimed that the desire for these new goods was so great that, if women were not permitted by their husbands to purchase these things, they would trade their petticoats or their husbands' breeches for them. It was presented as a joke, but the intent behind it was serious: the necessities of life were, it suggested, being recklessly discarded for useless luxuries. It is notable that most who indulged in this type of debate in Britain tended to see the desires of the groups below or above them as damaging; their own desires, generally, were assumed to be proportionate and reasonable.

In the colonies, however, consumer goods became a political matter. The American Revolution and its boycott of, especially, manufactured textiles, which were almost entirely imported, turned what had previously been dismissed as frivolities into items with a symbolic status. Now consumption was an engine of revolution, and women, as the managers of household expenditure and the makers of domestic choices, had moral as well as economic force.

It is possible to view the American Revolution as a revolution of consumption. The spark that ignited the revolt was after all the imposition by the mother country of taxes on items of consumption, such as glass and, most famously, tea. And one of the most effective weapons of rebellion was therefore a consumer boycott of imported goods. The list of proscribed items, as one historian has noted, sounds very much like the contents of a fashionable shop, including as it does 'hats…furniture, gloves…shoes…gold and silver and thread lace…gold and silver buttons…plate…diamond, stone and paste-ware…clocks and watches, silversmith and jeweler's ware, broad cloths that cost above 10 shillings per yard, muffs, furs and tippets, and all sorts of millenery [sic] ware…china ware, silk and cotton velvets, gauze, pewter…lawns, cambricks, silks of all kinds, malt liquors…' The origin of these items had made them politically unacceptable; the goods themselves, however, continued to be valued. By general consensus, purchasing a new table, or curtains, or pewter, or even a cambric handkerchief manufactured in Britain was aiding the oppressor; purchasing North American versions of the same items was an act of support for the rebel cause: consumption as patriotism.

Such patriotism, combined with the new mass market which increased access to well-made, well-designed items in a range of prices and styles for many more of the population, came to make owning goods seem a democratic right. Each generation possessed more goods, and better quality goods, than the one before. This proliferation, together with the development in the meaning of goods, produced a change in how they were valued. And the change in value, in turn, also changed the most basic element of the possession of goods: how they were stored. The Dutch had long shown off their china and silver on the tops of cabinets; in Britain, sideboards had had display spaces for tea sets and other pieces of status ware. In the colonies, however, many had continued to use chests as their primary means of storage, which meant that the new consumer goods could only be seen when they were in use. By the mid-eighteenth century, the spread and elaboration in design of that democratic luxury, inexpensive earthenware, provided the impetus for a new fashion for cupboards, where the dishes could be displayed even when not in use. These cupboards in turn became objects of display in their own right, as Diderot's fable had foretold.

Other objects achieved their status not simply because they were desirable luxury goods in themselves, but as a result of developments that took place a world away. Sugar was the first new mass-consumed foodstuff, its price dropping sharply as trade routes were regularized. In the late seventeenth century in England, sugar consumption was less than a kilo per person annually; by the 1770s, that had risen to just under a kilo per person every fortnight. (A rise that seems almost impossible, until today's annual consumption – 37.5 kilograms – is considered.) Tea and coffee were initially luxury imports, and only in the eighteenth century, with the establishment of plantations under European control, did the consequent drop in price see tea, in particular, change from being an exotic drink taken in a public place to a comforting drink made at home. Soon milk and sugar were added to the original oriental beverage; the result saw it become a panacea. Even those who could not necessarily afford a hot dinner could afford this hot, sugary substitute. For the poor, the drink was enough. For the rich, the objects used to make and consume hot drinks were also markers of status: kettles, spirit-lamps, tea caddies, teapots, hot-water jugs, strainers, sugar basins, sugar tongs, milk jugs, slop bowls (which held the dregs of emptied teacups), teaspoons, cups and saucers, and more.*

The new commodities, the increase in the number of people who could purchase them, and most importantly the status that derived

---

* Chinese teaware soon became entirely unsuitable for British tea-drinking, so radically did the drink alter. Chinese handleless cups were fine for their twice decanted, and therefore cooled, drink, but not for tea served, British-style, as hot as possible. A handle was therefore added. This, together with the inclusion of milk in the drink, made larger cups more practical. The addition of sugar necessitated a small spoon, the teaspoon, to stir it with, and once there was a wet spoon, a saucer was needed to rest it on.

from their ownership and display, meant that birth alone was no longer sufficient to establish a person's place in society. Joseph Cabell was linked by birth and marriage to many of the great families of Virginia. But by the 1780s, to maintain what had been his by right at birth, a friend advised, 'you should have a home...Until you do this you can have no real weight or influence in society'. That 'home', of course, would be nothing more than a house until it was furnished, and furnishings alone were not enough. Cabell would only maintain the necessary social cachet if the interiors and objects were displayed to the right people. By the early nineteenth century, a visitor observed a similar development in Britain, and not merely among the upper classes: 'custom demands many luxuries...as much...at a shopkeeper's house as at the Duke's; a handsomely fitted up house, with elegant furniture, plate...a profusion of dishes...True hospitality this can hardly be called; it is rather the display of one's own possessions, for the purpose of dazzling...' Display had become the essence of the house. This public display of the private was considered to have a moral dimension too. Immanuel Kant thought that 'No one in complete solitude will decorate or clean his house; he will not even do it for his...wife and children...but only for strangers, to show himself to advantage.' Without a public face, the private sphere would not be maintained.

This is not to suggest that people in previous ages had been unconcerned by the appearance of household objects, but now many more owned objects whose appearance could be valued independently of their utility. From the end of the sixteenth century, it is possible to discern a widespread desire to be identified with one's possessions: initials were carved on boxes and chests, dates into lintels and mantelpieces, plaques bearing their owners' names were affixed on houses and barns. And even in small, rude one-room houses, with unplastered walls or earthen floors, even there, possessions were decorated, cupboards and chests were carved or painted in cheerful colours – they were considered worth making beautiful. But in the new urban, mercantile world, these goods, and others, were more commonly purchased than inherited, purchased to establish, or maintain, status. Because now paintings, furniture, china and ornaments were no longer solely the status symbols of the aristocracy, but the products of the marketplace, trade and mass production. And with urbanization, and the anonymity an increasingly mobile population created, appearances had more value than they had had when everyone's family history was known. The question now was, what do people, who may not know me at all, make of me based on what they learn as they pass my house? What do relative strangers think when they call on me? And thus the question of style, which until then had been an issue for the very rich, became important to the middling classes too. Their houses were expected to reflect the qualities of those who lived in them, to present their owners as people of taste and cultivation, of 'sensibility', to use the contemporary idiom.

This increasing enjoyment of appearance for appearance's sake did not meet with unanimous approbation. Adam Smith, in 1759, was disturbed by the lack of utility of many new goods. 'How many people ruin themselves by laying out money on trinkets of frivolous utility?…All their pockets are stuffed with little conveniences. They contrive new pockets…in order to carry a greater number. They walk about loaded with a multitude of baubles…all of which might at all times be very well spared…' Daniel Defoe's objection was grounded in the perceived threat to honest English manufacture. He viewed these new luxuries as foreign invaders infiltrating the country to despoil the simplicity of the good old days: Indian chintz fabrics 'crept into our houses, our closets and bedchambers, curtains, cushions, chairs, and at last beds themselves', replacing what had previously been English wools and silks.* Yet to others, this new consumerism was beneficial, serving the national interest through both trade and manufacture. In 1821, in Baltimore, *Niles' Weekly Register* wrote, 'We never reflect upon the progress and prospects of that portion of the national labor which is applied to household manufactures, without feeling our hearts warmed with a national pride; for all the virtues, moral, religious and political, are interested in it.' It was a virtuous circle: buying goods was patriotic because it promoted industry, industry enshrined national virtues, the goods were burnished with those virtues, which made those who possessed them better people.

But patriotism, industry, status and even fashion were not the only forces driving the spread of commodities. Another equally intangible benefit, also played a crucial role: comfort. Luxury, or merely costly, items, had been valued by the rich; in the new commodity markets, taste and comfort, both infinitely replicable, won the day. Comfort is an elastic word, and there were different ways of acquiring it. Some comfort was directly purchased, in new houses, or upholstered furniture. Comfort was also achieved via new technologies: rooms were better heated; they were better lit; and, particularly in the USA in the nineteenth century, where labour costs remained high in comparison to Europe, a plethora of labour-saving devices, especially for the kitchen – potato-peelers and -mashers, raisin-seeders,

---

* To Defoe in 1708, silk was a native English product, its French origins forgotten. The Huguenots who had fled religious persecution in France from the 1680s had become so well established as silk weavers in Spitalfields in the East End of London that by the early eighteenth century silk was considered to be as English as wool. In fact, the Huguenots had not historically been weavers, but took up the trade on their arrival in England. In France Protestants had been barred from employment in the Grandes Fabriques that held the monopolies.

coffee-grinders, cherry-pitters, apple-corers, meat-grinders and egg-beaters – produced another kind of technological comfort.

Yet even as comfort and ease through technology, upholstery and improved housing standards became widespread, the display of status could in some strata of society also be expressed by their very rejection. In Britain in the nineteenth century, technology made warmth, for example, more readily available. New, improved Rumford stoves burnt fuel more efficiently, producing more heat at lower cost. But the upper classes, with their many fireplaces, and many servants to clean and tend them, felt no need to make the change, and kept the older, more inefficient open fires. The middle classes, in emulation, also rejected the comfort that new technology might have brought them, instead genteelly and emulatively freezing in their drawing rooms. So too with lighting technology. With servants to tend candles and oil lamps, the rich could afford not to acquire the more efficient, but smelly and dirty, gas lighting. Homes without the new technology were therefore considered to be of higher status, and in 1857 a character in a novel by Anthony Trollope is marked out as irredeemably vulgar for installing gas. Similarly the rich in large houses could afford to devote a room, or many rooms, to activities that occurred only infrequently; the middle classes, with their parlours, did the same, even though their comfort was diminished by reducing the amount of space available for everyday living. Similarly, parlour furniture was not created with comfort in mind, but was designed to be admired, imitating, in small, often parochial form, the grand architectural statements of the French courts.

This was the theory, at least. While the origin of these domestic display rooms was located in the French courts, the parlour also drew on commercial spaces, hotels in particular, for its decorative effects. Then, as world fairs and expositions became popular in the second half of the nineteenth century, a variety of model rooms gave 'glimpses of the surroundings of the classes who set the fashions' to those with far less money. The reach of these showrooms was extended first via engravings, and then, when photographs could be inexpensively printed, magazines became prime disseminators of the ideal of home, and the ideal home. (The magazine *Ideal Home* first appeared in 1909 in the USA, and 1919 in the UK.) In 1876, Britain's *The World* ran a series called 'Celebrities at Home', which presented biographies of famous people – Disraeli, Rowland Hill (of penny-post fame), the philosopher Thomas Carlyle, the sensation-novelist Wilkie Collins, and Tennyson, the poet laureate. This had been done before, but now the magazine offered in addition photographs of what their twentieth-century equivalents would come to call 'their lovely homes'.* Thus the display style of a previous age was reinterpreted through elements drawn from commercial premises and from the houses of the famous, combined to produce an ideal of what a parlour should look like, one accepted by millions who could only ever aspire to such furnishings, but who none the less believed absolutely in the social merit they represented: the drapery, the piano, the mantelpiece loaded with ornaments; the damask or silk or embroidered or velvet fabrics; and the all-important matching 'suites' of furniture.

For one of the precepts of the parlour was that items in multiples, and in even numbers so they could be arranged symmetrically, were superior to the same number of single pieces: six chairs were most frequently advertised, although a dozen was preferred if space were available, with two armchairs to match. Tables, sofas, mirrors, all

---

* The desire to see people in their own houses spread into many curious places. Mme Tussaud's waxworks had shown murderers from the beginning of the nineteenth century, but after the arrival of 'At Home' journalism, the company began, for the first time, to purchase not merely the clothes of the convicted criminals, but the rooms in which the crimes had occurred, to be reconstructed for the delectation of the public.

were designed for display rather than utility, while china was placed carefully on what was known as a buffet (or a boffett, beaufat or bowfat).* These parlour furnishings were available both at enormous prices for the rich, and at modest ones for the rest – in the USA in 1897, a three-piece suite was available from Sears, Roebuck for $18.50. But whether expensive or economical, these items shared a common feature: they were designed not to be used. The chairs were often higher than would be comfortable for most people, upholstered in fabrics that were impossible to clean; the tables were narrow, to be set against a wall. The symbolic value of these furnishings had become all-important.

Even for those with little, the possession of objects, and their display, was not necessarily merely a matter of fashion or status. Individual objects could suggest a higher standard of living than a family had achieved, a way of indicating their owners' hopes and dreams. The pioneer mother of Laura Ingalls Wilder, who from the 1870s moved from log cabin to sod house to claim shanty across nearly 2,500 kilometres, carefully transported a china shepherdess to each new house, placing it ceremoniously on a purpose-built shelf that the children were not allowed to touch. After one move it was unpacked only once a wooden floor had replaced the house's original earthen one. Then, with a 'red-checked cloth on the table', she sighed, 'Now we're living like civilized folks again.'

The tablecloth – even for this family where furniture was constructed out of tree-stumps – was another sign of 'civilized' living, one of the markers of the new emphasis put on communal meals. As late as the seventeenth century, while the rich ate off pewter,

---

* Along the northeastern coast of North America, the word 'hutch', to mean a display dresser, is still in use, almost 150 years after the last citation in the *Oxford English Dictionary*.

or, among the greatest, silver or even gold, most had no individual dishes, and helped themselves directly from a central dish, into which food had been ladled from the cooking vessel. Over time more households began to acquire wooden trenchers or pewter dishes, and where that happened, diners were now expected to take their portion from the main platter with a knife and fingers. Earthenware and stoneware then began to replace wood and pewter: three-quarters of households in London and half of country families in Britain owned some earthenware goods by the early eighteenth century, a five-fold increase over half a century. After that, different types of china and tableware spread widely. By the last third of the century, many of the German middle classes naturally expected to own pewter, earthenware or porcelain. One Hamburg merchant had all of these things, as well as fifteen knives, twenty silver spoons, and a fork, while even a humble blacksmith and his family owned a number of cups, coffee pots, jugs, bowls, plates and soup plates, as well as fifteen spoons and three serving spoons.

The single fork and the odd numbers of knives and spoons are telling. Spoons dated back to the Romans, and had been used across Europe forever after, while table knives had arrived in Europe with the 'barbarian' invasions of the early Middle Ages. Both of these implements were regarded as personal items, belonging to the individual diner, rather than being household goods held in common, and visitors routinely brought their own with them. This pattern of behaviour is still reflected in several languages. In Italian, cutlery is *posate*, from the verb *posare*, to place: diners were expected to place their knives on the table when they were ready to eat. In German, the word is *Besteck*, a sheath, the one that held the knife that diners carried to the table (the sheath later expanded to include a spoon and fork too).

During the Renaissance, the sharp points of table knives were blunted, domesticating them for household mealtimes. As this new round-ended implement was no longer capable of spearing food to lift it from the serving dish on to an individual plate, another stabbing implement was needed to replace it. The Romans had used forks for cooking and in food preparation, but not at table; the fork had then vanished entirely from the continent, not reappearing until the tenth and eleventh centuries, as an import from the Byzantine Empire, and it remained a foreign oddity, not embraced by the general population. It was in the thirteenth and fourteenth centuries that forks became objects of daily use in Italy, when pasta became a local staple: unlike spoons and knives, forks are perfectly designed tools for noodles. The fork may have travelled to France from Italy with Catherine de' Medici, who married Henri II of France in 1547, but a quarter of a century later their son, Henri III, was still trying, and failing, to encourage their use. In Tudor England two-pronged sucket forks were used to spear sticky sweetmeats, but otherwise (larger) forks were known only as agricultural implements. Later, James I used a fork, but few imitated him. The masses certainly didn't, and the practice of eating with knives and spoons was what was exported to the new world. At Plymouth colony, from its foundation to the middle of the seventeenth century, spoons were the most common eating implement. Even knives were rare, while forks were, says one historian, simply 'non-existent'.

In the Netherlands in the same century, even in the heart of the new commodity market, while forks were not unknown, they were confined to the very rich. A merchant boasted that, at his daughter's wedding, 'There were forty-two complete place settings for the guests – knife, fork and spoon, as well as glassware, plate and napkin'. It is telling that he itemizes each piece of cutlery, but not the other components of the table setting. For most of the population, in most places, however, it was the eighteenth century before the fork became more than a fanciful luxury for the wealthy. Even in London, the urban centre, only 14 per cent of households owned table knives or forks at all, and a scant 2 per cent of rural households did. Little had altered half a century later, when fewer than two households in ten in some counties of New York possessed a fork, and only half of the inventories in Massachusetts at the same date listed even a single knife or fork. The residents of Greifswald, a busy German Hanseatic port city, began to use knives and forks around this time, but as a trade hub, it was perhaps more open to new fashions.

As the fork had appeared in the Renaissance as a response to the changing shape of the knife, so its spread in the eighteenth century was also a response to changing fashion, this time to the increasing prevalence of earthenware. Wooden trenchers were slightly hollowed in the centre and had a rim around the edge, the perfect shape to allow the bowl of a spoon to gather food from the bottom and neaten it up on the edge before lifting it to the mouth. China and earthenware plates were flat, with at most a raised border, and those eating from new plates with spoons found themselves chasing their food around the plate. The solution was to add a spearing implement to hold the food in place while it was cut, or to raise an already bite-sized piece: the fork.* Not everyone accepted the novelty – the British Navy persisted in its refusal to accept new-fangled forks until 1897.

* In many countries, the arrival of the fork and the rounding of the knife-end occurred fairly close together in time, and so the fork naturally acquired the piercing element that the knife was losing. In the USA, the round knife was in use long before the fork, habitually paired with a spoon. Thus, it has been suggested, Americans eat with their forks upside-down (or right-side-up, depending on where this is being read) because, when the fork finally replaced the spoon, it took over the spoon's scooping motion, giving a three-stage eating pattern of pierce-cut, implement transfer, scoop, instead of the European single-motion pierce-cut-balance.

For others, it was not so much that they rejected the new implements, rather that they had simply never encountered them. In the USA, as elsewhere, the dissemination of these utensils was frequently confined to urban areas, or to relatively prosperous rural ones. A ferryman and his wife in Maryland in the middle of the eighteenth century still ate entirely as their ancestors had done, from a single wooden dish with their hands: 'They used neither knife, fork, spoon, plate, or napkin'. They were not unusual. Even when eating utensils became more common, and most no longer lived with quite such a minimal level of possessions, many still had far less than urban middle-class writers might lead us to suppose. As late as the 1870s, Laura Ingalls Wilder's family's table implements were personal: each person had a tin plate, a steel knife and a fork; the adults also had a tin cup each, as did the smallest child, while the two older girls shared one mug between them.

That the adults took more of the scant resources than the children was the norm. Adults automatically took priority, not only in possessions, but every other respect too. Adults had their own utensils, while children shared; adults were served first and, when food was scarce, most plentifully; and adults sat while children stood. The world was made by and for adult men, and children were required to adapt to their requirements, not vice versa.

For most of history, children had been treated as small, imperfect adults. This meant, on the one hand, that children were treated as inferior, but on the other, it also meant adults and children interacted together without the boundaries that, since the twentieth century, both age groups have expected. Play, for example, was rarely age dependent. As late as the seventeenth century, children participated in adult games: they bowled, gambled, or played at skittles or dice, just as adults enjoyed games – hide-and-seek, blindman's buff – that today are considered for children. Rather than produce items specifically designed for children, manufacturers merely produced smaller versions of adult goods, be they scaled-down whistles and rattles, bows and arrows, or battledores and shuttlecocks. Delft tiles from the late seventeenth and early eighteenth centuries show children not only skipping and rolling hoops, but also playing with skittles and miniature golf clubs. On Twelfth Night, whoever found the bean hidden in the seasonal Twelfth Night cake was named king of the evening. A painting by Jan Steen from 1668 shows a toddler with a paper crown being handed a glass of wine to drink the traditional toast; had an adult found the bean, the scene would have been exactly the same. The line between adults' and children's possessions, and adults' and children's play, was fluid. 'Babies', the English word for dolls until the eighteenth century, were, for the most part, not the ragged and worn objects of children's affections that have become familiar, but expensive adult possessions, usually manufactured to display the new fashions. In 1699, a fractious child in Warwickshire was lent a visiting adult's 'wax baby in swaddles', but the story ended unhappily: the little girl dropped it, and, being wax and therefore not a toy in the modern sense, it 'broke to pieces…[its] life was very short'.

The word 'toy' itself reflected the lack of age-defined expectations for play. From the sixteenth century, a toy was a trifle, or an inexpensive ornamental object. Shakespeare used it to mean anything of no value but great charm or cleverness ('Why 'tis a…knacke, a toy, a tricke…'), a funny story ('I never may believe These antique fables, nor these Fairy toyes'), or even a woman's cap ('Any Silke, any Thred, any Toyes for your head'). By the eighteenth century, it referred to an entire classification of small decorative items made of metal: shoe buckles, or boutonnieres, were toys. (But so, confusingly, was a button-hook.) Until the late eighteenth century, toys specifically designed to amuse children needed to have a prefix: 'playing-toys'.

Before 1750, few toys are mentioned in the colonies, almost none are depicted in portraits, and fewer still have survived. It was only as the century progressed that toys took a more prominent part in the lives of children. The popularization of the writings of the philosopher John Locke, who thought children learned through play, encouraged hopeful mothers to buy toys for their offspring. Eliza Pinckney, in South Carolina, bought her three-month-old son alphabet bricks, to 'play himself into learning'. As babies' and young children's dress was unisex, so too were their toys: rattles, hoops, Noah's Arks, jigsaws, pull-toys. And as children began to wear gender-specific clothes, so too were they given gender-specific toys. Running-about toys (hoops, hobbyhorses, balls, kites) were for boys, while girls had dolls and miniature versions of household objects. Boys had a wider range of toys, from variations on military themes (lead soldiers, guns, swords, bugles, drums and so on) to outdoor items such as wagons. In the new world, toys – and attitudes towards them – varied geographically. The south and the Middle Colonies saw children playing with kites, skittles, hoops and tops, as well as outdoor games – races, tag, blindman's buff and others – while in the more Puritan New England, many elements of play were distrusted as time-wasting and unproductive, and so ungodly.*

Girls' toys were intended to encourage the habits of nurturing – dolls or dollshouses, essentially. In addition their toys were often fragile, often not actually to be played with, but merely put on a shelf where they could be admired. Only towards the end of the nineteenth

---

* One modern historian notes that today Amish children are given, in place of toys, a calf or lamb to call their own and take care of, or a section of a garden to plant, similar, she suggests, to Puritan forms of 'play'.

century did manufactured dolls start to look like their owners – like children – instead of like their mothers. For those children who had no toys at all, it was usually the girls who went without (one historian suggests that, between 1830 and 1870, two-thirds of American boys had toys, while 80 per cent of girls had none). Although the cost of toys was diminishing, and their availability increasing, most dolls were still homemade, of rags. Books too were gendered: boys' books typically recounted adventures, while those for girls stayed closer to home, telling their readers of careless girls who broke their toys and learned a lesson, or good girls who played quietly and became good mothers – 'when', as Rousseau so depressingly put it, 'she shall be her own doll'.

Board games began to be sold in Britain at the end of the eighteenth century, to provide the educational element that some parents worried that unstructured play lacked, while jigsaws were invented by a schoolmaster to teach children geography and history as they pieced maps or historical panoramas together. But Maria Edgeworth, whose writings on children's education at the close of the eighteenth century were as influential as Locke's had been a century earlier, recommended games that improved hand–eye coordination, or encouraged children to run about: kites, tops, hoops and balls were, she believed, as educational as paper and pencils, while toy towns or dollshouses cultivated the 'power of reason', 'the inventive faculty' and promoted 'general habits…patient perseverance'.

Children did, however, have far more freedom than we can imagine today. Thus, whatever the adult expectations of education, most of their play was unsupervised. Rural children spent their days climbing, hunting for birds' nests, running races, playing hide-and-seek, flying kites, or simply roaming the countryside, while urban children played, equally unsupervised, in parks, cemeteries, empty lots or just on the streets. Outdoor play was encouraged. The tiny houses, and adults working at home, meant little space was available for children, while the dangers were no less inside than out: rooms were filled with tools of the adults' trade, sometimes machinery, and of course open fires.

At home, children were expected to adapt their lives to adults', not the other way around. Rarely were objects expressly designed for them – a house that had at most one or two chairs was understandably unlikely to boast specialized baby-items. From the sixteenth-century, some Dutch images depict miniature chairs, or, more often, wooden stools with a hole in the centre, for babies just starting to stand, or walk. These stools were the most frequently found items of children's furniture, possibly because they prevented children from crawling across earthen floors, which would dirty them and their clothes, and, more importantly, they stopped them from straying too close to open fires while other family members worked.

At a time when children were considered miniature adults, their clothes, too, were, once past babyhood, essentially small versions of adult clothes, not dedicated items for a distinct period in life. In the seventeenth-century Netherlands, babies of both sexes wore baby caps, corsets and skirts until they were seven; after that, boys wore miniature men's outfits, and girls wore women's. Babies in the colonies were little different, wearing petticoats, a pinafore and a special baby cap called a biggin; the only difference between genders was in the shape of their pinafore collars. The petticoats marked their inferiority, even boys being dressed in this item of women's wear. The petticoats were also extra-long, to prevent the babies from crawling, a physical characteristic that put them on the level of animals. From the age of five or six, boys, instead of directly adopting the clothes of adult men, went through an interim stage when they wore robes that resembled long frock-coats, the habitual dress of sixteenth-century men: they had achieved the status of men, but their clothes made it clear that they were yet to achieve equality with their fathers.

Before the eighteenth century, most household items that were specifically designed for use by children were those that imposed physical restraint: swaddling bands, cradles, walking stools. When babies were swaddled, they could be laid down anywhere, as they were unable to roll. As swaddling began to disappear in the sixteenth century, so cradles are found more frequently. They were often made of wicker, which was inexpensive, lightweight and therefore convenient for moving around in a multi-purpose room. In addition, they could easily be burnt in case of infectious diseases. More generally, however, special arrangements for the smallest members of the household remained unusual, or unknown. It was only in the second half of the seventeenth century that the high-chair arrived, and even then, it was at first just a chair with longer-than-normal legs; only in the eighteenth century was a restraining bar added. Until then, toddlers, as small adults, were simply expected to learn to restrain themselves.

In the eighteenth century, between the ages of three and five, boys from well-to-do families wore not the breeches their fathers dressed in, but the long trousers worn by working-class men. Their clothes still marked them out as inferior to adult men, but now as inferior in class, rather than gender or age: lower in the hierarchy than their fathers, and their mothers, who in turn outranked working-class men. (A typical threat for misbehaviour was a return to petticoats – to womanhood.) When boys turned seven or eight they finally took on the clothes of their fathers, although not their powdered wigs and cravats, which indicated their still less-than-full adult-male status. Girls had far fewer stages to accommodate. After they left baby-clothes behind, they were immediately dressed in tiny replicas of their mothers' clothes. Upper-class English children took on the accoutrements of womanhood even earlier: many two- and three-year-old daughters of the wealthy already wore whalebone bodices.

The nineteenth century, that century of specialized commodities, saw the appearance of dedicated baby-furniture. By the end of the century, high-chairs had a board added at the front, in effect forming a miniature space for the baby, its own eating area. Specialist children's furniture was always more popular in the USA than in Britain. British nurseries, for the upper classes, were in the private rather than public areas of the house, and so were furnished with cast-off items from other rooms. In the USA, children's lives in well-to-do homes were more integrated with the adults', and furniture was therefore, where affordable, made especially for them.*

As specialist baby-furniture spread, so too did specialist baby-clothes. No longer did babies wear miniature versions of adult clothing. Now, in addition to the petticoats, items such as bellybands, undershirts and nappies were widely worn. No gender differentiation was marked at this stage, and frequently, if not always, not at the next either, which included short skirts (that is 'petty' coats, little dresses). Unlike the older long baby gowns, which extended well past the infants' feet, skirts were now ankle-length, making it easier for the children to crawl and then walk on their own. Between the ages of three and ten, both boys and girls now wore an entirely new outfit, of half-length petticoats and pantaloons. It was adopted for boys first, but by the middle of the century girls too were wearing them. To modern eyes, the pantaloons look very feminine, being white and

---

* Although it is not always easy to tell: small chairs that today are identified as children's chairs were sometimes footstools for adults; little tables and chests-of-drawers were sometimes intended for children, but others were miniature models made by cabinetmakers to promote their wares.

trimmed with lace, but to their contemporaries they were, shockingly, trousers – men's clothes – and many considered it 'an abomination unto the Lord' that girls – little women – were dressed as boys – little men. In hindsight, it can be seen that, rather, the unisex outfits signalled that gender had, for this age group, been neutralized. These small beings were no longer being dressed, and treated, as nascent adults, nor even as boys and girls. They had become a separate group, *children* first and foremost.

As the idea of perfect womanhood became increasingly centred on a woman's reproductive role, so children became pre-sexual, angelic blessings to the household. Highlighting their gender differences would be to rob them 'of their innocence and happy ignorance'. Childhood was no longer primarily a stage for these small, imperfect adults to learn self-control, but had become almost a state of grace, and children in that state needed to be protected from the harshness of the outside world. Rousseau, in *Émile*, had prefigured the idea of keeping children well away from the pernicious influences of worldly society. Yet even he had never gone as far as suggesting that children's needs might be placed ahead of adults. But now that was beginning to happen. Childhood was becoming the centre of what a home was perceived to be, a place where children were kept apart from the contaminations of the world.

Yet even as they were being protected, their new importance ensured that the marketplace began to cater for them. Crawling-mats and blankets, high-chairs and prams: hundreds of commercial goods were now created for functions that had not previously been felt to need them, all to enable parents to provide their children with everything that might keep them cocooned from the outside world for just that little bit longer.

5

Building Myths

In the 1960s, builders renovating a house in north London found, bricked up behind a fireplace, a basket holding two shoes, a candlestick and a drinking vessel, as well as the skeletons of two chickens that had been walled up alive, and two more that had been strangled first: votive offerings to the house-gods of the sixteenth century, resurfacing in the twentieth. Houses, according to myth, folk tale and legend, have souls, and possibly even minds. While we may no longer subscribe to these beliefs on a conscious level, many small rituals based on those beliefs were performed until recently: clocks were stopped and mirrors veiled on the death of a member of the household, while on the day of a funeral window-blinds were habitually drawn, covering the house's 'eyes'. Even today, brides continue to be carried over the house's threshold, marking the ceremonial border between home and not-home. In 1870, a British clergyman stressed the fleeting nature of human life in a metaphor of household furnishings. 'Don't you sometimes look about you and say to yourself...those window-curtains are getting sadly faded... Those carpets must be replaced some day...These are...the things which come up in the strange, confused remembrance of the dying man in the last days of life.' For him, and his readers, the strength of the emotional resonances of their household goods made it natural to imagine they might be among the last thoughts of the dying.

Even the most mundane objects could embody resonances of

their owners, and their owners' lives. The actor Stanley Lupino, who had the same sort of impoverished south London childhood as the slightly older Charlie Chaplin, remembered how, when his mother died in 1899, 'the brokers came to take away the poor little home that she had struggled to keep together for so long…The full tragedy of her loss only dawned on me the day after her funeral, when…I was left behind to see stick after stick of our furniture being taken out'. This elision between a house's furnishings and the soul of its inhabitants achieved literary greatness in *The Great Gatsby*. The coloured lights Gatsby strings outside his house signify his presence. Then one day they remain unlit, and his rejection by Daisy, his lost love, and then his death, follow the house's physical darkness. Lupino's chairs, Gatsby's lights – or televisions, sofas and mixing bowls: all unspoken offerings to the gods of home.

By the nineteenth century, the centrality of domestic life had become so firmly entrenched, so all encompassing, that no one could remember a time when it had not held sway. In particular, said a German in London, 'The Englishman sees the whole of life embodied in his house.' Englishmen were not *flâneurs*, as Parisians were, finding the pleasures of life in the street, in cafés opening out onto the pavements from where they could watch the world pass by. Even those poor benighted men who had failed to marry, and thus had no home – for by this time, a house without a woman was a house, not a home – even they found homes by outsourcing their domesticity, eating in coffeehouses and chophouses, places that ran with such routine for their regulars that they barely had to speak, before spending evenings in their clubs, those commercial versions of home.* As the architect

---

* Ibsen satirized this conflation of home and marriage among the middle classes in *Ghosts* (1881), when the conventional Pastor Manders assumes that Osvald Alving, an artist, 'never had the chance of knowing what a real home is like', because his friends are

Ernest Newton said in 1891, 'the sacredness of home-life is…itself a religion, pure and easy to believe. It requires no elaborate creeds, its worship is the simplest, its discipline the gentlest and its rewards are peace and contentment.'

'Peace and contentment' – what many would consider to be the epitome of what home, of domesticity, was all about. Home as a haven from the outside world, a place where we are cherished and protected, where we find emotional sustenance, a place where we can be ourselves, and where, in addition, we can find literal, as well as spiritual, comfort – a word that, as late as 1859, gave the French philosopher Ernest Renan pause: 'I am forced to use this barbarous word to express an idea quite un-French.' If the word 'comfort' was un-French, what, one wonders, would Renan have thought about the even more comfortable 'cosy', or the Dutch *gezellig*, or the German *gemütlich*, or Danish and Norwegian *hygge*, all of which contain undertones of a comfort that is understood to be found only indoors when set against a real or metaphorical cold world outside?

The vocabulary of home expanded in English in the late eighteenth and early nineteenth centuries, when a number of new words come into popular use: homelike, home-maker, homey. Over a hundred years later, in Chicago in the 1970s, eighty-two families were asked to describe the houses they actually lived in, and the houses they wanted to live in. The words most often chosen were not architectural, nor even descriptive, but emotive: 'comfortable', 'cosy', 'relaxing'. German too has a range of words that evoke domesticity and comfort: *heimelig* and *häuslich* (home-ly and house-ly) are the

---

all artists, who cannot afford to 'set up a home', which he equates 'exactly' with marriage. Sherlock Holmes was merely one of a fictional range of middle-class bachelors who lived in a simulacrum of home, complete with professional 'angel of the house', a resident landlady.

most obvious, but *behaglich*, an emotional as well as physical comfort, has a sense of being inside (*hag* means enclosure), while another type of cosy comfort, *wohnlich*, comes from *wohnen*, to dwell. *Gemüt* was originally a philosophical term, a Romantic conception of mind and soul (*Gemüt* means soul), but by the middle of the nineteenth century, *gemütlich* had been domesticated, and democraticized. No longer the preserve of the literary and literate, the word represented an enjoyment of home that was now available to all. Art that had previously concerned itself with the rarefied emotions of exceptional men transformed itself, tamed itself, into a domestic idyll for all. And not just in Germany. The 'incidents and situations from common life', as Wordsworth phrased it, were the chosen subject for many poets and writers in nineteenth-century Britain too. The Dutch *gezellig* and *gemak* are synonyms for comfort, but many are adamant that the words are untranslatable because the sentiments are purely geographical. While each country embodies their own cosiness, with one aspect or another emphasized, they all tend to include an emotional range similar to *gezellig*, which, it has been suggested, means 'homely, cosy, informal, atmospheric, entertaining, civilized, courteous, modest, decent, generous and ceremonial'.

The increase in comfort words in northwestern Europe came first, but by the end of the nineteenth century, there was a tradition of reading emotional as well as physical comfort into architecture. Previously, houses were considered to be good if they kept the rain out, were large, or well built; they were bad if they didn't keep the rain out, were too small, or poorly constructed. Or houses were good if they were fashionable, built in the latest style. Now a house could be small but good if it conveyed feelings of emotional wellbeing not merely in the residents, but in a viewer. Words that emphasized aesthetic value, such as beautiful, increasingly gave way to words that emphasized moral value, such as honest, or truthful. Houses were no longer only reflections of the people who lived in them: now the right kind of architecture was also thought to imbue its residents with the right kind of thoughts. In 1776, the American who spurned imported British fabrics and clothed her family in homespun was expressing her household's patriotism; in the nineteenth century, 'The man who has a home, presenting comfort allied to taste…is…a good citizen,' wrote the editor of a builders' journal in Philadelphia in the 1860s.

By this time, the lifestyles of the rich and famous had become a familiar feature of American popular journalism. Magazines had, for half a century, been publishing accounts of the famous that also displayed them in their own homes. And it was their physical surroundings, suggested these stories, that reflected – that possibly even enabled – their successes, a popularization of the Romantic idea that a house is a physical expression of their owners. But the style that became the ultimate expression of Americana is, at first, surprising. From the start of the nineteenth century the English style known as Greek Revival had synthesized a variety of elements taken from the Doric and Ionic buildings then being uncovered by archaeologists, creating a public architecture most frequently used for museums (both the British Museum and the National Gallery), theatres (Covent Garden) and government buildings. The style was uncommon for residential architecture in Britain, except on occasion for the wealthiest. In the USA, however, Greek Revival was adopted first as it had been used in Britain, for public buildings such as the Capitol in Washington (1803), but then, after the War of 1812, it spread more widely, for houses big and small, including the White House when it was rebuilt after the British set fire to it on (briefly) capturing the city.

The peace that followed saw a complete assimilation of the style. Greek Revival was no longer viewed as British at all. The citizens of the new North American republic saw themselves to be in a direct line of descent from the birthplace of democracy, and thus the porticoes, the colonnades and the white façades of Greek Revival were reinterpreted as the embodiment of patriotic Americana, American houses fit for American success stories. While the style's references to Greece, as the birthplace of democracy, made it desirable, it became widespread for far more pragmatic reasons. The classical motifs – a columned portico, a pediment – were easily added to buildings that were already standing, a relatively inexpensive way of making an older house look modern. (The novelist James Fenimore Cooper gently parodied this trend when one of the settlers in *The Pioneers* is seduced into giving his old-fashioned gabled-roofed house a transformation in the name of Greek simplicity, and suffers correspondingly, as snow accumulates on his stylish but flat Greek roof.)

The adoption of an architectural style as an expression of patriotism was by no means confined to the USA. As industrialization brought uncertainty and change, many countries developed styles of their own, often using a number of symbolic motifs to represent what were seen to be the country's individual values, history and virtues, and most commonly drawn from a period thought to represent the values that the present day appeared to lack, or at least wished to emulate. In Britain, the assumption of Tudor as the default history style began in the unstable political world of the late eighteenth and early nineteenth centuries. Following the French Revolution, many British landowners, fearing the spread of revolutionary discontent, made sudden and hurried improvements to their workers' housing, as when the Rothschilds from 1833 built at Tring Park, at Mentmore, Wing and Wingrave, in Buckinghamshire, a series of estate workers' villages, all white-plastered and black-beamed, with tall Elizabethan-looking chimneys: Rothschild Tudor. Generic Tudor detailing became a shorthand for 'Merrie England', for an agricultural past when the local squire was the font of patriarchal benevolence, and industrialism was unknown. The appeal of a style that evoked a mythic past when all had been happy was obvious. By the end of the century, other magnates had followed. From 1888, Port Sunlight, outside Liverpool, was built in the Tudor style for the workers at the Lever Brothers' Sunlight factory; Cadbury's workers outside Birmingham were accommodated in the equally Tudor-esque Bournville from 1893. But the style was not merely for workers: many owners applied it to their own properties too, the newly rich especially building Tudor-esque country houses, perhaps to give the impression that they, and their houses, had always been there. Other landowners knocked down old houses and replaced them with ones that were intended to look older than those they replaced. In Kent, a wealthy hosiery manufacturer erected a new 'Tudor' manor where once a Georgian house had stood, surrounding it with matching black-beamed cottages for his workers.

Yet despite Tudor's ubiquity, and the familiarity now of its component parts, in reality the Tudor style of the nineteenth century and later was very different from the style as it appeared during the Tudor period itself. The black beams and white plasterwork that for the last century and a half have been an archetypal element of the Tudor building style were a nineteenth-century invention. In the sixteenth century, the beams were usually hidden under the plasterwork, which was generally buff-coloured, not white. When, occasionally, the beams were left exposed, they were never painted, which allowed the wood to weather into a silvery-white, only a few tones away from the plaster around it. In the nineteenth century, when black and white

became the hallmark of the style, surviving sixteenth-century buildings had their beams uncovered and darkened, to 'restore' them to
what was assumed to be their original state. This can be seen in a very
rare sixteenth-century survival in London, where nineteenth- and
twentieth-century photographs show the buildings before and after
they were 'restored' (see plate section, nos. 16 and 17).

Tudor rapidly established itself as the rural upper-class historical
style of choice, but other historical styles also played a notable role in
Britain's construction of the ideal home. Cottage style, a somewhat
vague, non-specific term, was a generic that drew on Romanticism's
delight in the picturesque. Romanticism tended to equate pastoral
simplicity with domesticity, expressed as a retreat from the world,
be it industrial, commercial or urban. In architectural terms, this
produced 'cottages' that were no longer the tiny, one-roomed,
earthen-floored hovels of the working classes, but now prettified,
faux-rustic suburban dwellings fitted with all modern conveniences
and large enough to suit the nineteenth-century middle-class family.
The façades of these buildings replaced classicism's symmetry and
balance with irregular and asymmetric features, and exposed wooden
beams and panelled walls inside, while modern sash windows were
discarded in favour of old-fashioned small-paned casements. As
Tudor was represented by black-and-white façades, so the idea of a
cottage was conveyed by a number of stylistic flourishes rather than
by its overall design. In the private areas of the house – the bedrooms
and studies – high ceilings gave way to low ones, to create a sense of
enclosure. Words that indicated a small size, when used to describe a
cottage, indicated approval: humble, cosy, snug.

Queen Anne style, which developed at the same time in towns and
cities, is, even today, so common that often it barely registers to the
British as a style at all. Superficially it appears to have no connection

to cottage style, but the impetus was the same, and so too were the references it drew on, assimilating from the Romantic picturesque a range of asymmetric features and quirky, quaint elements: overhanging eaves, front porches, decorative tiling, oddly shaped windows – bay or oriel in particular – and textured, red-brick construction materials, which aimed to give an impression of individuality.*

In the USA, elements of Queen Anne and cottage styles were adapted and developed to produce a new generic historical style, a purely American one, known as Colonial. In 1876, in Philadelphia, the Centennial Exhibition displayed objects that had been owned, or at least were thought to have been owned, by the first English settlers. Instead of showing them in a quasi-museum display, the exhibitors built a re-creation, one of the earliest reconstructions of a period room, a stage-set version of a Puritan house. A magazine illustration of the time shows one section, with a fireplace and a cooking pot simmering alongside a woman spinning. The exhibition's visitors were not shown the historic reality of the seventeenth-century past, a tiny, crowded, single-room house where beds, tools, cooking implements and storage nestled together, and furniture was primarily notable by its absence. And just as this 'Puritan' room was not a room any Puritan would have recognized, so too the Colonial style would have bewildered the colonists, who would have been entirely unfamiliar with the white-painted clapboard houses set in neat yards that, from the nineteenth century, have borne their name. Until then, the colonies' small, shabby houses had rarely been considered worth painting. Instead, the wooden façades gradually darkened with the

---

* Confusingly, there is only the most tenuous connection between this nineteenth-century style and Queen Anne herself (reigned 1702–14). The early architects of Queen Anne style were thought to have drawn their inspiration from seventeenth-century red-brick country houses, although in fact many of these houses pre-dated Anne's reign.

weather, turning a dull, muddy colour. Outside the cities, yards were unfenced, and rather than being planted, they were liberally dotted with middens and piles of waste. In the early nineteenth century, New York had become known for the first appearance of painted brick house-fronts, although they were not white, but gaily coloured red, yellow or light grey, sometimes with the brickwork outlined in white: the effect was, said many, like looking at a city of dollshouses. In the following decades the houses along the Hudson River, a prosperous location, were also painted, now most commonly white, but it was not until the 1840s that white lead paint became both affordable and readily available. Until then, white-painted houses were a fancy of the upper classes. At about the same date, in north Philadelphia, the first gardens began to be fenced in. It was only from the 1870s that what is now regarded as the traditional, Colonial, style became geographically widespread: the two-storey white clapboard house with painted shutters, front porch, centre door and pitched roof, all behind a neat picket fence, simply saying 'America'.

Thus Victorian Britain had Tudor and the USA had Colonial. The Netherlands had Oud Hollandsch, a style that featured rooms decorated to resemble the interiors in Dutch Golden Age art. As in Philadelphia's Centennial Exhibition, the style was promoted via 'authentic' display rooms that featured in the many exhibitions that flourished in the last decades of the century. One, in Amsterdam in 1876, advertised itself as a 'picturesque revelation of life in Amsterdam in earlier and later times', despite being newly laid out by an architect. Another showed what it called a *Kamer van Jan Steen*, a room decorated to resemble those in the paintings of Jan Steen, although the room on display actually drew on the decorative traditions of agricultural Friesland, in the north, while Steen came from the urbanized region of the central Netherlands. The exhibitors additionally decorated these supposedly peasant rooms with urban household possessions such as Delft tiles, copper pans and the other seventeenth-century commodity goods familiar to nineteenth-century viewers from the paintings. The purpose was not to create a precise historical simulacrum – the concept of authenticity was not yet a commonplace – but to produce a display that represented the quintessence of the past. And just as nineteenth-century Tudor subsumed the plainer reality of sixteenth-century Tudor, so nineteenth-century Oud Hollandsch formed the twentieth-century's misreading, still current, of the realism of Dutch Golden Age art.

In the early part of the nineteenth century, by contrast, both the German territories and much of Scandinavia had enjoyed a style of simplicity and lightness of decoration, using pale woods, a neutral palette and elegantly patterned drapery. This later became known as Biedermeier, although the term was not in use at the time.* It was only after German unification in 1871 that a neo-traditional style, Altdeutsch, developed. Altdeutsch exteriors had stepped gables and ornamental scrollwork, while inside massive furniture was dimly lit by stained-glass windows and *Lüsterweibchen*. These hanging lamps, in the shape of mermaids, looked back to a sixteenth-century style; the originals were rare, but they appeared in engravings by Dürer, and were thus reintegrated into modern interiors, as carpets on tables had been in the Netherlands. Other popular elements derived from German history included suits of armour (a company in Nuremberg made papier-mâché versions for home consumption), the *Lutherstuhl*,

---

* As with many art terms, it was originally an insult, drawn from a fictional character in a newspaper, Gottlieb Biedermaier (sic), a portmanteau name from two poems by Joseph von Scheffel, 'Biedermanns Abendgemütlichkeit' and 'Bummelmaiers Klage' ('Biedermann's Cosy Evening' and 'Bummelmaier's Lament'), which were merged to produce a satirical portrait of the self-satisfied middle-class man. So the term Biedermeier, applied to domestic interiors, was intended as a condemnation of bourgeois décor.

a wooden armchair, and, most prominently, the *Kachelofen*, the tiled stove, sometimes with an integrated seat, winsomely dubbed the *Schmollwinkel*, or sulking corner, all liberally embellished – like the Delft tiles in the Netherlands – with decorative objects that carried resonances of 'old' and 'local': stoneware, leatherwork, embroidery or weaving with peasant connotations.

Despite, or perhaps entirely because of, these rustic references, Altdeutsch was a style of the urban haute bourgeoisie. Initially Old Alpine, or Bavarian style, found favour with the tourist market, both inside and outside Germany, for those searching not for sophistication but for a lost ideal of home, as log cabins symbolized a simpler time in the USA, and cottages did the same in Britain. And as cottages had done, so Old Alpine quickly crossed the social scale, from its origins in the primitive houses of country dwellers to decorating the country houses of the affluent. Many who did not embrace the style wholesale nevertheless adopted some of the elements, be it the *Brettstuhl*, a splay-legged wooden chair, or textured pine walls. (These elements were also incorporated into public spaces such as beerhalls – the Old Alpine *Bierkeller* is to Germany what the Tudor-beamed pub is to Britain.) By the end of the century a new style for middle-class homes in Munich synthesized the motifs from Old Alpine with modern comfort and technology, and the original patriotic motivation had become almost invisible. As Colonial became simply the ideal of home in the USA, so urban Altdeutsch was identified as *gemütlich*, and also as *behaglich*, comfortable in an emotional as well as, or more than, a physical sense.

These heritage approximations and adaptations, whether Tudor beams, Dürer lamps or white-painted clapboard, subsumed the reality of history, and were both widespread and long-lasting. In a north London suburb in the 1910s, extras that could be added to new houses for an additional payment included faux-rustic fret-work wooden screens, wooden mantelpieces, floor tiles and leaded windows: all items to transform a newly built suburban house into ye olde country cottage. By 2013, a British timber-cladding company promised to create 'the authentic "New England" look with Cape Cod cladding', illustrated by a photograph of an accountancy office in the Netherlands. Tudor and Colonial are no longer history, or geographically fixed, just the embodiment of the ideal home.

These styles meant that it was no longer necessarily the size or fashionability of a house that were used as indicators of the virtue of the family within. Now small houses, country cottages and log cabins could be patriotic by virtue of their choice of symbols from the past, while, conversely, innovations in furnishings and technology could be seen as troubling. In 1852, an American architectural writer condemned the owners of farmhouses who replaced their old, wasteful and fuel-inefficient fireplaces with stoves. Stoves may have consumed less fuel even as they produced more heat, but, his book warned, they gave entirely the wrong impression: 'A farmer's house should *look* hospitable as well as *be* hospitable…and the broadest, most cheerful look of hospitality within doors…is an *open* fire'. Another book warned against replacing 'the hardest and homeli-est bench[es]' with upholstered chairs, the older style being 'more respectable'. A cheerful-looking hearth was, according to these experts, if perhaps not to the residents themselves, somehow better than actually being warm; furniture that evoked a rugged pioneering spirit was similarly better than furniture that made it possible to sit comfortably. Such attitudes were common across the home countries, the *Brettstuhl* being no more comfortable than that 'hardest and homeliest bench'. They were symbolic comforts. Once the Industrial Revolution had turned the world upside down, the past, with its subtext of generic happier days, was always the lost, longed-for ideal. It is not coincidental that the Dutch Golden Age painters returned to popular appreciation in a period when the images could be read as a clear articulation of a pre-industrial once-upon-a-time, now forever out of reach.

Technology and progress were always in tension with nostalgia and its corollary, that better times were always in the past. The Great Exhibition of 1851 in London looked wholeheartedly to progress, technology and the future, but the success of that exhibition spawned many others that chose instead to embrace the supposed simplicities of the past. In the USA the horrors of the Civil War created an increased desire for a simpler, and simplified, past, and found expression in model rooms, either generic, such as a 'New England kitchen' of colonial times, or supposedly more specific, such as an ostensible replica of the interior of the house in which Benjamin Franklin had been born in 1706. Here, with the addition of volunteers in olde-worlde dress posing among the pieces of furniture, were all the symbols of heritage: a cradle, a tall case, or grandfather, clock, a spinning wheel. The Colonial kitchen at the Centennial Exhibition in Philadelphia in 1876 also contained spinning wheels, cradles and an old-fashioned settle, as well as furniture thought to have been owned by specific historical figures – in this case, a desk that was said to have belonged to John Alden, one of the Plymouth colony's original settlers.* Superannuated technology – here the spinning wheel, and also, in paintings like John Frederick Peto's *Lights of Other Days*, a

---

* The need for a tangible link to the past, whether authentic or imagined, has not vanished. An analysis of the wood of a chair displayed in Pilgrim Hall, Plymouth, Massachusetts, and said to have been brought to the colonies in the *Mayflower*, shows that it must have been made in America.

shelf of lanterns, candlesticks and lamps – had become a shorthand for 'happy olden days'.

Throughout history, it was accepted as a matter of course that buildings were routinely altered as time went on, with rooms or even wings added, and modifications made to function and decoration. In the nineteenth century, for the first time, the 'authenticity' of buildings began to be considered, with later historical additions stripped out in an attempt to return the building to an original state. As industrialization was felt to be creating a new world, many clung hard to their perception of the old one. A Georgian wing on a Jacobean house was no longer viewed an organic extension, but *wrong*. Some people, particularly in places where Romantic notions held sway, went as far as suggesting that all old buildings should be allowed to decay and ultimately fall into ruin: any attempt even to repair them was to interfere with their history.

By the 1870s, the passion for stripping out later architectural accretions in order to return buildings to a more authentic past had become so strong that an opposition group, the Society for the Protection of Ancient Buildings, was formed, to counter the desire for what William Morris, its founder, called 'forgery' through overenthusiastic restoration. (Morris's family, tellingly, nicknamed the group 'Anti-Scrape'.) He passionately rejected these wholesale restorations, which all too often 'meant the reckless stripping a building of some of its most interesting material features'. His idea was to repair 'our ancient buildings', but then to impose a ban on all future alterations, leaving them 'as monuments of a bygone art, created by bygone manners': 'thus, and thus only can we protect our ancient buildings, and hand them down instructive and venerable to those that come after us'. So while he disapproved of removing earlier layers of history, he still fell into nostalgia's heritage trap. The accretions of the past were, from his nineteenth-century perspective, history; accretions from his own or any later time, however, were abominations.

Even as Morris was pleading for the preservation of British monuments, Artur Hazelius, a folklorist and language reformer, was working to preserve the material culture of everyday life in Sweden. He had founded the Nordiska Museet, or Nordic Museum, an ethnographic collection of peasant house-furnishings, children's toys, clothes and objects of daily life, but by the late 1880s his ambitions were greater. In 1891, Skansen, the world's first open-air museum, opened on the island of Djurgården in Stockholm. This was not simply a collection of chairs and jugs and dresses. For Skansen, Hazelius collected entire buildings – ultimately 150 farms and cottages from all over Sweden (and one from Norway) – as well as their contents, to build a museum of vanished or vanishing Swedish lifestyle and culture.

The feeling that houses – homes – needed to be preserved in an age of industrialization was one that was, like self-consciously archaic building styles, shared across many of the home countries at this time. Initially, the first house preservation groups were less concerned with the everyday, and more with conserving buildings that had once housed the great. In 1850, George Washington's headquarters on the Hudson, the Hasbrouck House, in Newburgh, New York, was opened to the public, followed by other houses belonging to presidents or great men, or houses with Revolutionary or, in time, Civil War connections. The purpose of these buildings was to serve as three-dimensional history lessons. In 1929, Henry Ford virtually industrialized the process, acquiring eighty-three houses with historic connections, re-siting them from their original locations to Green-field Village, next to the Henry Ford Museum in Michigan, to create a venue where visitors could walk through a single narrative of America's great men. Here the house where Noah Webster wrote his dictionary was conveniently hard by Thomas Edison's workshop, which was not far from the courthouse where Abraham Lincoln had practised as a lawyer, and so on.

But it was Hazelius's elevation of the everyday, not Ford's bricks-and-mortar hymn to Great Men, that came to dominate home-as-history museums, reflecting as it did the widespread perception that industrialization was steam-rollering the past. In Germany, in particular, the urban middle classes studied and collected aspects of the rural past as a way of allaying their fears about the urban present. Now the organizers of new Heimat museums adopted the methods of the emerging scholarly discipline of art history to attribute, classify and authenticate the impedimenta of home life. The Museum für deutsche Volkstrachten und Erzeugnisse des Hausgewerbes (Museum of German National Dress and Handicrafts, now part of the Museum of European Culture), which opened in Berlin in 1889, aimed to display everything connected to houses and their occupants – furniture and furnishings, clothes, food and kitchenware, as well as items of art, craft and trade. The same trend saw Britain's National Trust, originally established to preserve landscapes, acquire its first building in 1896: not a stately home, but a fourteenth-century farmer's modest hall-and-parlour house.

The struggle, which continues, was not whether small houses were worth displaying – there was, and is, universal acceptance that they are. Rather, it was, and is, how to display them. What can practically be displayed in a museum commonly takes precedence over what is accurate, or even what is 'suitable'. The frequently messy multiple realities of history have often been, and often still are, rejected as too crude for the more genteel showcases of heritage. One early Heimat museum exhibited what it labelled as a copy of a peasant house from German north Friesland, but added that an 'accurate' copy could not be shown, 'since such a house was hardly suitable for exhibition purposes'. Nineteenth-century, and some twentieth- and twenty-first-century, organizers of exhibitions in the USA found it difficult to accept the tiny size and multi-purpose rooms of the colonial era. Imaginary spaces such as 'borning-rooms', where women retired to give birth, were conjured up, the reality of the one-roomed house apparently more beyond comprehension than a room used, at most, once every eighteen months. Heritage had become an outpost of home nostalgia, a commercial, institutional packaging of an emotion.

This is not a problem confined to the nineteenth century. Today's sometimes almost fanatical desire for authenticity can itself, para-doxically, lead to inauthenticity, as it did with William Morris. Period-room displays might carefully confine themselves to items from a single region, or date, even though the contents of real homes have always been gathered over decades if not centuries, while trade routes from the sixteenth century onwards enabled goods to arrive from across the world, not solely the district in which a house is located. Even where houses or their contents are entirely authentic, the display may not necessarily be so. In many museums, décor and furniture are collected from numerous sources and locations to tell a story, whether a historical, an ethnographical or a decorative one. The National Trust furnishes the houses in its care from its central stores, not necessarily from the house to hand; it then places items where they can best be seen by visitors, or where they won't impede circulation, or contravene fire regulations, rather than where they might have originally been located. In the early twentieth century, English country-house style, a creation of a number of early-twentieth-century interior decorators (several of the most prominent of them American), leavened eighteenth-century upper-class domestic décor with the requirements of twentieth-century middle-class living. The success of this style was so far-reaching that by the end of the twentieth century it was treated as though it were a genuine representation of historical domestic arrangements, and houses and period displays that did not conform were condemned for historical inaccuracy.

Even the most careful modern scholarship has not entirely solved the dilemmas of authenticity. In 1990, with the help of the architect herself, the Museum für angewandte Kunst Wien (Vienna's Museum of Applied Arts) displayed a reproduction of Margarete Schütte-Lihotzky's famous Frankfurt kitchen, discussed more fully in Chapter 7. Although what was on display was clearly marked as a copy, it was, and is, not quite clear what it is a copy of. The Frankfurt kitchens of the 1920s, although theoretically mass-produced, were often handmade, each kitchen starting off fractionally different from the others; their owners then adapted them further over the decades, adding to them, adjusting the design to suit themselves. Had the museum chosen to show a 'real' Frankfurt kitchen, removed from one of these apartments, altered by time and its owners, counter-intuitively, it would not have been authentic either.

The most artificial – and it must be admitted, the most popular – heritage sites are the historic towns and villages that were 'preserved' in the twentieth century in America. Colonial Williamsburg is a replica of the capital of Virginia as it would have appeared in the 1770s, was established by John D. Rockefeller in 1926; Plimoth Plantation (note the carefully olde-worlde spelling) in Massachusetts was founded in 1947 as a re-creation of the original Plymouth settlement. (As we have seen, none of Plymouth's original houses survived.) Colonial Williamsburg has a few surviving pre-Revolutionary buildings, from which all post-1776 additions have since been removed; these are supplemented by many more reconstructions. Yet the highlights – the Capitol building, the Governor's Palace and the College of

William and Mary's earliest building, dating from the 1720s – are far from typical of everyday buildings of the period. And so the overall impression is that eighteenth-century Williamsburg was very much grander than it actually was. Some effort has been made to acknowledge the town's historical reliance on slave labour, but the story that is visible remains one of elegance, not poverty, of sunlight, not shadow, of relentless good cheer, presenting the classical, clean, upper-class housing of the elite as though it can stand in for the reality of the remaining 99 per cent.

The word 'nostalgia' was coined in the seventeenth century, when it was defined as a physical ailment to which Swiss soldiers fighting abroad were particularly vulnerable.* The recommended treatment was opium, an application of leeches and a visit to the Alps. Then, with the arrival of the Romantic movement in the early nineteenth century, this physical ailment was reinterpreted as a spiritual affliction: nostalgia became an indicator of a person's sensibility, their engagement with what a historian of the emotion has dubbed the 'romance with the past'. As industrialization spread, this past, reimagined as a slower, gentler place, a world of tight-knit communities, social cohesion and charming rural pastimes, was contrasted to the present's new, fractured, urban style of living. Nostalgia became not a longing for a lost place, but for a lost time, either of the nostalgic's own childhood, when things had been less complicated, or, more broadly, of society's childhood, an imaginary past.

And this past often centred on ideas of home and family, whether real or imagined. In 1950, more than ten thousand American families

---

* The Vatican's Swiss Guard is the last surviving relic of what was once Switzerland's major export industry: mercenaries.

were asked to describe their hoped-for futures. The majority of answers comprised a nostalgic reimagining of traditional living, most frequently finding expression in the desire for a Cape Cod house.* At the same time, most also acknowledged that really a Cape Cod was not at all practical: they were too small, the layout was not suitable for family life, or even for modern household technology. What the respondents desired, it became clear, was the emotional resonance that they attached to the style. As the nineteenth century found inspiration in Tudor buildings, or Dutch Golden Age art, or Dürer, to evoke the emotional resonances of the warmth and comfort of the ideal home, so in the twentieth century it was preconceptions of 'past times', an interweaving of motifs from history, and from newspaper and magazine descriptions of the homes of the famous, past or present.

In the USA, these sources combined to produce perhaps the most resonant example of mythic housing, fixing it so firmly in the nation's consciousness that dislodging it would be both impossible and unpatriotic: the log cabin. In 1857, the 250th anniversary celebrations of the founding of Jamestown, the first permanent English settlement in the Americas, were announced to have been held exactly on the spot where 'the first log cabin was built'. In reality, Jamestown's 1607 founders built with the methods they had known in England, and the settlement's earliest permanent houses were made of 'strong boards' – that is, sawn timber boards. The first use of the term log cabin can be traced back only to 1750.

For the log cabin was first brought to the new world by settlers from Sweden, where it was a traditional housing style. From 1655, these Swedes (many of whom came from areas that are today Finland)

---

* The main indicators of Cape Cod today are symmetrical construction in a house of one or one and a half storeys, a pitched roof and a central chimney.

settled on the Delaware and around Maryland's tidewater region. And it is here that the first contemporary references to houses built of logs appear. A court record in 1662 mentions a 'loged hows' that had existed four years earlier.* In 1679, a Dutchman stayed in a log house in what is now New Jersey, built, he said, 'according to the Swedish mode...being nothing else than entire trees, split through the middle...and placed in the form of a square, upon each other.' These and subsequent references to log cabins appeared always in areas with Swedish settlers.

One of those areas was what would become Pennsylvania, and by the time William Penn himself arrived, in 1682, there were already numerous log cabins in the region. Penn's English followers copied them, believing them to be the indigenous style, as did Scottish and Irish immigrants in the eighteenth and nineteenth centuries who saw them on their way south and west. (Today Pennsylvania Dutch architecture refers, as so often, to the stone houses of the wealthiest, another instance of the small house rendered invisible by the survival of the large.) Pennsylvania also drew immigrants from Moravia, the Black Forest, the German and Swiss Alpine regions and Bohemia, places where log housing was familiar, while at the beginning of the eighteenth century, a new group of German immigrants settled in the Hudson and Mohawk valleys. This second wave of immigration

---

* The terms log house and log cabin were used interchangeably, although in the nineteenth century a distinction was sometimes intended. A log cabin was built from round, unhewn logs infilled with moss, straw and mud, with no window and no chimney, smoke exiting through a hole in the roof. A log house used hewn logs, which were infilled with stones and then plastered; it had glass windows, a chimney and a shingled roof. In general usage, the main distinction was whether the building was made of round or hewn logs. Many who lived in a round-logged construction that had a chimney and windows still called it a cabin. Sometimes the choice of word indicated size – cabins had one or, at most, two rooms on one floor, or one floor with an unfinished loft; more rooms, or a finished second storey, turned the cabin into a house. As all these caveats indicate, both terms were fluid.

grafted German elements on to the earlier Swedish ones, and a third wave of log-house-building immigrants, the Norwegians, who settled in the Midwest, particularly Minnesota, brought still more small changes and modifications, even as they reinforced the basic formula.

As with so much new-world housing, log cabins were regarded at the time as temporary and makeshift. They were built by pioneers with little or no cash, out of materials readily to hand – the wood came from the forests that the settlers were clearing for agriculture anyway, and they required few, or no, nails, a rare commodity in the colonies. The expectation was that as soon as the crops from the first harvest on the newly cleared land were sold, the cabins would be demolished and replaced with houses of timber boards. Even that great mythologizer of the west, James Fenimore Cooper, considered that a settlement was permanent once stone houses replaced the original log cabins.

It was in the 1840s, the heyday of nostalgic housing styles throughout the home countries, that the log-cabin myth took definitive form. When William Henry Harrison ran for president in 1840, his opponents mocked his supposedly humble background by sneering that he lived in a log cabin. The canny Harrison embraced the caricature as the embodiment of his man-of-the-people roots. His supporters marched with banners depicting symbols of pioneer life – log cabins, ploughs and canoes – and floats built in the shape of log cabins. Daniel Webster, a constitutional lawyer and long-time politician, couched his endorsement of Harrison in the same terms: 'I was not myself born in [a log cabin], but my elder brothers and sisters were – in the cabin…which at the close of the Revolutionary War… my father erected on the extreme frontiers of New Hampshire…In this humble cabin amid the snow-drifts of New England, that father strove [sic], by honest labor, to acquire the means for giving to his children a better education, and elevating them to a higher condition than his own'. It's all there: the frontier, New England self-sufficiency, the War of Independence, social mobility and of course the log cabin. (Harrison was no more a child of hardship than Webster: contrary to his detractors' claims, he had been born in a mansion in Virginia; his sole connection to a log cabin was a house 'he had bought in Ohio, which had once been a one-room cabin, although by the time Harrison was finished with it it had sixteen rooms.) Within a year, the symbol had already made an appearance in literature: Natty Bumppo, the hero of Cooper's *Leatherstocking Tales* (the best-known of which is *The Last of the Mohicans*), although raised by Delaware Indians, lives in 'a rough cabin of logs'. With this, the log cabin was well on its way to becoming a symbol of the American spirit itself, essential, indigenous and simple.

Twenty years later its resonance only increased, becoming impervious to any incursions of reality, with the election of Abraham Lincoln and the rise of a real log-cabin dweller to the presidency. With Lincoln's murder in 1865, the log cabin came to represent the lost Eden that was pre-Civil War America. And this was only reinforced as, postwar, urbanization and industrialization swept across the eastern seaboard. The wilderness that Cooper had written about might have vanished, but the mythic log cabin not only survived, but flourished. Lincoln's log-cabin birthplace is on show in the Memorial Building at the Lincoln Birthplace Historic Site in Kentucky (see plate section, no. 18). Except that it isn't. The original cabin, like most buildings of the type, was demolished long before Lincoln became famous. Some of the logs may have been reused to build a neighbouring house. That house too was demolished, and a new house, which in turn may or may not have used some of the original logs, was built in its place. It was this third building that in the 1890s was toured around fairs and exhibitions as Lincoln's birthplace (and at this point some of the logs from that already-compromised building also vanished), before being installed at the Lincoln Birthplace site.*

From such fairs and exhibitions, the log-cabin symbol seeped into the everyday life of twentieth-century suburban domesticity: 1916 saw the production of Lincoln Logs, children's building blocks in the shape of logs (designed by the son of modernist architect Frank Lloyd Wright, and a century later still sold); tins of Log Cabin maple syrup, named in the 1880s for Lincoln's birthplace, bore a picture of a log cabin at least until the 1960s. (Its current squeezy bottle continues to gesture, if ever more vaguely, to the shape of logs.)

The log cabin, in common with other patriotic styles of architecture, represented not so much physical as emotional and psychological comfort, a national symbol of domestic belonging, of a shared heritage. It was less important that the buildings that provoked these emotions were artificial constructs. No English cottager of the sixteenth century would have recognized the warmth or plumbing or upholstery of a nineteenth-century English country cottage, any more than the Puritans would recognize these log cabins, nor the specific possessions attributed to them by their descendants.

Other key symbols of Americana – the spinning wheel and the patchwork quilt – are similarly mythological. In 1858, Longfellow's *The Courtship of Miles Standish* presents the prototypical Puritan maiden, Priscilla Mullins, sitting 'beside her wheel...the carded wool like a

---

* It must be noted that while the national parks are usually scrupulous in pointing out any inauthenticity in their historic displays, the Lincoln Birthplace National Historic Site sows a little confusion. As well as straightforwardly acknowledging that the cabin is not the original, it retains an early-twentieth-century plaque that proclaims, 'Here over the log cabin where Abraham Lincoln was born, destined to preserve the Union and free the slave, a grateful people have dedicated this memorial to unity, peace, and brotherhood among the states.'

snow-drift / Piled at her knee, her white hands feeding the ravenous spindle'. In reality, the evidence suggests that in the early days of the colony, only about one family in six owned a spinning wheel. Even fewer wove. Most cloth, from the earliest days, was purchased. For those householders who did spin, it was one task among many, and many who were heroically productive still did not spin nor weave. Spinning was simply not time-efficient: one wheel could produce only enough yarn to knit an average family's stockings. Mary Cooper, on a farm in Long Island in the 1760s, grew fruit and vegetables, made preserves and pickles, selling the excess to her neighbours, salted beef, kept bees, made the family's wine, candles, soap and clothes, and even combed flax, but she did no spinning. It was the Revolution first, then the War of 1812, with their economic boycotts of British goods, that turned spinning and weaving into activities with patriotic resonance. Thereafter homespun fabrics came to signify the self-sufficiency of the new nation. By the 1820s, northern citizens were once more relying on industrially manufactured textiles, whether made abroad or locally, but in the south and the frontier territories, homespun survived longer, as the availability of slave labour made its production more viable in the south, and the west's low- to no-cash economy made it essential. It was, according to Frederick Law Olmsted, the co-designer of Central Park, the clothing of 'half the white population of Mississippi' in the 1850s.

The proportion of the population who relied heavily on home-spun therefore suggests that the supposedly common homemade patchwork quilt must in reality have been a rare object in American houses before the nineteenth century. Patchwork is a product of surplus, of textiles which are abundant enough that large remnants are routinely available – large enough and routinely enough that they can be used to make another large item entirely. If the output of a single spinning wheel could only keep a family in stockings, how much more work was needed to spin enough to be able to weave a family's clothes, and still have more left over for scrap, to 'tear…into bits for the sake of arranging it anew'? In Britain quilts began to be seen in quantity once less expensive textiles from India became available in the eighteenth century. But in the USA, this was not the case. Throughout the nineteenth century, clothing for everyone except a minority of urban, cash-paid workers continued to be square-cut, precisely so as to utilize every scrap of what was valuable material. More fashionable patterns might leave more offcuts, but at a period when the majority of people owned one, or at most two, sets of clothing, daily and 'best', it would take years to gather enough offcuts to make a quilt. Patchwork was not a product of pioneer life, but of the industrial world, and with the spread of inexpensive textiles, new business opportunities were grasped: in Britain from the nineteenth century, pre-cut fabric squares were packaged up by manufacturers and sold as the raw material for quilts. Of course, basic quilts could also be made from scraps, or from a single, repurposed, worn-out item, or a combination of purchased and repurposed fabrics. But until there was plenty, and a textile industry, quilting was confined to the cash-rich.

Communal quilting-bees, too, if not entirely a myth, are nevertheless an elaboration of reality. The bulk of the work for any quilt – the cutting of the squares, their stitching, the lining, preparing the batting – was done at home alone, or by several family members working independently on different elements. Only the quilting, the final stage, was a joint effort. A quilting frame was enormous and in use took over a great proportion of a room: it was generally stored in an outbuilding, or shared among several families or a community. The purpose of the bee was to get the job done as quickly as possible so that the frame could be returned to its storage place and daily life resumed in the main room. A few contemporary drawings depict a frame raised to the ceiling on ropes, but this is more likely to have been a temporary expedient so that family life could continue during the time it took to finish a quilt, not a permanent location. Although there was certainly a party element to the event – food was provided, and for those who lived in sparsely populated districts, any sort of companionship was festive – sociability was not the motivating factor. And later writings that describe quilting-bees with music and dancing are frequently fictitious. If the frame took up almost all of one room, and people lived in one or two rooms, where did the dancing take place?

These are myths of national origin. Britain has comparable myths, of a fixed, rural population where everyone lived their entire lives in the same village, knowing their neighbours and handing down relationships and resentments through generations. In reality, to take one representative example, a seventeenth-century Nottinghamshire village saw more than 60 per cent of its population move in only twelve years. The upper classes were just as mobile, with great houses regularly changing hands: one Northamptonshire village recorded that three families had owned the village's manor house in a single decade. And as the squires came and went, so too did their servants. These were not the faithful family retainers beloved of novels and television period dramas. In the same village, only one of the area's twenty-six servants was still working there ten years later, and in the interim she too had lived in another village before returning and being employed in a number of different households. Half of those who employed a servant were obliged to find a new one each year.

But the most influential and widespread myth, the one that continues to be prevalent today, is that there was, at some point, a golden age of family, and the family home. This myth recurs like a refrain from the dawn of the Industrial Revolution and urbanization, and it is protean, changing and taking on new forms as troubling new elements of present-day life arise. Today's version of the myth appears as the frequently expressed proposition that the modern family is in decline from a past ideal, stating as fact what is, in truth, a feeling. The idea that there was a period when extended families lived in multi-generational harmony persists, even as we know that nuclear-family living arrangements have been the norm across northwestern Europe for half a millennium, and possibly much longer. Similarly, social commentators who decry the effects of divorce, worrying that the modern family's 'unprecedented' fracturing will have unknown (but always deleterious) effects should be asked to reflect for a moment on the realities of life expectancy before the twentieth century. Before the eighteenth century, typically around 40 per cent of children in England had lost at least one parent, well above the proportion of today's population affected by divorce. (Currently approximately 30 per cent of marriages end in divorce, although of course not all involve children.) And the death of a parent fractured a family in a much more permanent manner. In the eighteenth century in the Netherlands, it was so routine for children to be brought up by extended family members – grandparents, uncles and aunts or more distant relations – that many sources do not trouble even to mention the reasons. After the population devastation caused by the Black Death, and then the later plague outbreaks, life expectancy began to improve, only to decline again in the nineteenth century as a consequence of industrialization and urbanization. With it, the number of children with at least one deceased parent increased. While life expectancy was substantially higher in rural communities, even there the typical family for most of the century was a 'broken' family: up to two-thirds of all children in the American south had lost one parent before the age of twenty-one.

In 1860, the London *Morning Chronicle* warned its readers that Christmas, the traditional 'grand opportunity of reuniting the love of families', was endangered by rampant commercialism and a newly mobile population. Yet the population had long been mobile, while Christmas had only been celebrated as a family occasion for a matter of decades. Furthermore, until paid holidays arrived in the late nineteenth century, only the wealthiest had ever contemplated a seasonal family gathering. Other private family occasions that are today thought to be 'traditional' – marriages, christenings, funerals – were previously community events, participated in, and taking place, outside the home. Not even the tradition of a Sunday church service survives examination of the evidence. In London, in the middle of the nineteenth century, all the churches combined had enough seating for less than half the city's residents, and even so the pews were barely half-filled every Sunday. A special census was conducted one Sunday in 1851 to enumerate not those who said they went to church regularly, but those who were actually present. Of England and Wales's population of 18 million, just 6 million attended church on census Sunday, two-thirds of the population being otherwise occupied.

Today's symbol of family togetherness is not Sunday church, but the nuclear family gathered around a dinner table. Evidence of family breakdown is adduced from the millions of people who eat alone, often in front of the television. A survey reported in the *New York Times* in 1992 noted that 80 per cent of respondents with children claimed that their family had eaten dinner together the previous evening, even as observational studies indicated that the figure was closer to 30 per cent. The power of the myth can be seen, not merely in the desire of the respondents to imagine – or present themselves

– as a cohesive family unit through their eating habits, but also in the beliefs of the researchers, who concluded, in the same sentence, that family dinner-time was in decline even as they acknowledged that no comparative figures from earlier decades were available. Had the researchers been historians rather than psychiatrists, they would have known that their image of a family of the past gathered together around a dinner table was a novelty of modernity, and of plenty, not least because, historically, few sat around the family dining table for the simple reason that, as we have seen, most households did not have tables, or enough chairs.

For families, and homes, have always been in flux, evolving to meet the needs and circumstances of each era. The only permanency has been our belief that there is one unchanging reality, perhaps the strongest and most comforting myth of all.

Part Two

6

Hearth and Home

Heat and light, the two essentials of the technology of home. For much of history, both were provided by fire. Fire was the essence of home, the centre of the house. The Romance languages, languages with no separate word for home, often use some derivation from the Latin for hearth, *focus*, as a synonym for home: *il focolare domestico*, *le foyer familial*, *el hogar*. (And the centrality of the hearth survives in 'focus' in English, the centre of attention.) The hearth was so fundamental that legally it frequently represented the household: various places imposed hearth taxes, from the Byzantine Empire, through France in the fourteenth century, to England at the Restoration and Ireland until the nineteenth century.* These taxes were levied not on the building, nor the number of its residents, but on the quantities of chimneys and hearths each possessed. Church courts also used the hearth as a metonym for the household, permitting some couples legal separation *a mensa et thoro*, 'from table and hearth'. In parts of Italy, the basic rental space was a *camino*, meaning fireplace. The hearth might even embody citizenship: Britain and Ireland both had 'potwalloper' boroughs, where voting eligibility was extended to anyone with a hearth where a pot walloped, or boiled.

---

* The 1662 hearth tax in England, which was imposed to pay for the newly restored monarchy, engendered riots by those outraged at a levy 'exposing every Man's House to be entered into and searched at Pleasure', almost the language of physical violation.

The hearth's centrality was also expressed in folk sayings and proverbs – 'a home must have a wife and a fire', or 'a hearth of one's own is worth gold' – and it long continued to symbolize the family gathered around it. The nineteenth-century MP and journalist William Cobbett thought servants should always have their own fire. Sharing the family's fire, he said, was 'downright bigamy': the family was, in effect, married to its hearth.

Throughout the Middle Ages and beyond, hearths had been not merely figuratively central, but literally so: when the hall was the main, or only, room of the house, at the centre of that room was the open hearth. In the absence of chimneys or flues, smoke rose through the rafters of the unceilinged room, or through shuttered smoke-holes, or louvres, aided by drafts from carefully positioned doors and windows. The smoke, far from being considered a nuisance, was valued. Meat and cheese, fruit and grain were stored under the roof, preserved by the smoke as it rose; when the roof was thatched, the smoke also served to fumigate it and control insect-life. Below, around the fire, all daily and nightly activities transpired: the hall was the place of food preparation, of eating, sleeping, work and entertainment.

The date of the creation of the first chimney is uncertain. The earliest fireplace we know of may have been one built into the side wall of a building in Venice in 1227; others think traces of fireplaces appear as early as the ninth century, when the monastery of St Gall, in Switzerland, was recorded as having what might have been something like a fireplace in its walls. Whenever it occurred, the arrival of this new method of fire-control shifted the fire from the centre of the room to its edge. By the thirteenth century, we know that chimneys had been constructed in some great houses in France, because they had complete second storeys, which was impossible as long as smoke from open fires needed to escape through the roof. Henry III of England had fireplaces built in his private chamber in the same century, but the custom was barely known: a royal fancy, not yet the commonplace of the populace. Throughout the fourteenth and fifteenth centuries, central halls, and central hearths, remained standard.

It was in the late fifteenth and early sixteenth century, with the political stability brought by the end of the dynastic struggle known as the Wars of the Roses, and the accession of Henry VII and the establishment of the Tudor dynasty, that the function of the great halls in England began to change, enabling alterations to the architecture. No longer did nobles need to quarter soldiers in their halls to defend their lands. Wealth and status were no longer measured solely by the number of men one had under command; now a display of luxury goods, using the hall as the setting, performed a similar function. In the mid-sixteenth century, not merely the function, but the physical layout of these halls was modified, as the central hearths moved to the side of the room. The fire was not yet embedded into the fabric of the wall, but now flues were, and a great overhanging hood swept down and out into the room and over the fire to guide the smoke upwards.* Over the following half-century, in the houses of the great, and even many smaller houses of the lesser, fires were built into the walls of new houses, ventilated by flues, particularly in England, where the prevalence of brick as a building material encouraged the construction of what became standard, the brick chimney.

This in turn encouraged the Great Rebuilding, that period of widespread construction. Houses, no longer constrained by the

---

* A later version of such a hood is illustrated in the plate section, see no. 9. Hearths by partition walls, covered by hoods, or in bays, survived well into the twentieth century in both Scotland and Ireland.

physical limitations imposed by central fires, gained second storeys; windows, freed of the need to act as ventilation controls for smoke, were enlarged, re-sited and more frequently glazed; and in wealthy houses in the south, the number of rooms rose from an average of three per house to six or seven. All this was dramatic enough that, although the term Great Rebuilding is a coinage of the twentieth century, contemporaries were vividly aware of the novel landscape around them: towards the end of the sixteenth century, 'old men' were said to have remarked on 'the multitude of chimneys lately erected, whereas in their young days there were not above two or three, if so many'. It is notable that for this speaker, chimneys were a defining feature of the house. The new central, or just off-centre, placement of chimneys was guided by pragmatism – it allowed hall and parlour to have a fire in each room from a shared central chimney – but its position swiftly made it symbolic too, a sign of prosperous and comfortable living.

In the seventeenth century, some of the less well-off were also able to join this rage for rebuilding, acquiring the new luxuries of light, warmth and privacy. In the American colonies, even the first one-room huts often had chimneys: their builders had grown up during the Great Rebuilding, and took chimneys for granted as an integral part of any house, albeit constructed from clay-covered logs rather than brick. For those on the frontier, however, well into the eighteenth century, methods of heating were a step back into the past. These houses frequently lacked both fireplace and even a hearth, householders laying their fire on a collection of stones, the smoke once more exiting, as it had habitually for centuries, through a hole in the roof.

Most home countries developed their own heating methods, based on considerations of climate, fuel availability and local technologies and industries. By the sixteenth century, many countries in northern Europe had replaced open fires with the superior technology and convenience of closed stoves, whether made of stone, brick or, later, tile. The two most common methods, stove and fireplace, unusually, were not distributed evenly between home and house countries: the British Isles, the Netherlands, Italy, France, Portugal and Norway favoured fireplaces; the Scandinavian countries, much of central and eastern Europe, Switzerland and Germany preferred stoves, while Spain went its own way with braziers.

Stoves were usually set into a wall that separated two rooms, surrounded by benches or other sleeping furniture. In the seventeenth century, cast iron became the material of choice, and stoves became widespread. The new technology did not necessarily mean that smoke vanished from the house. On the contrary, as in the medieval halls, smoke was useful. The layout of many German houses featured a *Küche*, or hall, which contained an open, chimneyless fire, from which the smoke rose to the room above, the *Rauchkammer*, or smoke-room, where food was stored. The *Stube*, or main room, was heated by a stove fuelled from the *Küche* next door, and thus the high-status public room remained smoke-free. Although stoves were more efficient than fireplaces, houses were still very cold. Wooden walls were infilled with wattle-and-daub, or clay-daubed straw, for insulation, but despite this the *Stube*, with its stove, was often sited next to the stables, the animal heat being a welcome addition.

The newly built Dutch city houses of the time were little warmer. The *voorhuis*, the room that opened on to the street, had no fireplace, although the inner rooms might, depending on the prosperity of the family. These fireplaces projected into the room, with an overhanging hood supported by columns and open on three sides. The hood was, as mantelpieces later became, a status symbol, and in the richest households they might measure as much as 2 metres wide and 2 metres high. While the fire surrounds could be imposingly large, the fires they contained were not always of equivalent size, or even heat. The largely unforested Netherlands was forced to rely primarily on peat, a fuel that burns poorly, needing careful ventilation just to stay alight. In the seventeenth century, the Dutch used metal firepots set inside their hearths, in which stacks of peat were piled in thin, round pillars. Even with these specialized items, the houses, rich as well as poor, the most modern as well as the most basic, were cold, and households therefore contained a number of items to ameliorate the impact of this indoor frost. Footwarmers, pierced metal boxes that held burning peat, were common, as were the *zoldertjes*, wooden platforms designed to create a buffer between the sitter and the chill of the floor.* (A *zolder* is a loft, the insulating space between the roof and the rooms below. The diminutive '*je*' ending makes a *zoldertje* a 'little attic', a little insulating space.)

In the British Isles, regions without plentiful timber also used peat, or animal fuels – dried dung – or, failing these, even dried gorse. In urban areas, timber was the main fuel until the seventeenth and eighteenth centuries, although improved transportation saw coal become steadily more common. When the coal tax was repealed in 1793, many switched to that fuel. But by modern standards, houses remained cold, for most rooms in all houses were entirely unheated. Even among the wealthy, it appears that heat was considered a luxury rather than a necessity. In seventeenth-century Cambridgeshire, even in large houses of up to six rooms, houses that had recently been

---

* Footwarmers in art could symbolize amorous preoccupations – one engraving of a footwarmer is entitled '*Mignon des Dames*' [favourite of the women]. The shoe slipped off in Metsu's *Woman Reading a Letter* (see plate section, no. 3), encourages a symbolic reading there too. Despite this symbolic reading, there is good evidence to suggest that footwarmers and *zoldertjes* were used by both sexes.

rebuilt and had owners worth a substantial £200, even here, half these houses had a single fireplace. By the end of the century in Norwich, a flourishing urban centre at the time, houses with up to six rooms still averaged only two fireplaces, and in the early eighteenth century, half the parlours – the best room, the showpiece – had no fireplace at all. The greatest residences were little warmer. As the eighteenth century began, the wine on the king's dinner table at Versailles was reported to have frozen. And it was often the case that poorer households, with their smaller rooms and fewer and smaller windows, were warmer. A house of twenty rooms might average four fireplaces, while a two-room lodging might have one.

By the nineteenth century, many of the comfortably-off in countries that used stoves, particularly Germany and the USA, lived in houses with extremely efficient heating systems, and the inhabitants often commented on those, particularly in Britain, who remained emotionally attached to fireplaces, which used more fuel while producing markedly less heat. Hermann Muthesius, the architect-trained son of a small building contractor from Thuringia, served as a diplomatic attaché in London from 1896 to 1904, and his appalled fascination with English domestic arrangements is telling.* He mentions the poor quality of the weather-proofing of housing: the thin walls, the lack of insulating cellars, double-glazing and entrance porches, the poor-fitting windows and doors, all of which he attributed to the mildness of the climate. Then he moves

---

* Muthesius (1861–1927), the author of *Das englische Haus* (*The English House*, 1904), was socially as well as professionally connected to many of the architects of the Arts and Crafts movement, and his work has been profoundly influential. It is important to bear in mind that, despite its title, his book is not about 'The English House', but about 'The English Houses of the Rich'. Sentences such as 'An English kitchen without a gas stove is unthinkable nowadays' reveal his unconscious bias, for at the date he was writing only 33 per cent *of those who had gas at all* used gas cookers. As late as the 1930s, 40 per cent of all working-class housing had no access to gas for lighting or cooking.

on to fireplaces. He acknowledges that, given the damp climate, the ventilating element of fireplaces, which suck up air voraciously, is useful, although he clearly finds bizarre the phlegmatic English acceptance of the resulting draughts. 'The many advantages the fireplace is deemed to possess (not least its aesthetic advantages, some of which, it must be admitted, exist only in the imagination) so completely convince an Englishman of its superiority to all other forms of heating', he notes, that the superior efficiency, and value, of stoves is passed over. By the 1870s, hot-water central heating was widely used in greenhouses, and in some public buildings that were not suitable for fires, such as church halls and civic spaces, but the cheapness and easy availability of coal meant that these other forms of heating were rarely if ever considered for domestic purposes. Fires remained totemic for the British: in World War I a popular patriotic song urged the populace to 'Keep the home fires burning', and at the start of World War II, coal fires still heated the houses of three-quarters of the population.

The harsh climate across swathes of North America made it necessary for residents to be far more pragmatic when it came to heating, and as the population was drawn from many northern European countries, knowledge of other technologies was readily available. From the 1840s, cast-iron stoves were the standard heating method, initially in the form of the popular Franklin fireplace, which had metal sides and was open at the front, later with the closed stoves of Europe gaining popularity. An amateur watercolour shows the dining room of a doctor's house in Rhode Island in 1815 with its Franklin stove and, beside it, a figure in heavy clothes (see plate section, no. 25). Whether this was intended to suggest the man has come in from outside (a pair of boots sits beside him), or whether the room is, despite the stove, still bitterly cold, is impossible to say.

Central heating began to appear in the USA in the 1890s, but until the 1920s, like so many domestic improvements, initially it remained the preserve of the wealthy, or at least those of the middle classes who lived in new houses. Installing it involved major construction work. A basement had to be dug to house the furnace, and pipes and ducts run behind walls and under floors. Just as the spread of chimneys had reoriented the design of buildings, allowing not only changes to house layouts, but also to the behaviour of the houses' inhabitants, so too the adoption of central heating changed more than just the temperature, altering both room use and permitting new ideas of privacy to flourish. With fireplaces and stoves, the cost and labour of heating ensured that as many members of the household as possible would naturally gather in the room where a fire burnt, irrespective of the number of activities being undertaken. With central heating, there was only a small difference in fuel consumption when additional rooms were heated, and there was no increase at all in labour. There was therefore little reason not to heat several, or all, of the rooms, irrespective of which were occupied at any given moment. There was no longer an economic or labour-saving reason for many people to gather in a single room, and so the members of the family, and their activities, began to spread across the different rooms of the house.

Where the USA did follow many other countries, both house and home, was in sharing an emotional response to the hearth, and in associating the fireplace with the idea of home, and family life, as a whole. In the 1860s, an American outlined to his fiancée his 'visions of [our] future years fraught with happiness', years 'when we should sit together by ourselves in "our home" on the winter evenings by our bright fireside'. In Britain, this emotional reading of a physical architectural element was so reflexive that it was generally noticed only by foreigners. At the end of the nineteenth century, Muthesius wrote that 'All ideas of domestic comfort, of family happiness, of inward personal life, of spiritual wellbeing, centre around the fireplace.' By this date, if anything, that focus had now increased. Earlier, at mid-century, Gothic Revival architects took their inspiration from churches and public buildings, not natural locations for fireplaces, or domestic associations. Nevertheless, their domestic designs frequently highlighted a symbolic over a pragmatic function for the hearth. The houses designed by Augustus Pugin often incorporated the chimney-breast into the exterior walls, in a style reminiscent of the Middle Ages. This was deeply fuel-inefficient, causing far more heat to escape than even traditional fireplace construction did. But the style announced to the world at large the presence of the fireplace, and the value of the symbolism apparently weighed more strongly than the value of the heat.

Later, the architects of the Arts and Crafts movement were equally focused on the fireplace as a locus of home emotions. For interiors, they revived the inglenook, a feature last seen in the days when fireplaces had first moved to the walls from the centre of the hall. Then benches had been placed under the great overhanging hoods that loomed over the hearth area, forming a seating area in the warmth. When the fireplaces were set into the walls themselves, the hanging hoods had given way to the mantelpiece and the inglenooks vanished. Now, at the end of the nineteenth century, this reactionary architectural style produced recessed seating areas around the fire once more, creating artificial inglenooks and re-centring household life on the fireplace. On the exterior of their buildings, Arts and Crafts architects such as Edward Lutyens also frequently designed chimneys that were much taller than was necessary for smoke dispersal, ensuring that these symbols of home were visible from afar.

7. The nineteenth century's Tudor architecture was very different from the sixteenth century's. Then, beams were rarely exposed, and never painted. Instead they weathered to the same buff shade as the ?beside them, creating a unified façade. In the nineteenth century, authentic Tudor buildings were ?d' to what was assumed to be their original state, using paints and colours unknown earlier, as can be ?these photographs of Staple Inn, in London, before and after their transformation.

18. & 19. The newly industrialized world created a desire for a simpler, imagined past, and in the nineteenth century in the USA, the log cabin became a symbol of this desire. Abraham Lincoln's early homes had long vanished by the time he became president, but this did not stop his supposed birthplac being put on show (*top*). In Britain, the architects of the Arts and Crafts movement emphasized architectural elements that were redolent of enclosure to create ideas of home and the past, as in Charle Voysey's 1908 house-plan, *above*.

21. For much of history,
[w]e we regard as essential was
[luxur]y. As late as the seventeenth
[century], few households had enough
[chairs] for everyone to sit. In Jan
[Steen's] *A Peasant Family at Meal-time*
[(1665?,] *right*), only the man of the
[househ]old has a seat, while the rest of
[the fam]ily eats standing up. A century
[later,] a scene that appears to us
[frugal], Joseph van Aken's *Saying*
[Grace, c.1720, below*) is in reality a
[celebrati]on of prosperity, with its display
[of candl]es, earthenware, pewter and
[glass. (]There may even be running
[water,]suggested by the pipe at the top
[of the c]himney-breast.)

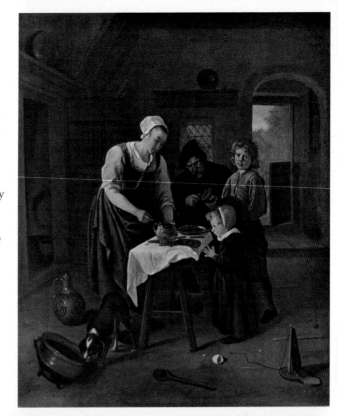

22. & 23. Lighting technology barely chang[ed] for centuries. The woman in Judith Leyste[r's] *Proposition* (1631, *above*), in the technologi[cally] advanced Netherlands, sews by the light of [a] lamp that consists of a wick floating in a d[ish,] the only development from Roman lamps [a] millennium earlier being the clamp enabli[ng the] light source to be raised or lowered. In the eighteenth- and nineteenth-century betty [lamps] (*left*) were little different, simply replacing [the] clamp with a chain.

24. Most households had multi-functional rooms. In this anonymous portrait of *John Middleton with his Family in his Drawing Room* (*c.*1796, *above*), the prosperous shopkeeper and his family worked and ate in their elegant sitting-room, as indicated by the dining table that pulls out on the left, and the dresser, at the rear, *right*, which holds a knife-box, for cutlery.

ing technology was slow to develop, even in the harsh North American climate. *The Dining-room of —ridge's, as it was in the Winter of 1814–1815* (1814–15, *above*), in Rhode Island, shows a Franklin stove, an — with a metal surround. The bundled-up figure beside it indicates the room's probable temperature.

26. & 27. Lighting was expensive, therefore often used as a symbol o or even profligacy, as in Hogarth's depiction of a gambling den in *Th Progress* (*above*). Quiet domesticity well as new technology, is illumin Georg Friedrich Kersting's *The Ele Reader* (1812, *left*), where the new lamp sits on its own special stand.

& 30. What looks to us like abject poverty was actually the result of the abundance of consumer
ewly affordable to the masses. But as late as this 1910 photograph (*top*), the design of many
ds had not kept pace with the increasing number of items they contained. In 1869, Catharine Beecher
ined her dream of a kitchen where there was 'A place for every thing, and every thing in its place'
ft), but her rationalization of household space would have to wait for the twentieth century for most.
hütte-Lihotzky's famed Frankfurt kitchen (*above right*) of 1926 was the ancestor of many more
chens.

31. & 32. Objects of luxury and
display changed in type, but pr[...]
of ownership remained consta[...]
whether it was the newest porc[...]
tea-service painted so carefully [...]
Arthur Devis in *Mr and Mrs H[...]*
(*c.*1750–51, *left*), or the televisio[...]
that two centuries later replace[...]
fireplace as the focal point of e[...]
sitting-room (1957, *below*).

Others favoured roofs that swept down low, with overhanging eaves, to create a sense of safety and enclosure, the emotional resonance of home in physical form (see plate section, no. 19). And yet, powerful as these symbols were, these same architects frequently displayed a lack of engagement with the practicalities of home. Charles Voysey's houses were notorious for their poor heating and plumbing, for kitchens that were both unattractive and inconvenient, and frequently decades behind in their provision of basic facilities. The style's emotional impact appears to have been bought at the cost of physical comfort: the appearance of homeliness taking precedence over the reality of home-making.

The same emotional impulse drew these architects to return to old-fashioned casement windows fitted with small, leaded panes of glass, overturning three centuries of improved glazing technology. By this stage, of course, windows were regarded as par for the course; in earlier centuries, they had been a concern. Windows might let in thieves, or just the dangerous night air. Witches might also enter: doors, chimneys and windows were all vulnerable points, and witch bottles were buried under doors or hearths, and horseshoes hung over windows to protect them. (One London house was found to have had its window protected thus as late as 1790.) On a more practical level, too many windows also caused a central hearth to smoke uncontrollably. Northern climates had to balance the benefits of additional light against the consequent loss of heat; southern ones against the influx of additional heat. The Anglo-Saxon words for window – eye-hole, wind-door, eye-door – suggest tiny size, and that they were for ventilation, or at most for peering through the way peepholes are used in apartment doors today. As 'wind-door' suggests, windows were originally also open to the elements, with no shutters. Even in the Middle Ages, a window was primarily for ventilation, not light: the word referred to any opening that was not a door. For much of the subsequent centuries, most housing was built to an unspoken rule, that each wall had at most one opening, be it a chimney, a door or a window.

The first known reference to glazing in England dates from 675, when French glass, and the French glaziers who knew how to fit it, were imported to install church windows at Jarrow, in Northumberland. (The monastery was also the first stone ecclesiastical building in the British Isles.) But this was singular. Glass began to be used more routinely in ecclesiastical buildings only from the twelfth century; it was the middle of the thirteenth before secular buildings followed suit, and then glass was confined entirely to the houses of the wealthy. The windows of the less well-off, depending on their location, were covered with shutters, or with wooden latticework; or with waxed or oiled paper or linen, or fabric rendered opaque by soaking it in turpentine. In the British Isles the church continued to be at the forefront of glazing innovations: in the thirteenth century Lincoln Cathedral was the first to use wooden frames to hold the glass, and to set its shutters on hinges – previously the boards had been nailed in place. In the fourteenth century, in the halls of the aristocracy, the two purposes of windows, light and ventilation, were commonly treated separately. Generally, the top section was glazed, for light, and did not open, while an unglazed lower section was covered with shutters, for ventilation. Some were mixed, the fixed glazed panes interspersed with small panels of lead, known as ventilation quarrels, that were designed to open, letting air in and smoke out. But a division between functions remained standard in the Low Countries in the fifteenth century and then spread across northwestern Europe, with modifications: fixed glazing in the upper section of the window, sometimes an unglazed, shuttered mid-section, and a lower section with a wooden lattice, or wooden shutters, or both (see plate section, nos. 10 and 11).

Early glass was the most fragile of materials: a pane might shatter in strong winds or heavy rain. When wealthy owners travelled between their houses, therefore, these delicate, and valuable, panes were routinely removed from their frames and carefully wrapped and stored, or they were packed in their baggage along with other valuables such as tapestries, jewels and plate. Because of this, until the early years of the sixteenth century, the glass panes and the windows they were fitted into were considered to be separate items: legally the frames were an intrinsic part of the building, while the glass those frames held belonged to the owner of the house, to be sold or bequeathed like any other personal possession. Then, as the cost of glass dropped dramatically over the course of the century, the builders of Elizabethan and Jacobean great houses embraced glass as a building material, using it in a way previously unknown, and to an extent that went far beyond any need for light. It became, for the first time, an object of conspicuous consumption. Hardwick Hall in Derbyshire (1590–97) was the most extreme example, so extreme that there was even a little ditty about it: 'Hardwick Hall, More glass than wall.' The sheer acreage of glass there created numerous problems, from intolerable glare indoors, to awkward arrangements of furniture, owing to the paucity of solid walls. Hardwick was built by the Countess of Shrewsbury, one of the great aristocrats, and the richest woman, of the day, but the mercantile rich also participated in the fashion for what might be described as seventeenth-century curtain-walling. By the end of the century, the rapid acceptance of what had previously been a rarity had produced a new legal standard: 'without glass', ruled the courts, 'it is no perfect house'. Glass was henceforth an integral, and integrated, part of the window.

Integral, but still a luxury rather than a necessity, even for the comfortably-off. Many who could now afford glass still saw no particular reason to glaze their windows. In Oxfordshire in the sixteenth century, less than 4 per cent of the inventories of the poor and the averagely circumstanced mention any glass windows at all; even among the better-off, it was less than one in ten. As the seventeenth century began, prosperous farmhouses in the Midlands often had glazed windows only in the hall, or just one glazed window per room. It was not until the end of the seventeenth century that three glazed windows per room became typical.

In the American colonies, glass, and even windows, long remained the rarity they had been in Europe in earlier centuries. In the early years of colonial settlement, windows were primarily seen as creating vulnerabilities. Physically, windows would open up houses to potential attacks from indigenous peoples; emotionally, there was a sense that they opened the colonists up to the wildness of the new world more generally. Then there was the climate, in most places more extreme than the home climates of the early immigrants. Whether for heat-conservation in the north, or protection from the sun in the south, shutters did a better job than glass. And for all in those early days, the technology, even at the most basic level, had to be imported. In the middle of the seventeenth century, advice to would-be settlers continued to tell them to 'bring paper and linseed oil for your windows'. Flowerdew Hundred, a Virginia plantation that existed from at least 1619, had one of the earliest stone foundations in English America. One of the later houses on this site had at least some glazed windows, for archaeological finds there have included English lead window-bars inscribed 1693 (although there is no telling when they were shipped to the colonies).

It is notable that in colonial America, as had earlier been the case

in England, window-glass, and the frames, were not part of the building, but pieces of furniture, along with the shutters, or the household
furnishings, or even 'the bedstead matt'. The older legal distinction
mirrored the older emotional response to windows, and to many in
the new world they were neither necessary nor desirable. In 1637, one
householder instructed his builder: 'For windowes, let them not be
over large in any roome, & few as conceivably may be.' And as late
as 1751, many considered them a fashionable addition, a luxurious
extra. A New England minister's new house had thirteen windows,
which caused 'very Sharp' comments to be made about 'the pride of
Ministers', he reported dolefully. He hastily professed himself 'griev'd
that the windows were so large and I have often said it that I wish'd
they were less'.

Into the nineteenth century, half of the houses in the USA had
either no glazed windows at all, or just one, and that one usually no
more than the size of a single small pane. Instead many continued to
use slatted shutters, which were 'universal' by the nineteenth century,
and had the benefit of letting in fresh breezes while excluding dust
and some insects, as well as providing shade in the warmer areas of
the country. In 1853, Frederick Law Olmsted described, with all the
astonishment of a sophisticated urban northerner, a house owned by
a southern planter. The landowner was more than solvent, owning
between twenty and thirty slaves, and yet, wrote Olmsted, amazed,
his house was nothing but a 'small square log cabin' with 'no window,
nor was there a pane of glass' anywhere on the property.

Olmsted was representative of many prosperous city dwellers, who
were the beneficiaries of the revolution in window design that, over
the previous two centuries, had transformed the buildings of much
of northwestern Europe. The first development was at Versailles,
halfway through its transformation under Louis XIV, and already

known across Europe for its grandeur. In 1673, when the innovative Swedish architect Nicodemus Tessin visited the court, the palace's great series of *grands appartements* were complete. Tessin, however, gave his first consideration not to the interiors, to the overwhelming grandeur of the designs, but to a technical novelty: casement windows set in pairs, and now extended to reach from floor level nearly to the ceiling, which in English are still designated 'French' windows. These clearly fascinated him, and he detailed their workings – how they opened and closed, how the frames were built, their size and decoration. He was not alone. The windows were widely admired, and by the 1690s several aristocrats had arranged for these novelties to be featured in their new Parisian mansions. But incorporating the style into older buildings required major structural work to the walls, and was not something to be undertaken lightly. French windows, instead of bringing light to the many, remained a luxury of the wealthiest few.

It was, instead, the English and the Dutch who most thoroughly domesticated light, in the seventeenth century creating a new style that was quickly emulated across the home countries, literally enlightening the homes of millions. The sash window consists of two identical frames, or sashes, set one above the other, with a double tier (or more) of glass panes in each. Instead of opening outward on a hinge, as casement windows do, one frame slides up or down over the second one. Simple sliding windows that could be propped open with wooden blocks, struts or pins had been in use in France by the end of the sixteenth century, usually in corridors and service areas where limited space restricted the use of casements. The revolutionary feature of the English sash window was not the sliding element, but the weight-and-pulley mechanism inside the frame. The weights counterbalanced the two frames as each was raised or lowered, allowing the window to remain open in any position. Upper sashes could, for example, be left open only a few inches at the very top, above the level of the three-quarter shutters then common, ventilating a room at night even as the shutters kept the house secure. Furthermore, the new wooden frames could be fitted more tightly than a casement's metal frame, keeping out both damp and draughts far more efficiently. (It is notable that sash windows were most frequently first installed in bedrooms and chambers, rooms where draughts were easily felt.)

The first sash window that can be firmly dated was installed in the royal apartments in Whitehall, in 1662. But unlike the French windows of Versailles, the style did not long remain a luxury of the great. Sashes' space-saving, lighting and ventilating qualities made them hugely desirable, while, unlike French windows, sash windows could conform to the dimensions of the older casements, and could thus replace the old-fashioned windows without wholesale rebuilding. By the 1670s, several of the great landowners in England had installed sashes in their houses, and the prosperous swiftly followed suit, as did the Dutch.* As in England, in the Netherlands the windows were first adopted in royal palaces (the indefatigable Nicodemus Tessin also reported seeing them in Het Loo, William III's palace, in 1686), but they were so eminently suited to the unique social and geographical circumstances of the Netherlands that their spread was almost immediate. As we have seen, the Dutch were pioneers of modern urbanization, and the scarcity of land made terraced

---

* In the nineteenth century, the Dutch term for them was still 'English windows', but the speed of transmission between the two countries clouded the origins of the invention, and it was long thought that the windows were Dutch in design, brought to England with the court of Charles II on his restoration in 1660. (Modern Dutch simply calls them 'sliding windows', *schuiframen*.) The architectural historian Hentie Louw has, however, definitively shown that the windows' movement was in the opposite direction.

housing – housing that is typically both narrow and deep, with no exterior side-walls – the national style, a style that puts a premium on large windows at front and rear. By the eighteenth century, this type of housing, complete with sash windows, had spread to become the standard in many urban areas across the home countries. As early as 1701, a Boston merchant installed sash windows in his new house, although he had had to import both the glass and the frames, as there were no manufacturers, or even joiners, who knew how to make and install the counterweighted pulleys in North America at that date.

The new technology increased the amount of light indoors; at the same time, the problem of lighting more generally was one that was being addressed. Across Europe, as cities expanded, and buildings grew taller, as population density increased, and as streets therefore became darker and more filled with strangers, how to light the streets became a civic preoccupation. Some cities tried to rebuild their narrow medieval streets, either widening individual routes, or, more ambitiously, replacing the meandering medieval roads with streets laid out in a grid pattern, to allow more moonlight to penetrate. But improving artificial lighting was a simpler, and cheaper, solution.

As we have seen again and again, the Low Countries, the first in the modern world to experience high-density urban living, were also the first to address many of the problems consequent on these conditions. Dutch cities instituted a night watch, or street patrol, which operated from 10 p.m. to 4 a.m., checking that doors and shutters were properly closed and helping anyone who was lost or drunk.* The patrol also had the power to arrest anyone on the streets

---

* Rembrandt's famous *Night Watch* looks both more glamorous and more martial than these mundane duties suggest; its real title, *The Shooting Company of Frans Banning Cocq*, makes clear that the men portrayed were members of a militia company, not the street watch.

after dark without a lantern, which was now a legal requirement. Similar regulations were enacted in parts of France, the British Isles and Prussia, with night-walkers obliged to carry their own lighting on pain of arrest. But developments in the Netherlands went further, and occurred earlier, than in other countries. From 1595, civic regulations required that the façade of every twelfth house be fitted with a bracket for a lantern, and a century later Amsterdam pioneered the use of an oil street lamp, thereby becoming, almost literally, a beacon for other cities. In the final decade of the seventeenth century, Amsterdam was far more brightly lit than Paris – the city of light was still in the future. Amsterdam's streets contained 2,400 lamps; Paris, with twice the population, had just 2,736. And while Amsterdam's street lights were fixed to the houses, Parisian street lights hung from ropes that ran across the streets, illuminating the thoroughfares more clearly, even if the areas near the houses remained in the shadows. By 1750, the streets of Paris were lined with more than eight thousand lights. In 1680, Prussia, too, started to experiment with street lighting, adopting yet another system. Here the lamps were hung from poles erected for the purpose, a precursor to lamp posts. Of all northern Europe's major urban centres, London lagged furthest behind. Late into the eighteenth century, its civic authorities only required lamps to be affixed to houses, without regulating the type of light, nor attempting to enforce technological improvements, as Amsterdam had. It was 1736 before London's local parishes took control of the supervision of street lighting. Funded by taxes, minimum standards could finally be established, and maintained.

Parish control suggested that lighting was now considered to be a civic good for all London's citizens. In Paris, by contrast, it was the police who set the standards and supervised street lighting, all falling under the remit of crime prevention, and swallowing a remarkable

15 per cent of the money spent on policing and security. In London, breaking a street lamp was a civil offence, a crime against private property; in Paris it was a crime against the state.* In both cases, lighting, no matter which the supervisory body, still had to be supplemented by private enterprise. Throughout the eighteenth century, most major cities, as well as smaller towns that had no official arrangements for lighting, continued to rely on link-bearers – men carrying torches of burning pitch – to cover areas where there was no street lighting, or where the dark was so profound that the lamps were inadequate. The sources of funding for street lighting predictably influenced public attitudes to link-bearers, even though these men were not paid by the city, or the government, but were in business independently. In Paris, where lighting was a police matter, the bearers were widely believed to be informers who sold information about night-movements to the police. In London, where lighting was civic, the link-bearers were on the contrary assumed to be in the pay of criminals, accepting bribes to lead unwary pedestrians into lonely places where they could be relieved of their possessions.

It was, however, only the major cities that had populations large enough for street lighting to be practical. In smaller towns, and in the countryside, throughout the eighteenth and into the nineteenth century, people relied on the oldest lighting of all, moonlight, and the nights of the full moon were nights of sociability. In *Sense and Sensibility* (1811), a landowner apologises for the small number of

---

* One historian has very plausibly suggested that it was the state's control of street lighting that led to enemies of the people being *lanterné*, hanged from street lamps, after the storming of the Bastille, rather than from shop signs, or trees, or other easily available high points. He also explains that the hangings were not, as many imagine, from lamp posts, which did not yet exist in France, but from the ropes that held the lamps. Some larger squares had lamps attached to wall-fixtures, and these were also used, but they were the exception.

guests at his impromptu party: 'He had been to several families that morning in hopes of procuring some addition to their number; but it was moonlight, and every body was full of engagements.' Even in the more prosaic surroundings of a Baptist chapel in Lancashire, one minister declared himself available to lead evening prayer meetings at any time, before clarifying that he meant those on moonlit nights.

The arrival of gas in the nineteenth century produced a transformation, both on the streets and at home. Gas street lighting was first demonstrated in London in 1807, and then spread rapidly across the cities of the western world – Baltimore in 1816, Paris in 1819, Berlin in 1826. London, by the eighteenth century the commercial centre of Europe, already had in place legislation that could be adapted to permit the wholesale excavation of the streets to lay gas mains, and it therefore became the first city to establish uniform lighting as a civic obligation. From the first small experiment in a single London street in 1807 – thirteen lamp posts were erected along Pall Mall for a three-month trial period – sixteen years later fifty-three British cities had gas mains, and by 1868 1,134 did. By contrast, Paris adopted gas for home lighting only in the late 1820s, and it took another two decades for pipes to reach other French cities. By the 1860s, London's 3 million residents were consuming as much gas as 50 million Germans. The USA was even slower to adopt what was there initially regarded as an outdoor form of lighting, for the most part holding out until the mid-1860s. From the first, gas was understood to be a revolution, not just a technology that made the night streets safer. 'What,' asked an anonymous reviewer of a book on the new gas lighting in 1829, 'has the new light of all the preachers done for the morality and order of London, compared to what had been effected by this new light...It is not only that men are afraid to be wicked...but they are ashamed also.' And by the end of the century, a walk down a street at night was regarded as little less dangerous than a trip across one's sitting room. 'Mankind and its supper parties,' wrote Robert Louis Stevenson, 'were no longer at the mercy of a few miles of sea-fog; sundown no longer emptied the promenade; and the day was lengthened out to every man's fancy. The city-folk had stars of their own; biddable domesticated stars.'*

Before the stars became biddable, developments in lighting had been a matter of evolution, not revolution. Oil lamps had been in use since classical times, as had candles and rushlights. The candle is an ancient technology, with only two basic forms, beeswax and tallow. The disadvantages of tallow are legion: rendered from animal fat, its melting point is half that of beeswax; it produces more, and much hotter, wax as it melts, and so requires a larger wick to burn up the excess; the larger wick in turn produces a bigger flame, which lacks oxygen at its centre and therefore makes the unburnt carbon smoke heavily. (Houses in northern Europe often had tiled niches for a candle or a rushlight, which could be easily wiped free of soot.) For all these disadvantages, tallow had one great counter-advantage in the home countries: it was readily available in northern Europe's sheep- and cattle-farming regions, and it was, therefore, cheap. The relative scarcity of domestic animals in colonial America meant that tallow was scarce, although those living on the frontier made use of bear- or deer-fat tallow. Otherwise as northern Europeans used resinous pinewoods to make torches for exterior lighting, or small splints for interior, so colonists relied on candlewood, or on wax from bayberry trees. (Bayberry grew only by the sea, but was one of

---

* It is interesting to note that some twenty-first-century cities, motivated by energy-conservation and light-pollution concerns, as well as cost, have been experimenting with a return to dark night streets. Preliminary reports suggest that these produce lower crime rates, belying centuries of fears.

the few natural saps that smelt pleasant as it burnt.) Most resinous woods smoked heavily and leaked pitch, and so like tallow were used by those who had few alternatives.

Even beeswax candles, which had a more pleasant smell, and burnt more cleanly, had problems. Until the end of the eighteenth century, all wicks were made of twisted cotton. As the candle burnt, the carbonized section of the wick had to be regularly and repeatedly snuffed, or snipped away: without snuffing, increasing quantities of black smoke plumed out, and a tallow candle lost 80 per cent of its light in half an hour, before finally it extinguished itself. Beeswax had a higher melting point, and beeswax candles therefore could be made with thinner wicks; these did not need to be snuffed quite as much. Today to snuff out means to extinguish, possibly because snipping a burning wick without also putting out the flame is difficult.* Before friction matches were invented early in the nineteenth century, that might mean hours of darkness. Late one night in 1762/3, the diarist James Boswell accidentally put out his candle, and, 'as my fire… was…black and cold, I was in a great dilemma'. He crept downstairs to the kitchen of his lodgings to see if the stove there had any embers, 'But, alas, there was as little fire there as upon the icy mountains of Greenland'. Nor could he locate the kitchen tinder-box in the dark.† Resigned, 'I went up to my room, sat quietly until I heard the

---

* The little conical hats on rods that many today call snuffers are properly known as extinguishers. Snuffers were adapted scissors, with a small box on one blade that caught the burnt section of the wick as they were snipped. Snuffers were luxury items from the sixteenth century, appearing in ordinary households at the end of the seventeenth century.
† These boxes hung by every fireplace. Each box was divided in two. One side held a scrap of fabric, a flint and a striker. The flint was struck over the fabric, the sparks setting it alight. A candle was then lit from this small blaze before the damper, in the second compartment, was used to put out the flame. A modern historian estimates that if the user was proficient, it took three minutes to get a flame; the less skilled might need half an hour.

watchman…I then called to him to knock at the door…He did so, and I opened it to him and got my candle relumed without danger.'

The first technological advance on wax and tallow candles came at the end of the eighteenth century, when spermaceti, the fat from sperm whales, was found to burn more cleanly than tallow, and began to be commercially processed. By the mid-nineteenth century, stearine, extracted from tallow, but less smelly, was also available, as were palm- or coconut-oil candles. These all burnt at higher temperatures than tallow, and this, combined with new types of wick with a tighter weave, made it possible for the wicks to burn away completely and be consumed by the candle. Snuffing was no longer necessary.

Even before the appearance of these new technologies, candles had always been a luxury. In most agricultural, and even many urban districts, well into the nineteenth century, most tasks were performed by firelight, including many involving skills that today are thought to require a bright light, such as sewing or reading. Given both the relative scarcity of windows, and, in North America, the continued use of shuttered, unglazed windows, artificial light was frequently needed indoors during the day as well as at night. As fires were necessary for cooking, they were often the primary light source as well. Candles were used chiefly to provide light when moving from one room to another, and it is not coincidental that their use spread at precisely the time when sash windows, which reduced draughts, were being installed in many middle-class houses. Even at the top of the social scale, there is an observable increase in the use of candles with the advent of sashes. Ham House had candlesticks only in its kitchens in 1654; twenty years later, there were so many scattered throughout the house that an inventory just listed them as 'numerous'.

This was despite the fact that in Britain most artificial light was legally categorized as a luxury good at various times in the seventeenth and eighteenth centuries, and was therefore subject to tax: coal was first taxed in 1667, and while many of the domestic levies were lifted in 1793, some remained in place until 1889; from 1709 to 1831, both wax and tallow candles were taxed, and had to be purchased from licensed dealers. Wax candles carried a higher tariff, although some country dwellers were permitted to make their own tallow candles, and, in a few carefully legislated circumstances, supply their neighbours.

Only rushlights, the poor man's lighting, were never subject to tax. Rushlights could be produced at minimal expense by anyone with access to rushes, found on common land. Towards the end of the eighteenth century, eleven hours' worth of rushlight cost a halfpenny, while the same halfpenny bought just two hours of candlelight. For most people, therefore, for most of the time, rushlights were the primary source of artificial light. In the early nineteenth century, William Cobbett reported that his grandmother had never used any other form of lighting, had 'never, I believe, burnt a candle in her house in her life'. In autumn she, like many others, gathered rushes, soaked and then peeled them, before drying the pith and dipping them in tallow or fat. For daily tasks, Cobbett said, rushlights were 'carried about in the hand'; for working or reading they were fixed in clamps of varying heights.

Many, like Cobbett, regarded candles as a mark of wastefulness, even sinfulness in their sheer profligacy. Churches had been the first to use artificial lighting routinely, but in secular contexts candles had come to represent not merely wealth, but louche living. Hogarth's engravings depict, possibly unconsciously, this pervasive distrust. In *The Rake's Progress* (1732–5), the lodgings of the rake's father, a prudent, careful man, have a fireplace and a single pricket candle-stick (this had a spike on which the candle was speared, rather than a socket, and was by then very old-fashioned). There is a single wall sconce for a candle, and that is empty. After his death, the rake begins to dissipate the inheritance his father had so carefully accumulated, and he is shown spending his time in a tavern that is lit by four candles, with mirrors behind them to enhance their light; later he patronizes a gambling den that has three candles and a lantern – profligacy heaped upon profligacy (see plate section, no. 26).

A Salem clergyman in 1630 drew up a list of 'needful things' that settlers should bring with them to survive their first year in North America. He included foods, spices, weapons, armour, clothes and tools, but no type of artificial illumination at all. And this was not because the settlers made candles themselves: the absence of candle-sticks in New England inventories makes it clear that they were simply not in daily use. In the early part of the eighteenth century, only one in four Pennsylvania estates valued at up to £400 owned any candlesticks at all, and even among the seriously wealthy, the figure was still no more than 40 per cent. It was not until the last third of the century that candles were routinely found in most households in the colonies. By then, three-quarters of the inventoried estates in the thirteen colonies had candlesticks, although there was considerable geographical variation: half of the households in South Carolina and Virginia, but between 80 and 90 per cent in New York and Boston. By then, some of the wealthiest households had become every bit as profligate as the moralists feared. In 1770, the household of Lord Botetourt, the Governor of Virginia, contained 114 'lighting devices', 952 'illuminants' and 31 snuffers.

As with all technologies, not everyone followed suit, even among those who could afford to. The extremely wealthy Landon Carter, a Virginia contemporary, owned a plantation of more than 50,000 acres and 500 slaves. Yet his entire household rarely consumed more than two candles a day. His nephew, more urbanized, used more artificial lighting, but still always with due care. His household ate dinner in daylight, and the bulk of social engagements – parties, dancing, visiting neighbours – were also scheduled before 'day-light-End'. The hours after dusk and before bedtime were reserved for leisure activities that needed some light: reading, conversation and music. The most festive occasions in this sophisticated household still used far less light than we might imagine. One party for seven adults and an unspecified number of children was described as having a 'splendid' appearance, owing to the seven candles that illuminated the room. This was not unusual, as the comment of a prosperous woman in Charleston, South Carolina, in 1791 inadvertently makes plain how low the level of lighting usually was. One supper party she attended, she marvelled, 'was so well lighted we could see every body'.

Candles and fires were not the only pre-industrial sources of artificial light. From classical times, oil lamps had been in daily use in many households across Europe, more frequently in the olive-growing regions of the south, while tallow candles predominated in the northern pasturelands. In Judith Leyster's *The Proposition* (1631), a Dutchwoman sews by the light of a lamp that consists of a wick floating in a flat dish, little different from the lamp a Roman would have used a millennium before. The only visible development was that the seventeenth-century dish now had a holder, a clamp that enabled the light source to be raised or lowered to suit the task in hand. In Pennsylvania a century later, the technology had barely altered, the local betty lamps (probably from German *besser*, better) merely replacing their ancestors' stick-stand with a hook or chain for suspension. (For both, see plate section, nos. 22 and 23.)

The first important technological developments in oil lighting emerged at the end of the eighteenth century. Patented in 1780, the Argand lamp included improvements that allowed the flame to burn more brightly, and more cleanly. This new flame was, for the first time, now enclosed in a glass cylinder, called a chimney, which not only protected the flame from draughts, but further increased its brightness by creating an up-draught. A winding mechanism for the wick made it easier to use, while a reservoir to hold the oil was gravity-fed, giving a more constant supply, and therefore a more constant light. (G. F. Kersting's *The Elegant Reader* (*c*.1814; see plate section, no. 27) shows an Argand lamp, in which this reservoir, above the shade to the left, can be clearly seen.) The success of this new lamp encouraged other manufacturers to work on improving efficiency, ease of use and, of course, brightness throughout the nineteenth century: wicks were repositioned, oil reservoirs repositioned, pumps added. From the 1830s, different types of oil were also becoming available. Colza, or rapeseed, was popular in France (although heavily taxed in Britain, so less common there), while the USA favoured camphene, distilled from turpentine and mixed with alcohol – cheap but on occasion dangerous. From the 1860s, paraffin, first distilled in 1846, began to be manufactured in commercial quantities. Both less expensive and less smelly than animal and vegetable oils, it was also less viscous, which allowed manufacturers to dispense with expensive pumps. (It also had a low flashpoint, which meant it exploded spectacularly, and spectacularly often, but its merits were felt to outweigh this liability.)

As these constant small improvements suggest, while the light oil lamps gave was better, the lamps themselves were in many ways as troublesome as tallow candles. The reservoirs needed to be refilled and the wicks trimmed before every use. The glass chimneys, despite an extreme fragility, nevertheless had to be washed daily, or they grew so black with soot that no light penetrated. If not broken in handling, they were as much at risk each time the lamp was lit, cracking in the heat unless they were warmed very slowly and carefully. In Salem in

1835, one cautious housewife borrowed a pair of candlesticks (note, also, that she didn't own any herself) every time she entertained, in case her lamps failed. They worked perfectly for weeks, she grumbled, and then, without warning, 'They went out, they smoked, the oil ran over.' The reservoirs also routinely leaked, and many women made lamp rugs, small mats made out of scraps or, after its invention, oilcloth, to place under each lamp to protect their furniture.

In retrospect, lighting technology appears to have followed a simple trajectory: first oil, then candles, then gas, then electricity. The reality was more complex. No household used only candles, or only gas, or only oil. A single family may well have used an Argand lamp for those who sat sewing or doing similar types of close work at the family's central table, while others read or drew or played the piano by the light of the fire; an older person might have needed a candle to read by, and, where affordable, candles were always used to light the family to their bedrooms at the end of the evening; poorer households used rushlights for many of these tasks. Different rooms, too, were better suited to different types of lighting: gas was good for a front hall, as it wasn't easily extinguished by draughts; it was also ideal for children's rooms, where the brackets could be placed high on the wall, safe from little fingers; elegant candles were for drawing rooms and company; sewing tables needed bright oil lamps. Yet even with all the new technology of the nineteenth century, older forms long remained in daily use. When in *The House at Pooh Corner* Tigger wakes Winnie the Pooh in the middle of the night, Pooh 'got out of bed, and lit his candle' as a matter of course. Household gas had been available for nearly a century by the time A. A. Milne wrote this in 1928, and electricity for thirty-odd years, but a candle was either his own default assumption, or was the bedroom illumination he thought would be familiar to the middle-class children who were his readers.

Given the range of options, technologies and costs, no one type of lighting predominated. Gas was welcomed for its ease of use, but it remained expensive, and many districts were beyond the reach of the gas mains. Even when it was accessible, gas had many drawbacks. It smelt, it corroded metals and destroyed fabrics; it was dirty and left a sticky residue over everything. By 1885, gas was used in just 20 per cent of British households. It spread more widely only with the popularization of the incandescent gas mantle, invented by the Austrian Carl Auer von Welsbach in 1884. Gas mantles were small tubes filled with metallic salts that, when heated by a gas flame, gave a light which was ten times brighter than an Argand, while using a third of the energy. Gas mantles also had pilot lights, which meant that no longer were matches needed to light them. Safer, cleaner, brighter: once the mantles began to be made commercially, their benefits led to a marked increase in the adoption of gas lighting. By World War II, almost half of Britain's working-class housing had access to gas, even as electricity was spreading at a similar rate.

Like gas, electric lighting was initially expected to be an outdoor technology. In 1878, the avenue de l'Opéra in Paris was illuminated for nearly a kilometre by arc lights.* In London there was a temporary installation on the Thames embankment; the population of Sheffield watched football played under arc lights; and Godalming, in Surrey, had a plan to install electric street lighting as early as 1881. But while arc lighting was very bright, and very focused, its lack of diffusion left large areas in darkness. Hilaire Belloc was characteristically succinct:

---

* Arc lighting, first demonstrated by Sir Humphry Davy as early as 1802, is produced by two electrodes separated by a gas: the light is created when a voltage is pulsed across the gap. (Fluorescent lights are arc lights, although they use mercury rather than the carbon electrodes of the nineteenth century.)

This system (technically called the Arc),
Makes some passages too light, others too dark.

Indoors, it was too glaringly bright to be used at all. It was only with
the invention of the incandescent filament that light bulbs began to
be tamed, domesticated, and therefore to win favour for electricity:
by 1881, a great house in Scotland had been fully electrified. Initially
light bulbs were prohibitively expensive, greatly hindering the adoption of the new technology. Not until the patents expired in 1893 did
prices drop. From then, the comfortably-off could afford to think
about installing the new technology. But in Britain electrification
remained patchy – some rural areas were not fully electrified until as
late as the 1960s.

As so often, technological innovations had repercussions that were
both unexpected, and extended far beyond the immediate impact of
the inventions themselves. The various forms of improved lighting
technologies may well have played a role in encouraging the trend for
furniture to be moved away from the walls and placed permanently
throughout a room, for example. There is no danger of stumbling
against furniture in the dark when a room can be illuminated with
the rasp of a match. There is no evidence for this one way or another,
but it is notable that continental Europe was slow to adopt both the
changing furniture layout and gas lighting, as was America.* Decades
after the British had become used to furniture arranged throughout
their rooms, one of the USA's most influential household manuals

---

* Another prosaic reason suggests itself. When furniture was arranged against the
walls, the most routine job for cabinetmakers was mending broken table- and chair-legs,
weakened by the constant pulling and pushing. Did householders simply decide that
leaving furniture in place would cut down on damage? No evidence survives to suggest
this, but then, nor does it for the light-switch theory. Changing patterns of everyday
behaviour are rarely clear-cut in origin.

rejected what it reported as a new fashion for arranging rooms, which made it look as if the furniture was 'dancing a jig'. (There is a faint implication of rowdy drunkenness, or at least improperly decorous behaviour in this phrase, one that perhaps would not have been there with brighter lighting?)

As is often the case, the design for each new technology was drawn from the design of older ones. With electricity, the method of turning lights on and off was adapted from gas, and so at first each lamp, or sometimes each branch of a chandelier, had its own switch. It was some time before it was realized that switches could be separated from the light source, and moved to the walls of each room. (It was even longer before the wall-switches were routinely placed by the entrance. That it is sensible not to have to cross a room in the dark is obvious only in retrospect.) The conceptual leap, from light fixture to wall, was enormous. Just as windowpanes had once been furniture rather than part of a building, so too had lighting been before gas and electricity. Today we no more think of selling a house without glazing than we think of removing the wiring and taking it with us when we move. Lighting became, for the first time, not an independent unit, but part of the fabric of the house.

There is always a gap between the lifestyles to which people aspire, and the means, financial or technological, by which they might achieve those aspirations. Many of the changes spurred by technological improvements affected the daily routines of millions who never lived in houses directly touched by the innovations themselves. Soon after World War II, the Office of the Military Government in US Occupied Germany mounted an exhibition called *Amerika zu Haus* (America at Home); its centrepiece was a life-sized model six-room house, complete with an up-to-date complement of American appliances. Guides extolled the 'household miracles' of toasters, washing machines, electric ovens and vacuum cleaners to the sell-out crowd of 43,000 visitors who walked through it over the next fortnight. None of these eager viewers, especially the 15,000 from East Berlin, had any expectation that they would ever own a house like this, or ever acquire its consumer durables. The house itself was twice the size laid down for housing by postwar West German legislation, and the consumer goods were similarly oversized for the European market. They were also both unaffordable and unavailable, not least because they were wired for US voltages. Nevertheless, those thousands of visitors were keen to see these technologies, and these commodities, even if they would probably never own them, for while the individual elements that made up this American dream-house were almost entirely unachievable, the ideas of home they represented were not.

7

The Home Network

If market demand drives supply, it can also drive invention. In the seventeenth century, servants in the Netherlands were a highly taxed luxury: under 20 per cent of households could afford to employ a servant, and for all but the very richest or most nobly-born, housework was something that was undertaken by family members. By contrast, in the eighteenth, and especially the nineteenth century, even the middle classes of northwestern Europe could draw upon a large and relatively inexpensive service economy. In the USA at this time, low-density populations kept the cost of labour high. Countries that relied heavily on paid labour, such as Britain, where one in four women were in domestic service at the end of the nineteenth century, tended to have householders who, understandably, saw little need for technology. If someone could be employed for a (relative) pittance to carry hot water for baths, why spend a (proportionate) fortune to install a hot water system? The rich clients of Arts and Crafts architects such as Lutyens or Voysey had fully staffed households, so they were unconcerned by the lack of attention these architects paid to the service areas of their houses, their modern, forward-looking façades masking old-fashioned and inconvenient back premises. Dutch housewives had been their own labour force in the seventeenth century, and a revolution in how houses were run was the result; so too in the USA did American women in the eighteenth and nineteenth centuries drive another household revolution.

As we have seen, for much of human history, cooking had taken place in the main living space. In the days of central hearths, a chain suspended the cooking pot from a pole over the fire, closer or further away, depending on its contents and the amount and type of fuel being burnt. When fireplaces were moved to the walls, an adjustable chimney-crane, of wood or iron, improved matters. The pot was lowered and raised as before, but the crane also now swung out into the room, which meant the cook no longer had to lean over the fire to stir the food. But the food, and the method of cooking, barely altered. Solids and a liquid were put in a pot to be boiled or stewed. It was rare that there was space for more than one pot over a single fire, and so more elaborate meals were made by placing different ingredients in nets in the single pot, hooking each one out of the liquid as it was ready. This remained the standard cooking method until stoves appeared in the industrial age, making it easier to cook using several pots and pans at one time.

Most who lived in relatively well-populated districts did not bake at home, but relied on public bakehouses or bakeries for their bread. Those who lived in areas with clay industries might have small freestanding earthenware ovens, some dating from as early as the seventeenth century (and some still in use in the 1930s, in countries as distant as Wales and the USA). Otherwise, for those who lived too far from bakehouses, bread was baked by setting a breadstone and a pot to heat in the fire before the dough was placed on the breadstone and covered with the pot, to cook on the hearth in the residual warmth. Bread ovens, brick cubicles in which peat or wood was burnt, were the preserve of the very largest and richest households. Some were freestanding or, later, were built into the sides of fireplaces. These also cooked by indirect heat: after the fuel was consumed, the ashes were swept out and the dough placed inside to bake on the hot bricks. The relatively low temperature of these ovens was reflected in the length of time it took the contents to bake: two and a half hours for bread, two hours for a cake or a pie. (For non-cooks, a modern oven bakes these in 30–45 minutes.)

As with baking, roasting began as an upper-class luxury. Few could afford the large cuts of meat, few could afford the fuel, and few could afford the labour, or the time as a joint was skewered and then turned in front of an open fire. In the seventeenth century, dogs, or servants, usually children, were stationed beside the spit to turn the meat steadily for the five hours it took to cook through by this method. With the arrival of coal fires, the skewer was repositioned over the grate bars, or given its own stand in front of the fire, with a dripping-pan underneath to catch the fat so it could be poured back over the joint to baste it as it cooked. By the eighteenth century, the disappearance of hooded chimneys and the arrival of the mantelpiece led to the creation of the bottle-jack, which clipped on to the mantel, with the roast suspended beneath; it had a clockwork wind-up mechanism, which removed the need for constant attention, thereby putting roasting within reach of more families.

Apart from these innovations, however, cooking methods for the masses barely differed from those of the Middle Ages. Real change came only as coal became the primary domestic fuel; in England this frequently coincided with the development in room-usage that saw cooking migrate from the main room into its own dedicated space, the kitchen. It was in the eighteenth century that the first enclosed cooking range was created, but it was well into the 1800s before even middle-class households began to accept the idea. The range enclosed the heat source, the fire, most commonly by an iron surround. With that came the possibility of resting pans directly on the heat source, rather than over or in front of it. (In the regions of

Europe that heated their houses with closed stoves, this was less of a novelty, of course.) Trivets were now fixed to the grate, and frying and sautéing broadened the earlier repertoire of boiled and stewed dishes. Gradually these ranges became more elaborate, with interior spaces for baking in ovens that were regulated by flues and dampers. For the first time too the temperature food was cooked at could be controlled. These closed stoves, as they were known, were for a long time the province of the wealthy, and only a few of the middle classes. In New England in 1848, Catharine Beecher, famous as the author of books of household management, 'the American Mrs Beeton', dismissed them as confined to 'the settled areas'. She was almost certainly correct: while many books both in the USA and Britain refer to the new saucepans and pots that were available for use on these ranges, most recipes continued to give directions for cooking over an open fire. And indeed, most of the population did continue to cook that way, those in communities of any size using commercial cookshops and bakehouses for everything that could not be cooked in a pan or a pot over a small fireplace.*

Although Beecher had considered it unlikely that her readers would own a modern closed range, it was she who took the first steps towards the idea that a kitchen could, or even should, be designed around its user's tasks. The architects of houses for the great had not concerned themselves with how kitchens were organized – very often, on plans, the room is simply an empty square. Kitchens of the wealthy

---

* Given the prevalence of gas in British homes, it is surprising that it was barely used for cooking before the twentieth century. It may be that the range, which also heated water in a side-boiler, and provided heat for the room, made it more obviously useful. It was the installation of gas meters from the 1880s that first made a place for gas cookers. Until the twentieth century, cooking with electricity, too, was almost unknown in Britain. Being much more expensive than either coal or gas it was seen as a gimmick, best confined to gadgets such as toasters and kettles.

were used by servants, so it did not matter, while the rooms of the less wealthy had been so multi-purpose that little single-function planning was possible. By the nineteenth century, however, middle-class housewives had, or wanted to have, a separate room dedicated to food preparation, and Beecher, writing as a housewife, wanted that room adapted to suit her needs and convenience, not to have to adapt herself to suit the room. She grouped equipment not by appearance, but by the requirements of a cook or housekeeper. Her ideal kitchen had shelves near the workspaces, so that routine tasks could be performed without fetching and carrying: 'half the time and strength is employed in walking back and forth to collect and return the articles used'. Her innovative layout included putting a dish-drainer beside the sink, with space underneath for towels and cleaning equipment; a 'moulding board', or worktop, was set above bins that contained the most frequently used ingredients, and more shelves were located overhead (see plate section, no. 29). She was similarly pragmatic about other elements, giving instructions on where to site the stove for maximum heat efficiency, which way doors should be hung to keep smells away from the living areas, and so on. Beecher was, in effect, delineating the outline of the fitted kitchen of the twentieth century.

Such an organizational approach is taken for granted today, but it was slow to catch on. In the late 1880s, the kitchen in Laura Ingalls Wilder's new house had a series of shelves along one wall, with a bread drawer, space for her milk-churns, and bins for flour, graham flour and corn meal, much as Mrs Beecher had proposed. But its owner's amazement – 'you could stand...and mix up anything, without stirring a step', she marvels – suggests that this was the first time she had seen anything like it.

In the 1910s, an Indiana company marketed a 'Hoosier Kitchen', which joined a dresser, a table and a larder together to form a continuous workspace. While superficially this mimicked some elements Mrs Beecher had described half a century earlier, it misunderstood her intent, which had been to collect together in one place all the necessities for activities generally performed at the same time. Instead, the user of the Hoosier Kitchen was forced to traipse up and down one long narrow area, which was too narrow for a second person to work there as well, even as other parts of the room were under-utilized. Despite the poor design, the Hoosier Company's contribution was important. It was the first time a commercial organization had seen that there was money to be made in selling, not furniture nor consumer durables, but the very way a room was arranged. As we have seen, the new 'science' of industrial efficiency was, just at this date, expanding from its origins in the factory, and moving into the housewife's workspace, the home. Now many – domestic-manual writers, efficiency experts, architects and the population at large – began to consider space management not as a matter best decided by each individual household, but as an opportunity for profit, even if they had never heard of Mrs Beecher.

And while in Europe it is almost certain that Mrs Beecher was entirely unknown, the work of American industrial efficiency experts such as Frederick Taylor, and especially Christine Frederick, was being translated and avidly studied. By 1919, Germany was facing an acute housing shortage. House-building had been brought to a halt in the war years; the end of the war saw marriage rates rise as soldiers returned home; and peacetime populations were swollen by large numbers of refugees. The new Weimar Republic made social housing a primary goal in its 1919 constitution, with municipalities responsible for creating affordable housing in each region. From 1920, many German cities drew up plans for standardized apartment buildings, designed to meet local housing needs, and now also, for the first time, taking health into consideration and setting out legal minimums for space, light and ventilation. And thus most postwar advances in kitchen planning and design came from Germany. These new apartment buildings were intended to be mass-produced and 'rationally' organized; distinct spaces were allocated to the various functions of daily life, turning the traditional *Wohnküche*, or multipurpose living space, into three rooms: a living room, dining room and kitchen.

Many of the architects and urban planners were inspired by leftwing ideas; at the same time, from the opposite end of the political spectrum, living conditions were also a matter of concern for many conservative women's groups, worried by the 'decline' of the German housewife, and the consequent effect that the decline was said to be having on the birth rate. Home-making, said one activist, was 'a form of citizenship': good housewives would raise the next generation of citizens, but they needed to have the homes in which to do so. Women from these groups therefore worked alongside public housing officials, city-planners and architects in this postwar period. Many were influenced by American experts such as Taylor, and as a result the German National Productivity Board produced a series of time-and-motion studies on daily routines such as dusting and washing floors. Kitchens therefore became a major preoccupation for many designers. In 1923, a compact kitchen, the Egri-Küche, was advertised, while the Bauhaus exhibited what was to become a key contribution to kitchen design. Its L-shaped room featured unbroken counters all at one height, with eye-level cabinets above – a single workspace incorporating the room's three functions: cleaning, cooking and storage.

Most influential of all was the Frankfurt kitchen, designed in 1926 by Grete Schütte-Lihotzky (1897–2000), the first woman to study architecture at Vienna's Kunstgewerbeschule, or School of Arts and Crafts (it took a letter of recommendation from Gustav Klimt for her to be admitted). Schütte-Lihotzky's reading of Christine Frederick led her to apply scientific management to daily life and design, and she was one of dozens of architects who put theory into practice in the years of the social-housing boom, working under Ernst May, Frankfurt's city-planner, to build standardized, health-promoting public housing.* She began her work by considering how the layout of traditional kitchens wasted time and effort, and how many, in addition, were simply unhealthy environments. The Frankfurt kitchen (see plate section, no. 30) was long and narrow (less than 2 metres wide, just over 3 metres long), with areas organized by function: storage containers next to the work surface, which was beside the oven, not far from the dining table, and close to the counter beside the sink, all allowing the housewife to move seamlessly from food preparation to cooking, cooking to eating, eating to washing-up, and finally to putting everything away, in order to avoid what Frederick referred to as 'wasted steps', which had quickly become a catchphrase in design literature. Schütte-Lihotzky estimated that in a traditional kitchen a woman walked 19 metres to prepare each meal, over 20 kilometres a year. The Frankfurt kitchen reduced that to 8 metres, or 8 kilometres a year. Its single-level, connected workspaces made cleaning easier, and space was maximized by the use of built-in features, including a fold-down ironing board and a

* Schütte-Lihotzky's life would have the makings of an action-drama, if only films were made about kitchen designers: a committed Communist, she lived in the Soviet Union from 1930, before fleeing the Stalinist purges in 1937. In World War II she worked for the Resistance until her capture by the Gestapo; after the war, her Communism and vocal support for female emancipation ensured that she could not earn a living in Austria, and most of her later commissions were abroad. It was 1980 before she and her work were formally honoured in Vienna, more than half a century after her pioneering kitchen design was first manufactured.

folding dish-rack. Dried goods were stored in lightweight drawers that pulled out, with spouts at the back to enable the contents to be poured directly into a bowl, removing the need for a scoop. This was a kitchen designed by a woman who performed household tasks for women who performed household tasks.

Yet the Frankfurt kitchen was not admired by all. The room was designed on sound ergonomic principles, but it failed to take other aspects of life into consideration. Many women disliked the single-function nature of Schütte-Lihotzky's room: family members could no longer occupy the same space while the women were working, and even the new dining room increased their sense of isolation. The kitchens were also planned for electricity, even though many who lived in the buildings that housed these new kitchens could not afford such a luxury. The rooms were long and narrow, with little exterior lighting, and women therefore found themselves spending many hours every day in the near dark.

In the USA, despite first Beecher's, then Frederick's pioneering work, changes to kitchens revolved more around technology than ergonomics or time-and-motion planning. Until the twentieth century, much of what is now regarded as basic equipment was entirely lacking. As late as 1881, manuals made no mention of dish-racks to drain dishes, while soap, by then available in bars, still had to be grated for dishwashing; detergents and steel-wool for scouring had yet to be invented. Yet only forty years later, the amount of time US housewives spent on housework had dropped by a fifth. In the quarter century after 1905, when the first electric iron was marketed,* American housewives gained the tools of modern housekeeping:

---

* It had to be unplugged after it was heated, and plugged in again every time the heat dissipated, but it was still much better – cleaner, and more efficient – than an iron heated on the stove.

vacuum cleaners, thermostatically controlled gas ranges, electric sewing machines, washing machines, ice-boxes, even dishwashers. Meanwhile, the availability of tinned, dried and prepared foods had reduced the time spent cooking; and the new technologies of detergents, gas and electricity had similarly reduced the time spent cleaning up. By 1926, three out of four working-class houses in one Ohio town had electricity, 60 per cent had an indoor lavatory and bathtub, while more than nine in ten households had running water and piped gas. Even some of the poorer houses had hot and cold running water.

As we have seen, even small technological developments can make a substantial difference to the way people live. In this period, minor changes to cleaning technologies produced a marked shift in attitudes to what constituted 'dirt'. For centuries, floors in many home countries had been plain wood, or stone, or brick. In the seventeenth century, the Dutch commonly scattered sand across brick or tile floors, as did the British on their wood floors into the eighteenth century in less urban areas. In the USA floors were sanded in a house's public rooms into the nineteenth century. The sand soaked up grease from open-fire cooking, as well as wax and oil from lighting, and was easily replaced. (Sawdust was scattered on the floors of butchers' shops to soak up the fat and blood; it can still occasionally be seen today, although now it is merely a nostalgic flourish.) Most used twig brooms to sweep away the dirtied sand; then fresh sand was scattered either from a sieve or by hand; for holidays, or in the best room, a decorative pattern might be traced out using a special hair broom. Twig brooms were unable to collect the finest dust and silt, which was allowed to remain – it was not considered to be dirt. Then, at the end of the eighteenth century, industrially manufactured corn-straw brooms appeared, quickly replacing hand-tied twig ones: by 1833 half a million were being sold annually in the USA, and by the end of the century they were so common that even prairie homes had a 'boughten' broom. These corn-straw brooms swept up more, and more efficiently. Now the silt and dust residue that they were able to gather, but that twig brooms were not, was no longer something that could be overlooked. It had become dirt. Equally, houses in the USA were once filled with insects, flying and crawling, covering food, eating utensils and chamber-pots. At mealtimes a child or, in the south, a slave, was told to 'mind…the flies' when the food was set out on the table, but apart from this the clouds of insects were little remarked. Once relatively inexpensive screens became available, from the 1870s, insects swiftly came to be considered not merely inconvenient, but unhygienic.

Dirt has memorably been defined as 'matter in the wrong place'.* What constitutes dirt is frequently a cultural matter, decided by mutually agreed views of what is 'wrong'. It is unsurprising, therefore, that the most vivid descriptions of waste and dirt come, not from residents in any society, but from visitors to that society, bringing with them different expectations. They notice the dirt because it appears in unexpected places, or there is more, or it is of a type with which they are unfamiliar; at home, the same levels of dirt, in familiar form, or in familiar locations, pass without comment. Our dirt is the way things are; their dirt is filth. It takes extraordinary circumstances for people to notice, and to comment on, their own dirt. As a result, it is all too easy to assume that the norms of any given period also applied in the past.

In 1666, Charles II's court took refuge in Oxford, hoping to evade the plague then raging across the country. On their departure from

---

* The original quotation has been attributed to John Ruskin, William James, the anthropologist Mary Douglas and Sigmund Freud (of course). Lord Palmerston is now generally accepted as the phrase's originator.

their temporary accommodation, piles of faeces were found in every room and on the landings of every staircase. Even contemporaries were horrified, and a range of suggestions looked at ways to avoid such situations in future. Most of the proposed solutions were architectural, in particular concentrating on the shape of staircases. If there were no landings, ran the irrefutable logic, people would not be able to defecate on them. That people might simply not defecate in public areas was not at the time obvious to all, or possibly even to anyone. The situation in Oxford had been exacerbated by circumstances – a large court based in a small town for months on end – but otherwise it was unusual only in degree. At the same date, as Dutch Golden Age artists lovingly painted maids scouring already-gleaming floors, local legislation outlined the levels of compensation to be paid to pedestrians whose clothes were soiled when human waste was thrown out of windows. Again, there was no sense of the possibility of a society in which human waste was not thrown out of windows.

These were the very streets that the English admired as 'wonderfull Nett and cleane', but it was where they expected to see waste, and so it was effectively invisible to them. As late as the eighteenth century, the English regarded as unclean the Scottish custom of keeping chamber-pots in every room; better, they thought, was the southern English usage, where chamber-pots were confined to the bedrooms and dining rooms (where they were stored in sideboards, for use during after-dinner drinking sessions). Visitors from cities were similarly shocked by conditions in agricultural districts, where animals were housed cheek by jowl with humans. A Swedish proverb from the 1770s commented wryly on this urban distaste: 'He who scorns the pig-dung smell, can live without the pork as well.' It was not, however, only a matter of pig dung. A Swedish stonecutter's daughter remembered her rural childhood as late as

1910, where chamber-pots sat under beds, and 'little heaps' formed outside the door: these mostly consisted of refuse, but the children used them for their own waste, and adult men urinated there too.* In Skåne, in Sweden's south, farms were built around a courtyard where the animals were penned at night, ensuring that visitors and residents alike walked through manure before entering the house, while further north, in Dalarna, manure was also disregarded when women did their spinning in stables and barns to benefit from the animal warmth.

Until the twentieth century for the most part, hygiene was not primarily a matter of removing waste products. It was, instead, largely an aspect of personal appearance, presentation of self: for people and their clothing to make a fine show was more important than that they, or their owners, or their houses, were what today we think of as clean. Before the seventeenth century, clothes for all but the highest in society were mostly dark-coloured, and made of wool or leather. They lasted for decades, and were handed down the generations. The expansion of the linen industry in the seventeenth century introduced white items – shirts, collars, cuffs, petticoats, caps, handkerchiefs, neckerchiefs – into daily use for the prosperous. As more became available, the marker of status was now less a matter of owning such garments, than it was in keeping them white – that is, visibly clean. And visible hygiene was not merely an indicator of rank, or cash. It had become yet another way of distinguishing public and private. Towards the end of the eighteenth century, La Roche-foucauld, visiting Britain, observed that while the public areas of the houses he visited were 'constantly washed', the behind-the-scenes

---

* This was no doubt considered beneficial: the nitrogen in men's urine (women's is more acidic) speeds up the decomposition of kitchen refuse, and is still recommended for compost heaps today.

areas such as the kitchens were 'indescribably' dirty. The spread of industrialization made cleanliness a more pressing concern, as more crowded cities made access to water more difficult. Many no longer lived near the springs, rivers or wells that had previously supplied smaller communities, and were forced instead to rely on rainwater, and on piped water, which until the twentieth century was variable in both availability and quality.

The Netherlands was particularly poorly served. Geographically much of the country was below sea-level. In addition, it was the first country where the majority of the population lived in urban rather than agricultural communities, and so had few precedents to guide it. Dutch cities, as well as agricultural land, largely relied on rainwater and communal wells, neither of which were fully adequate. In France, among the nobility and the very wealthiest, some new buildings had piped water in the following century, and newer Parisian mansions occasionally had rainwater cisterns. A French engraving from 1732 shows a bathtub connected to two small tanks of water (hot and cold, the hot heated by a fireplace). Architectural treatises might grandly present arrangements for separate rooms for a water-heater, an airing-room, a room for the bathtub, a room for attendant servants and more, but it is doubtful that more than a handful of houses boasted such luxuries. The ideas were present, but the reality was very different.

In England, the first civic system of piped water was built in Derby in 1692, but it was limited in its reach. A painting from c.1720 of a family and servants eating dinner, by a Dutch painter living in England, shows, at the very top of the chimney-breast, what looks like a water pipe bringing water into this rather spartan house (see plate section, no. 21). There is no way of knowing if the image represents a reality, or is a painterly improvement on life: given the lack of other evidence, it is impossible to judge. The wooden pipes that existed at the time were both inefficient and expensive. At their widest, the pipes measured around 20 centimetres in diameter, and so a single pump or tap required dozens to supply it; the wood decayed rapidly, with pipes having to be replaced every two or three years. There was thus little reason for the experiment to be repeated elsewhere. It was only towards the end of the eighteenth century, with the arrival of cast-iron pipes, that piped water became a practical proposition. Cast-iron pipes could be wider, so fewer were needed, even as they lasted years longer than wood, all of which made them less expensive to install. As with heating, though, a constant water supply was regarded as a luxury, not a necessity, and irregular daily supply was typical until the twentieth century. Prosperous households had cisterns that filled every time the water company turned on the mains, but even these were rarely sufficient, and most households that could afford it also routinely supplemented their piped water by buying water from water-carriers, who walked the streets selling from barrels, or hiring caddies, as they were known in Scotland, people who were paid to wait at street pumps.

Although regular supplies of piped water were not to become standard until the twentieth century, over the course of the nineteenth century campaigners had persuaded the British government that sanitary reform was not a luxury. Cleaner cities, they urged, would lead to a reduction in epidemic disease, which would benefit the economy as a whole. Hygiene was a civic good, and water and sewage should therefore be regulated by legislation and paid for out of taxes. The industrial heartlands, with their fast-growing populations, were among the first to turn their attention to this problem. At mid-century, half of the households in Manchester were found to be using water contaminated by waste. The local government established rates to be levied to finance the cost of reservoirs and pipes, and within twenty-five years, 80 per cent of households in that city had piped water. New filtration plants also ensured the water was cleaner than it had ever been. Yet still there was no sense that access to clean water was in any way a universal right. It was, instead, a commodity, like any other, to be bought and sold by private firms. And as is so often still the case, those who could buy in bulk, via pipes into their houses, paid much less for their supply than those who could not afford to do so: at mid-century 36 gallons of piped water cost less than a quarter of a penny; the same quantity of river-water, brought by water-carriers, cost 4d; and well-water was even more, at 8d.

The USA, predominantly rural, was not as badly affected by the epidemics that had devastated so much of urbanizing Europe in the nineteenth century, and therefore its civic water systems were slower to develop. Where epidemics did occur, water improvements generally swiftly followed. A wave of yellow fever swept Philadelphia in the 1790s, and the city became a pioneer in water supply on the continent. A hundred years later, many American cities had municipal water supplies, although that did not necessarily mean that the water was piped. More typically, cities stored water in tanks and delivered it by wagon to individual houses: across the country, more than three-quarters of all households still had no running water, and those that did were almost entirely urban. Most rural houses had no running water until after World War II.

Many cities also managed without civic sewage systems. Instead, waste disposal was a matter of private enterprise, with householders paying contractors to empty their cesspits. Rural areas had even more makeshift arrangements, or none. In the south, slave quarters rarely had privies, nor did most small farmhouses. Many people simply emptied their waste out of the windows or doors. It is unclear how many households had lavatories connected to the mains – higher charges were levied on those households, and so there may well have been a level of under-reporting – but as late as 1890, in Muncie, Indiana, a city of 11,000 people, fewer than two dozen houses contained bathrooms that included a bath and lavatory. Given the rarity of piped water, it is unsurprising that 'washing' usually only referred to the face and hands, and soap was not necessarily part of the procedure: scrubbing with a rough towel was considered sufficient to remove the dirt.

In rural districts, fortunate householders could rely on nearby wells or streams; others simply had to walk long distances. The weight of water combined with the quantity needed for even minimal health made multiple daily journeys inevitable. In 1886, a North Carolina house was located just 55 metres away from a spring. But it took ten trips daily to provide enough water for the household, nearly four kilometres a week, half of that burdened by heavy pails. The centrality of water-collection in daily life may be judged from the fact that, while many poorer nineteenth-century households possessed almost no furnishings or technology by today's standards, they tended to own and use many, and many different types of, specialized containers for carrying water. Buckets and pails were ubiquitous, as were smaller jugs, pans and other less specialized implements. Many districts also had their own distinct equipment. In Aberystwyth, in Wales, in the eighteenth century, women balanced large pitchers on their heads. In the nineteenth century in Surrey, women walked inside hoops that distributed the weight of the hanging pails, called stoups, more evenly. In the north of England, skiels were tub-shaped containers, wider at the bottom than the top, with a single long wooden stave for a handle. In Orkney, water tubs were hung from sticks and carried between two women on their shoulders.

The quantity of water a household consumed was thus dependent not only on what was available, but on the strength of the women (it was almost always women, or children) who carried it, and the amount of time they were able to give to the task. It frequently took several hours to reach the front of a queue at a public pump in many nineteenth-century English cities, a wait that might lie somewhere between difficult and impossible for women who worked twelve- to fourteen-hour days. Consumption therefore had almost nothing to do with how much water was available; it had everything to do with how much manpower and time each family had to carry the water. Where possible, most houses owned a rainwater butt, but the run-off from a small house averaged little more than 10 litres a head per day for a household of five. In Paris by the end of the eighteenth century, the average consumption of water for all purposes was 5 litres per person per day, which weighs just under 5 kilograms; in Glasgow in the 1850s, it was as little as 3.73 litres per head per day. (The minimum recommendation for health today is 54.6 litres per head per day and average use in England and Wales is between 133 and 154 litres per head per day.) And as there were rarely any drains in working-class housing, everything except the drinking water had to be carried out again to be disposed of.

Little had changed by the early twentieth century. In much of urban and suburban USA, new houses for all but the most impoverished were now being built with running water, and even bathrooms. But older houses were not widely upgraded: back in Muncie, as late as 1925, a quarter of the houses had no running water, and a third were still not connected to the sewers. Britain was little different. At the start of the twentieth century, half of Scottish houses had no running water, and yet many of these were still more than a kilometre away from a regular water supply. Half the working-class housing in London in 1934 had no water supply, the residents relying on outside standpipes, while in the countryside a third of the population had no access to piped water even at the end of World War II. Ireland had less still: over 90 per cent of rural households in Ulster had no piped water as the 1950s began.

For as with lighting, technological development did not follow a linear progression, with one improvement succeeding another. At any one time, a variety of systems of water supply coexisted. The wealthier could select the most advanced if they chose, while many might still have no access, and others only partial access, whether through careful planning, happenstance (plumbing in housing provided by an employer, say) or sheer good fortune. And what today would be considered the minimum requirements were not necessarily a priority to those at the time who had the means to choose. In Muncie, in the first two decades of the twentieth century, twenty-one of the twenty-six families who owned a car had no bathroom.

Piped water was in itself a great convenience, but it altered more than merely hygiene. Cooking had been moving from multi-functional rooms to dedicated spaces, kitchens, long before the kitchen range appeared: ranges merely speeded up a process that was already under way. New bathroom technology, by contrast, provoked an entirely new development in room use. Until running water arrived, washing was something that might take place anywhere in the house: in Britain, at the household's single sink, often located in the scullery or kitchen, or in a tin bath that could be moved as convenience dictated; in the USA, in New England it was more commonly in the lean-to at the rear, or in the south in a detached kitchen, or in the west outdoors at the pump or a well. In the nineteenth century, the middle classes had turned washing from something done in public spaces to something done in private areas of the house, by confining it almost entirely to bedrooms. Furthermore, where possible, each family member was allocated a ewer and basin of his or her own. Now those living in technologically advanced houses could take this further. A range of hitherto disparate water and cleaning activities, which had taken place across the household, were gathered together in a new space, the bathroom, creating in effect a Frankfurt kitchen for sanitary activities. Manufacturers introduced householders to the 'suite': a sink, bath and lavatory, typically all in white, and designed to be plumbed in together not just in one room, but along one wall, with standardized fittings produced, in the USA, by the eponymous American Standard company.

Water, sewage, gas, electricity – these technologies connected the house to the networks of modern life around them, and they also enforced standardization on them. Builders now had to use pipes of a fixed size, and, eventually, to conform to new safety regulations, to wiring of a specific type installed in accordance with legislation. Initially water and waste pipes, breaching the nineteenth-century ideal that houses were 'castles', separate from the world about them, were seen by many less as a welcome way of moving dirt away from and out of the house, and more as a troubling innovation that allowed public dirt to enter private homes. An 1877 book intended to guide British householders through the new world of sanitary improvement warned: 'There are a "thousand gates to death!" Few are wider, or open more readily' than those that permitted 'noxious gases' or 'bad air from drains' to enter the house. It was not only waste pipes. Any feature that physically connected the house to the outside was seen to bring danger. Many householders turned the gas supply off at the mains every night in the same way that they bolted the doors and closed the shutters, isolating the house from the outside world, pulling up the drawbridge. It took time for the convenience of waste disposal, of water – both its arrival by tap, and its disposal by drain – of light at the flick of a switch, to outweigh such fears. The dissemination of the knowledge of germ theory of disease helped, as did new legislation that established basic safety standards for plumbing, wiring, gas lighting and heating systems. Defying Pitt's certitude of a century earlier, the government was now absolutely obliged to enter the 'poor man's cottage', in pursuit of dangerous wiring.

By the twentieth century, these very technologies, and the legislation relating to them, came to be seen, not so much as invasions of privacy, as the very means to promote it. And this renewed sense of privacy, of withdrawal from the world, in turn encouraged a raft of new purchases for the home to make it even more a place of refuge. These were a new type of commodity, however. They were purchased on the market, as bedding, or curtains, or kitchen units had long been. And, like parlour furniture, they conferred status on their possessors. But unlike these objects, the new goods could not be physically displayed. They were intangibles, what might be termed invisible commodities, and they included hygiene, nutrition, health, transportation, even tidiness and space. By the late nineteenth century, and gathering pace into the twentieth, these invisible commodities joined earlier items of display: all now were used to confirm the status of the household.

The display of possessions had always been moderated by social attitudes. The choice of goods, and how those goods were presented, were as important as the objects themselves. One of the purposes of good housekeeping, advice manuals and public opinion had long agreed, was to enable families to live within their means. Were a household's decorations and furnishings appropriate for the income and class of their owners? Too showy, too expensive, or too frugal, too modest? Either was a serious error. Display above one's financial level was a clear indication of profligacy in the wife, and the husband's ignorance or lack of control; below one's income, of insufficient ability to navigate the social world. Thrift was not a matter of saving regardless of income, but of judging exactly the right amount of spending, indicating that the family was a good financial proposition: if more money were available (if the husband were to expand his business, gain more clients, or more credit), the wife and children would be able to adapt to the increased status. These judgements were not passed only on those lower down the social scale. In colonial America, houses represented the colony's survival, ultimately its success, yet John Ratcliffe, briefly the president of Jamestown colony, was described as 'sillie' for having built 'an vnnecessarie pallas in the woods', a 'thing needlesse'. 'Silly' in the seventeenth century still retained some of its older meaning, naïve, lacking in judgement, but by now it also meant foolish. It was 'needlesse', unimportant expenditure that was condemned: not whether someone had the wherewithal to buy something, or use something, but whether what was bought or used was appropriate for that person's status. Three hundred years later, such an attitude had been well learned by the German child shocked to discover that his grandfather spread his breakfast *Zwieback* with butter: 'We had been told that whoever did this, would be put in prison'.

At times, painting made a direct connection between thrift and household happiness. In the Netherlands *banketjestukken*, paintings of 'little banquets', were popular in the 1620s and 1630s, promoting in still-life form the pleasures of sufficiency over excess: a herring, a piece of fruit, or bread and cheese on an earthenware dish, alongside those markers of domestic prosperity and felicity, clean napkins and shining pewter. In eighteenth-century Britain, painters produced a different kind of homage to thrift. As the commodity market exploded, genre-painters immortalized householders in the best, public, rooms of their new houses, resplendent in new silks and velvets, sitting behind new porcelain tea sets. Yet we now know that these paintings frequently did not depict reality, which was of rooms filled, even crowded, with many possessions. Instead they depict almost puritanically bare imaginary rooms, with, as the highlight, just one or two exquisite items of luxury consumption: a sort of super-consumption of restraint (see plate section, no. 31).

The promotion of thrift even as the number of commodities available, and affordable, increased vertiginously as the nineteenth century progressed, endowed the *choice* of objects with a moral dimension. Magazines assessed the attractions of many of the consumer goods available to their readers, but instead of presenting them as purchases that would cement status or bring pleasure, they gave the acquisition a moral dimension. Commodities might be described as an 'important agent in the education of life', suggesting that a family would be improved merely by living with it.

The perfect home was filled with objects that were neither too expensive, nor too cheap, too stylish, nor too old-fashioned. Equally, poor selection could take an otherwise ordinary family and make it into one that was simply not respectable: the husband unsuitable for promotion, the children dubious marriage-partners. Well into the second half of the twentieth century, the difference between respectable and not-respectable working-class households 'concern only household economy, which is largely the wives' affair', and was measured by whether the family ate off a bare table or used a cloth, or used china dishes or tin, had 'cooked meals, clean clothes' or managed without owing money to the local tradesmen, a list that slides almost imperceptibly from purchased goods to the intangible, invisible commodities of nutrition, hygiene and thrift.

For much of the nineteenth century the miasma theory of disease transmission – that illnesses bred in decomposing matter and were then spread through droplets carried in the air in the form of a mist, or miasma – was generally accepted. At mid-century, in the Surrey countryside, life expectancy for men was forty-five years; in London, thirty-seven years; and in industrial, overcrowded Liverpool, just twenty-six. (Once the very high child-mortality rates are filtered out, an adult who reached the age of twenty-one could expect to live longer, but the relative differences between town and country remained.) The germ theory of disease, and the knowledge that cholera and typhus were water-borne, won widespread acceptance only slowly in the second half of the century. In 1854, Dr John Snow had identified the source of a localized outbreak of cholera as the contaminated water from a single pump in one street in Soho. But while he was persuasive enough that the parish officers disabled that particular pump, more generally, the miasma theory continued to hold sway. Fortunately, the civic authorities' campaign to eradicate miasmas led them to adopt the same strategies that would have been the case had germ theory been more generally accepted: improvements to the water supply. During the Mexican–American war of 1846–8, for every death in battle, six soldiers died from disease. By the time of the Civil War in the 1860s, the army had instituted a Sanitary Commission, and deaths had fallen to three deaths by disease for every two in battle.

The campaigns against miasmas turned cleanliness from being a status indicator to being a health issue. And, in the eyes of popular opinion, the central role in this new campaign was to be played by the woman of the house. Housekeeping was no longer a simple matter of keeping the family clean, providing sufficient water to drink. While housewives had always been responsible for food allocation, ensuring that those who needed scarce resources received most, this was no longer enough: meals now had to be nutritionally balanced. Refrigeration, transport, and new methods of food preservation and processing had improved access for many to foods that, in previous centuries, had been unavailable to almost everyone, whether for seasonal or geographical reasons. Fresh fruit and vegetables could now be transported hundreds of kilometres far more cheaply; or tinned and purchased at any time of year; meat could be frozen and transported thousands of miles. And so preventing diseases of nutritional deficiency, such as rickets, pellagra or scurvy, as well as more routine illnesses, became another task for the middle-class housewife. It was she, and not providence, who had now become responsible for what the president of the British Medical Association referred to, in the 1880s, as 'domestically produced health'.

Yet for the working classes, as well as those who were outright impoverished, good nutrition was an unimaginable luxury, and most continued to eat according to much older patterns, with very different diets in winter and summer. In winter, there was little apart from root vegetables, cabbage, apples, corn or rice pudding or bread, and a few preserved vegetables, in America, most commonly stewed tomatoes; in northern Europe, pickled cabbage or cucumbers; in Britain, little more than onions. Those who could hunt, or who could afford it, ate meat as well. During the 'hungry gap', the period when the winter root crops had been exhausted, but the spring vegetables had not yet arrived, the already limited winter diet contracted still further, and many suffered from what was known as 'spring sickness', which tonics promised to cure, along with everything from boils, scurvy, scrofula and eczema, even as they 'purified' the blood, or the liver, or, more vaguely, helped with conditions such as 'sluggishness' or 'general debility'. The enormously popular Morison's Pills at mid-century promised more: 'Morison's Pills Cure All Curable Diseases'. But all tonics were, in reality, simply attempts to ameliorate the results of poor diet, in particular the widespread lack of fresh fruit and vegetables.

For until the twentieth century, the housewife who was seasonally occupied in bottling or preserving fruit and vegetables (called canning in the USA) was yet another mythical construct. The cost and availability of sugar and the jars, as well as the cost of the fuel, and the amount of time required, put jam- and pickle-making out of reach for many who were low paid or who worked in low-cash economies. Vegetables and fruit were for the most part dried, or simply stored in a dark, cool place. (Books from the nineteenth century did give instructions for all types of preserving, but so do cookbooks today, and only a small minority of people actually do it.) World War I, and its 'victory gardens', promoted home preserving as 'a patriotic duty' on both sides of the conflict ('We Can: Can Vegetables and the Kaiser Too') just as the invention of the pressure cooker and the ever-decreasing price of sugar and glass put this type of food preservation within the reach of many more. As more women withdrew from the labour market, they began to have the time too. Even then, it was a realistic task only for the at least modestly prosperous, or the rural: the urban working classes could not spare the time, had no access to the fruit and vegetables, and little space to store the finished product.

Preserving was, in any case, increasingly less necessary. New transit networks and the more widespread availability of processed and preserved foods in the later nineteenth century improved nutrition without the necessity for home preserving. Public health also improved, as sewage systems and in time the internal combustion engine cleansed cities of dung. These developments were well outside the control of any individual, yet as health improved generally, it became a commodity to be sold back to the housewife, putting the responsibility for her family's welfare firmly back into her lap. As electricity and gas replaced fires, cities were becoming cleaner than they had ever been, so clean that soap manufacturers faced a crisis: their product was being bought less, and used less, because there was less perceived dirt. In the early decades of the twentieth century in the USA, several manufacturers came together to promote 'the business of cleanliness', ostensibly an educational programme, more realistically a commercial strategy to boost demand for their products. They funded pamphlets that extolled the benefits of hand-washing, supplied free 'Cleanliness Teaching' packs to schools, and they published the *Cleanliness Journal*, available at no charge to teachers and civic leaders. At the same time, their advertising promised financial success only to those who reached new levels of cleanliness – bad breath, or (a new term) 'body odour', or yellow teeth, would, they warned, stand in the way of promotion, or salary increases, or even any employment at all. These advertisements were not, however, aimed at men, but at their wives at home. It was their job to send their men out to work each day meeting the new standards advocated by the companies, and swiftly assimilated by consumers as a societal norm. By the 1920s, daytime radio shows were sponsored by soap companies and manufacturers of cleaning products: the soap-opera was for the buyers of soap, and for those who enforced its use within the home. Cleanliness – soap – and the housewife had become inextricably linked. By the 1940s, middle-class hygiene, both personal and household, had changed beyond recognition. Deodorant, soap and toothpaste were the bare minimum – no more quick rubdowns with a towel. And that was on the personal level. In the home, too, all the rooms were to be cleaned out once a week, bathrooms and kitchens scrubbed down daily, while laundry occupied at least two days a week.

For those not yet of the middle classes, cleanliness was promoted as an enabler of social mobility. In the USA it also promised assimilation, whether of class, race or nationality. The African-American educator and rights leader Booker T. Washington (1856–1915) preached what he named the 'gospel of the toothbrush', a way, although he didn't articulate it as such, perhaps even to himself, for African-Americans to demonstrate their Americanness. Christine Frederick held a similar view. In *The New Housekeeping* she lauded 'domestic science classes, model kitchens and tenements...night schools and mission classes', all of which taught 'the poor how to transmute their old-world ignorance into the shining knowledge of the new hemisphere'. She automatically assumed that the poor were of the 'old-world', that is, immigrants, which by default suggested that native-born Americans were prosperous, and modern, and not in need of teaching. To be clean was to be American.

In Germany, too, it had long been received wisdom that German houses were cleaner than those of other countries. After unification in 1871, the superiority of German housekeeping became part of a new sense of nationhood. Belonging was inculcated by the disparagement of housekeeping in other countries or cultures: 'Polish management', or 'It looks like Hottentots live here'. Housewifery had long been part of German girls' formal schooling, after which many worked in the house of a relative or friend to refine their skills. From 1913, girls did an additional mandatory school year, in which they studied 'those virtues that should adorn every housewife: cleanliness and orderliness, thriftiness and industriousness, simplicity and good taste' to the exclusion of everything else. World War I brought the government into every kitchen, as rationing, food distribution and central control of both prices and ingredients – the government's K-bread was named for both *Krieg* (war) and its main ingredient, *Kartoffel* (potato) – made housekeeping an act of 'service to the country, defence of the country, and a form of citizenship'.

The connection between good housekeeping and good citizenship only grew stronger as the century progressed. Bad housekeepers might be viewed as immoral, criminal, even politically suspect. Under the Nazis, the Mother Cross was awarded both to women who had borne a specified number of children (the Soviets celebrated their Heroine Mothers in a similar fashion), and to women who reached high standards of housekeeping; there were campaigns to 're-shape household consumption'; and, more horrifyingly, the Hashude Educational Settlement was established in Bremen. This 're-education camp' forcibly detained 'asocial' families behind barbed wire in order to inculcate the women with right-thinking methods of 'household management, particularly how clean they keep their homes'. Domestic arrangements were checked daily, and families were not released until the husband was in regular work and the wife kept house in a manner deemed satisfactory by her supervisors, the two pillars of a 'respectable' household.

This was an aberration, but it was a natural development (if unnatural application) of half a century of laying an ever-rising importance on the invisible commodities of hygiene, nutrition and good housekeeping. The wellbeing of a house's residents was increasingly seen as a matter that could be controlled through hard work, or the application of scientific knowledge. By the middle of the nineteenth century, the site of the house itself had also become a factor to be considered. The coal fires of the Industrial Revolution had created cities with notably poor air quality, and health was therefore to be found in a visit to the seaside, or the mountains, or just the countryside more generally. Such trips were thought to be sure routes to ameliorating many of the ailments caused by poor air, poor water and the other inconveniences of urban living. If visiting the country was good for the health, obviously living there was even better. The arrival of new modes of transport as the century progressed – trains, omnibuses – and better roads made living further away from their new places of work possible for some of the middle classes. And as the idea of separate spheres for men and women, public and private, developed, so did this new ideal of home, away from built-up areas, seem to be a way of achieving segregation. Within half a century, for many, the suburban idyll had become the template of the ideal home.

The earliest suburbs were not extensions to cities, built on their outskirts, but were separate developments, as garden-city developments were later to be. In the USA, enclaves of upper-middle-class housing had existed from the 1850s. Home countries had similar settlements, but these mostly on city outskirts. All of them, however, were limited to those who could afford their own transport, always a very small proportion of the population. Over subsequent decades in the USA, a sharp increase in population after the Civil War gave an impetus to new building. For the first time, the choice of housing for many more of the population was not limited to a stark choice between rural and urban. Instead suburban living was seen as a desirable halfway house, offering the benefits of country air, lower rents and less crowded conditions, together with relatively quick access to shops and offices via the constantly expanding forms of mass transit. New roads were built to open up previously inaccessible land and the railways made commuting possible for those who could never have afforded their own carriages.

The attractions of suburbia were not merely a matter of health, or cost, but had an emotional resonance that went far beyond the reality of any suburban 'cottage'. And the source of this was derived in part from changing attitudes towards the land. In the USA, in fairly recent history the wilderness had first been a place to be feared, then one to be tamed. By the nineteenth century, even as new tracts of the country continued to be settled, the idea of the land was now being reimagined, and artists and writers such as Frederick Church and James Fenimore Cooper were – to great popular success – hymning the wonders of the unspoiled natural world, as the Romantics had done in Britain a few decades earlier. By 1864, as Yosemite Valley came under governmental protection, to be preserved 'for public use, resort, and recreation', it was possible to believe that all the wilderness might one day be regulated, no longer frighteningly limitless, but legislatively bounded. In Britain, allowing for smaller distances and a tamer wilderness, a comparable shift in attitudes was under way. The countryside had been the province of the elite – first owned by the gentry, then adopted intellectually, if not physically, by middle-class professionals, the readers of the Lake Poets, who venerated these unbuilt spaces as their own Arcadia. As the century progressed, railways and mass tourism opened up regions such as the Scottish Highlands and the Lake District to a mass market, turning them into holiday locations for a wider populace. In both countries, the taming of these areas was a joint enterprise of government and private industry. In the USA, railway companies and the army frequently operated together in opening up and managing the land, and the National Park Service came into being in 1916. In Britain, the Commons Preservation Society was founded in 1865, which aimed to protect open spaces being encroached on by urban building, and included Hampstead Heath, Wimbledon Common, some 3,000 acres of Epping Forest and parts of Ashdown Forest and the New Forest. The National Trust for Places of Historic Interest and Natural

Beauty, a private trust, was founded in 1895, initially also concerned with protecting open spaces. By the early twentieth century, it was a commonplace that access to the countryside was something that benefitted everyone. Outdoor living was encouraged for city children, to make them hale and responsible citizens. The Woodcraft League in the USA (1902), the Boy Scouts (from 1908) and Girl Guides (1910) were just a few of the groups that promoted this equation.

Although the countries are dramatically different in size, population density and therefore in the levels of wild and domesticated landscapes, the ideals of suburban living in Britain and the USA developed in tandem, and each influenced the other. The father of the garden-city movement, Ebenezer Howard (1850–1928), as a young man abandoned his job as a clerk in the City of London and sailed to the USA. He attempted to settle a homestead claim in Nebraska in the 1870s, and when it failed, he moved to Chicago just as the city parks were being laid out, the town reimagined as a 'garden city'. By 1889, Howard was back in London and planning a community, first named Unionville, then Rurisville and finally Garden City. It was 1903, however, before his First Garden City company raised the money to buy land in Hertfordshire, and work on the first British garden city, at Letchworth, commenced. Howard's ideas were more widely popularized in his book *To-morrow: A Peaceful Path to Real Reform* (later retitled, and more famous as, *Garden Cities of To-morrow*), where he outlined his vision for the garden city. The ideal community, Howard wrote, was one with space for industry, for commerce and for housing, a community that was purposefully limited in size, and that would always remain surrounded by large swathes of green, unspoiled land.

Howard's dream had, in some elements, been preceded by those model workers' villages established by a handful of benevolent, patriarchal industrialists who had also been persuaded of the benefits of a combination of fresh air and employment. Saltaire was established in Yorkshire in 1851 by the woollen industrialist Titus Salt, and at the end of the century Port Sunlight near Liverpool, and Bournville, outside Birmingham, were built by the owners of Lever Brothers and Cadbury respectively. This was not entirely new. In the eighteenth century, Matthew Boulton's Soho Manufactory near Birmingham had provided workers with housing, as had Josiah Wedgwood's Etruria Works in Staffordshire. The difference between these villages and the garden cities was one of scale, and that now these working-class enclaves were being mirrored by settlements for the middle classes.

But working-class enclaves, dependent on employment with a specific employer, were not what most people meant when they spoke of suburbs. Early suburbs in Britain that were planned, rather than those that had simply evolved, were intended, as Howard had hoped, as mixed housing for residents with a range of incomes. This was the initial intention for Bedford Park, in west London, designed in the 1870s by the architects Norman Shaw and E. W. Godwin. But, like many such projects, idealism proved to outrun the money available from private investment, and the area was ultimately entirely populated by the professional middle classes. Even Howard's own Letchworth garden city was to see financial considerations outweigh its visionary origins, as high infrastructure costs ensured that the houses were entirely bought by the middle classes. Similar housing projects in the USA, clustering outside Boston, Pittsburgh, Washington, Cleveland and across the country to Los Angeles, soon produced communities that were remarkably uniform in background and income. Many suburbs had their own individual profile – in type of workers, average salary, location of work, commuting routes, class, race. There were suburbs for clerks, suburbs for professionals, suburbs for the wealthy, all newly constructed communities of homogeneity.

Furthermore, Howard and his two influential designers, Raymond Unwin and Barry Parker, had not only envisaged a mixed community, but had also expected to integrate housing with commercial and light industrial premises. This, too, rarely became reality. The standard nineteenth-century suburb was far more frequently planned, in Britain often by a single landlord, as entirely residential, with all industry and commerce – indeed work of any type, including shops – firmly kept outside its borders. Many suburban leases even contained clauses that prevented householders from conducting any professional activities at home. William Morris despaired of the subsequent deadness of rows of 'villas and nothing but villas save a chemist's shop and a dry [non-alcoholic] public house'. This was the notion of separate spheres made a physical reality: nothing that was public was to impinge on these rows of private spaces.

Yet just as the home, the private sphere, was in reality commonly a place of work, so too these suburban communities, superficially so isolated and inward turning, the model of independent living, were built on – and dependent on – networks of connections to the greater world. The suburb was presented as a freestanding community, a place of privacy and chosen isolation for its residents. Yet without governmental involvement, suburbs simply could not exist. From the first communities, government investment in irrigation, canal-building, sewerage, roads, mass transportation, gas supply and electrification laid the foundations for the deep infrastructure without which suburbs could neither come into being, nor survive. And in the twentieth century, government involvement in suburban development expanded even further. By the end of World War I, the British government played a part in building nearly 60 per cent of all housing in the country; twenty years later, of the 4 million new houses erected, the government was directly responsible for building 1.5 million, and had financed many hundreds of thousands more. In Germany, as we have seen, new social housing was one of the Weimar Republic's driving forces. And in America, suburbs existed at all only because of intensive, and expensive, government involvement. There were the same infrastructure investments as in Britain: roads, sewers, gas, light, transport. In addition, the government increased its financial support of suburbs throughout the twentieth century: in the 1930s, low-income loans to remortgage the houses of families devastated by the Depression saved thousands of communities; after the war, returning soldiers were eligible for government loans for down-payments on their first homes; and wartime government production and research – the development of aluminium, prefabricated construction techniques – were turned over to private companies, the equivalent of a $50 billion investment by the government in private home-building industries. Over the following decades, the government funded architectural designs and drew up business plans for small developers, which it made available to builders at no cost.

This involvement had implications for the overall appearance of the new suburbs. In the nineteenth century, the preferred style for suburban housing had been a highly modified Gothic, a style that, under the influence of the Romantic movement, had become associated with the natural world. Neo-Gothic housing, however, was neither particularly utilitarian, nor did it lend itself to mass replication. Once suburbs were no longer confined to the upper-middle classes, therefore, the style was no longer viable financially, nor by this time aesthetically desirable either. By the early twentieth century in the USA, most of the financing of suburban building was predicated on the economics of prefab housing. Everything possible was done in the factory – the plumbing assembled, the lumber cut – and 80 per cent of the building work was completed before the contractors arrived at the building site. With the houses built on concrete slabs with no, or only a small, cellar, onsite work took as little as two weeks. Most builders were small contractors, building fewer than 100 houses a year, but William Levitt, the 'King of Suburbia', was the mighty exception. His company built 17,000 houses on Long Island in the late 1940s, as homes for returning GIs; another 22,000 in Pennsylvania and New Jersey in the following decade; and more in Illinois and Maryland. By his saturation of the market, Levitt's architectural decisions became the standard, many others following his lead, and making the Levitt visual style virtually an American shorthand for 'suburb'. Levittown, on Long Island, reduced choices to a minimum, offering two styles, a heavily simplified Cape Cod, and a ranch house, which the English call a bungalow. With a single storey, usually covered in wood, stucco, shingle or clapboards, a wide, low, pitched roof often overhanging a porch, the ranch house was a rejection of Victorian two- and three-storey houses, which were now widely viewed as overly formal, even staid. Despite Levitt's and his fellow builders' reliance on prefabrication and mass production, the ranch house was nevertheless read as 'natural', or 'informal', an epitome, even in its suburban rows, of 'country living'. This reading enabled it to be perceived as both anti-commercial and anti-consumerist in a way more traditional houses were not, even though the single-storey buildings required more land than traditional two-storey houses did, and were thus ultimately more expensive.

In Britain, the equivalent suburban style was initially a detached house, or at least a semi-detached one, a pair of houses sharing a central party wall. Bedford Park and the earlier upper-middle-class suburbs had assumed the Queen Anne style of the period, but most suburbs adopted the more 'rustic', and therefore comforting, Tudor motifs. By now, Tudor was a style that had apparently always existed, and was viewed as entirely ahistorical, belonging to no particular place – Tudor flourishes might coexist alongside Indian-inspired verandas, for example, or Arts and Crafts tiled entranceways – just as it belonged to no particular time, not even the sixteenth century. It reflected instead generic 'old' values such as community, continuity, and a world (always benevolent) that had vanished. As the suburbs were planned to join town and country, so Tudor joined modern suburban dwellers with their semi-mythical ancestors.

The Tudor, the Gothic, the ranch house – all were architectures of rejection, bricks-and-mortar repudiations of the lives that their inhabitants did not want to live. Their owners did not want to be modern, nor urban, they did not want to live in densely populated town centres, nor in mixed communities, which all seemed to represent a turning away from the now well-developed idea of what 'home' meant. Instead they sought a mythical past, a time when things had been simpler, easier. Articulating their desires in architectural styles allowed those living in a Tudor suburban semi to imagine that they were party to some form of exclusive, unusual domesticity. Yet the very universality of these desires altered the nature of the suburban experience. From the 1920s, the 'flight to suburbia' was a well-recognized pattern. By 1970, more Americans lived in suburbs than in either rural or urban environments; by 2000, more Americans lived in suburbs than in cities *and* rural areas combined. To consider that suburbs were somehow special, self-selected communities was no longer tenable. Suburbia was now for traditional couples with 2.4 children. And for singles. And the widowed. And the divorced. Suburbia was everywhere, and for everyone.

As a result, suburbs were transformed, even if, thanks to their reliance on mythological styles of domesticity, those transformations have barely been noticeable as they occurred. As more and more women returned to the workforce in numbers not seen since the nineteenth century, the lack of services and commercial premises near home ceased to be an acceptable, or even desirable, inconvenience, and became intolerable. So, steadily but surely, suburbs transformed themselves from residential satellites of nearby employment centres, and became employment centres themselves, complete with shops, services, offices and entertainment venues.

As this economic balance shifted, so too did ideas of what suburbs were, or what they should look like. If they were no longer isolated, protected residential communities, what were they? Developers in much of the English-speaking world answered that question with a new category of invisible commodity: suburbs, too, had become 'heritage', communities packaged to look old. They had become a means of representing the myth of the happy family times of olden days in architecture. Sometimes the trend for individual houses developed spontaneously, with a population buying into the nostalgia package, and being drawn to building styles that matched a prevalent myth. In suburban Santa Fe, in New Mexico, many houses are cement-covered, timber-framed buildings that have merely been decorated to resemble adobe, rather than actually being made of the region's indigenous clay. Other suburbs, however, were from their inception designed as a single heritage unit, as structured and planned as any garden city of Ebenezer Howard. Celebration, a suburb in Florida, was financed and designed by the Disney Corporation in the 1990s; Seaside, in the same state, was designed by its private owners in the 1980s in an amalgam of small-town motifs and styles chosen from a variety of Victorian, Classical, modern and postmodern options.* In Britain, Poundbury, under the patronage of the Prince of Wales, is a Dorset suburb masquerading as a pastiche olde-worlde village (which particular historical period it references is left carefully vague). In keeping with modern economic and social realities, many of Poundbury's 'houses' are actually banks, building societies, offices and the like, while all the signifiers of modern life – plumbing, gas, electricity, phone, television – are covered up, as if they were dirty secrets. Instead, the centrally heated buildings have false chimneys that produce no smoke.

It is not at all surprising that the heritage industry, the rise of the home-museum and the popularization of mythologized and patriotic styles took off as industrialization spread ever wider. In the twentieth century, many of the men who made their fortunes from technological modernity were great promoters of commercial depictions of idealized pasts: Henry Ford built Greenfield Village, John D. Rockefeller was instrumental in the establishment of Colonial Williamsburg. Heritage is an expression of fear of the future by taking refuge in a simplified past, a rejection of uncertainty by refusing to engage with variety, evolution and change. The revolutions of the eighteenth and nineteenth centuries made the simplifications of Altdeutsch and Colonial attractive, styles of safety. As the nineteenth century turned into the twentieth, the revolution of modernism, with its love of surface and its recoil from the past, made many cling harder than ever to their suburban dreams.

---

*   Seaside was where *The Truman Show* (1998) was filmed, this satire on reality television appropriately located in a confected town.

Coda:
Not at Home

In 1925, the Exposition Internationale des Arts Décoratifs et Industriels Modernes was held in Paris. This was one of a long line of such exhibitions, all drawing their inspiration from London's Great Exhibition of 1851, at the height of the Victorian age. Art Deco was the style of the moment, but if the Exposition of 1925 is remembered at all, it is as a birthplace of modern architecture, for it was here that the ideas of the Swiss–French modernist Le Corbusier were made concrete, in the Pavillon de l'Esprit Nouveau. Here, in three dimensions, the visionary father of architectural modernism demonstrated in bricks and mortar the theories he had set out in his manifesto, *Towards a New Architecture*, two years earlier. These stylish, sleek rooms displayed his 'five points' of modern architecture in action: that the structure should be raised off the ground; that it should have a flow of windows giving views of the outdoors; that it should have a terrace where nature comes into the house; that it should have non-supporting walls, allowing the architect to design by eye, rather than for structural necessity; and that it should be organized on an open-plan.

This five-point plan was to be hugely influential. But while the history of modernism has a literature rich in the theoretical, economic and philosophical underpinnings of the movement, it is worth considering for a moment the possibility that modern architecture was propelled not by Le Corbusier, or any other Great Man of the twentieth century, but by a housewife of the nineteenth.

Catharine Beecher was of course more than a housewife. As well as being the sister of the more famous Harriet Beecher Stowe, and the daughter of a celebrated preacher of the day, she ran schools and established the American Women's Educational Association in 1852, which trained teachers for frontier schools. It was in her books on domestic management, however, which at first glance appear to be the most conservative part of her work, that she set out the ideas that in retrospect can be read as the first proposals for the rationalization of household space. 'A place for every thing, and every thing in its place' was her motto, and to make that possible for people with even modest amounts of space, she formulated the concept for what is today called a built-in cupboard, but then was a novelty without a name. She combined this with many other ideas that later time-and-motion experts would adopt, and which enabled the creation of the twentieth century's open-plan household. She moved the broom cupboard into the kitchen, the linen cupboard to, or at least near, the bedrooms, the medicine cabinet to the bathroom. Such arrangements appear so obvious now that it seems inconceivable that someone had to propose it, but as Dutch linen-cupboards in reception rooms show, it had not historically been the case. In 1912, Christine Frederick adopted Beecher's 'every thing in its place' and her built-in cupboards to create built-in units of shelves, storage and seating. From there, ergonomic arrangements of both rooms and their furniture followed naturally.

Unlike Grete Schütte-Lihotzky, today neither of these women is recognized as a pioneer of modernism. High modernism has tended to focus its attentions more on appearance than utility, both in architecture and in product design, even as the most successful built their careers on the design and decoration of vernacular housing, whether the private houses of the rich, following the practices of the architects of earlier movements, such as Aestheticism, Wiener Werkstätte and the Arts and Crafts movement, or the apartment buildings of entirely new cities. Office buildings, or places where the public gathered, generally played a smaller role.

Architects, as we have seen, historically engaged little with the concerns of daily life. It was not, quite simply, considered to be their job. It would be unfair to blame the modernists for continuing along this separate path, were it not for their famous dictum, 'form follows function', which gave the illusion that function was, finally, to become a part of the architectural vision. As it transpired, however, few practitioners were interested enough in function to discover how form might be made to follow it. In *Towards a New Architecture* Le Corbusier has a great deal to say about the form a house should take, how it should look, but little on its function, on how it was to be used: nothing on how a house was to be kept warm, or the processes by which food was put on the table, from getting the shopping in, to cooking, cleaning and eating. And modernist architecture and house-holders continued to diverge over the essence of home – how people experienced their domestic spaces. Le Corbusier's slightly older contemporary, Adolf Loos, if apparently unintentionally, dismissed the entire ambience of a household, hominess, as an 'effect' which the architect 'wishes to exert upon the spectator'. Not only did he perceive domesticity merely as an effect, but he thought it was one the architect imposed – and not even on the residents, but merely on a 'spectator', a bystander. Others valued it even less, seeing the very idea of home as the enemy of modernism. As the philosopher Theodor Adorno said simply, 'The house is past'.

This was the case from the movement's very inception in the nine-teenth century. In 1863, in his essay 'The Painter of Modern Life', the poet and critic Charles Baudelaire had described the perfect *flâneur*, or man about town, as one who lives 'in the ebb and flow, the bustle, the fleeting and the infinite... to be at the very centre of the world, and yet to be unseen [by] the world' is his ideal. For Baudelaire, and for the readers of his essay, the *flâneur* was anonymous and solitary, detached from both family and home. It may be no coincidence that modernism took root most easily in house countries, in places where the life of the streets had always been paramount. In home countries by this date, the house, no matter how small or inconvenient, or how divided up into multiple occupancy, was the central focus of desire, the imagined site of the good life. In house countries of Europe, life was most agreeably passed in the public sphere – the café, brasserie and restaurant. But of course, no division is absolute. In the first half of the twentieth century, the German philosopher Walter Benjamin rejected nineteenth-century domesticity as physically and mentally cloying, conveying his distaste in metaphors of upholstery, which swaddles and swallows, or spider's webs, which ensnare. A man has two choices, he suggested. He can sit on a sofa, and leave the impression of his behind on the cushion. Or he can live in the city, the streets, and leave his impression on history. Adolf Behne, an avant-garde architect and critic in the Weimar Republic, thought that the solution to what Benjamin had called the nineteenth century's 'addiction' to home life was material, not psychological. Architects, he said, should build with glass, which 'has an extra-human, super-human quality'. That housewives had rejected it as too uncomfortable was, he enthused, what made it perfect: 'And that is not its least advantage. For first of all the European must be wrenched out of his cosiness [*Gemütlichkeit*]. Not without good reason does the adjective *gemüt-lich* intensified become *saugemütlich* [swinishly comfortable]. Away with cosiness! Only where cosiness ends, does humanity begin.'

The nineteenth century had barricaded its homes with the physical embodiments of comfort, physical and emotional, to protect them from the harshness of the rapidly evolving industrial world. Modernism wanted to tear those cosy barricades down again as it presented itself as the antithesis of bourgeois comfort, instead representing social equality and a belief in progress, of mankind striding into an enlightened future.

Le Corbusier's pronouncement, that a house is a 'machine for living', initially suggests an engagement with the nineteenth century's embrace of mass-produced, technological domesticity. As the spread of public utilities had rendered the deep structure of housing – the pipes, the wires – homogeneous, so modernist architects and designers embraced standardization and mass production for the goods that would fill the house. William Morris, a lifelong socialist, had advocated better design for all, although his hand-crafted aesthetic had kept his designs out of reach for all but the wealthy. In the twentieth century, those who shared his political views saw that better design for all could be achieved by harnessing technology and mass production. The Bauhaus architect Walter Gropius was vehement: 'The vital needs of the majority of people are essentially identical. A home and domestic utensils are important things for everybody, and their shape can be determined by reason rather than by artistic imagination.' For Gropius and his colleagues, unlike Morris, mass-produced objects could be 'better than those made by hand'. But just as Schütte-Lihotzky's Frankfurt kitchen layout had imposed her own political and economic views of how daily life should be lived on sometimes unwilling residents, so too the assessment of what made an item 'better' was not made by those who were going to use it, but by designers and architects and city-planners. Meanwhile, industrial technology was producing a stream of innovations that were making houses easier to maintain: linoleum flooring that needed only a quick wipe rather than intensive polishing; toughened, later ovenproof, glass – Duran glass in Germany in 1893, Pyrex in the USA in 1915; non-stick pots and pans after World War II. But these products were of little interest to the pioneers of modernism. The tableware, textiles and furnishings that they designed were not easier to use, nor easier to care for. They just looked good.

It is possible to view these designers as throwbacks, having a great deal in common with the grand architectural theorists of the Baroque age. Le Corbusier's primary aim in his houses was to create a dramatic visual statement, just as it had been the aim of Le Vau when he laid out the *grands appartements* at Versailles. The rooms designed by both architects were, to paraphrase Gibbon, for ostentation rather than use. The modernism of Le Corbusier was a modernism of the eye. The technology that underlay appearance, which governed people's daily lives, was of next to no interest to him. If a house looked sleek and streamlined, it was modern. If a wall had no electric sockets showing, it was modern, even if it left the residents nowhere to plug in a lamp; if the room had no skirting-boards, it was streamlined, even if mops and vacuums then marked the walls. As with the Baroque architects, too, furniture for the modernists once more became part of the overall design scheme of a house, not an aid to the sociability or comfort of its residents. If a chair enhanced the design, it was good, even if it was too low, or too narrow; if a table looked right, it was right, even if it was too heavy to move into position as needed. Comfort, utility, function – these had rarely been the architects' concern, but few had spoken as frequently as the modernists of utility, of building entirely new ways of living.

Le Corbusier was perhaps an extreme example. But he was also extremely influential. His open-plan layout in the Pavillon de l'Esprit

Nouveau was widely admired. It was also widely adapted, although in large part for reasons that had little to do with any underlying artistic, political or philosophical beliefs. That the architects working on public housing were followers of the modernist school played a small part. But this was overall of less significance than the need to resolve the acute housing shortage created by the two World Wars. Governments and local authorities were suddenly required to build large quantities of working-class housing in densely populated cities, striving to achieve standards to create maximum health and social welfare in the minimum amount of space. At the same time, land values and construction costs soared (in Europe after World War I, in the USA after World War II), and so houses became ever smaller. Three rooms – a living room, dining room and kitchen – occupy considerably more space than one mixed-use area. To compensate, technological advances such as replacing radiators with heating through wall-vents were deftly combined with the pragmatic arrangements of Catharine Beecher and Christine Frederick to turn the space that had been freed into wall-units and storage. As the century progressed, better heating and improved glass technology made it possible to install wide patio doors and large windows, which gave the illusion of more space as the outdoors visually infiltrated the house. These commercial necessities and technological opportunities were glossed with a superficial coating of modernist theory as the open-plan housing of the 1950s through to the 1970s returned families to patterns of communal living last experienced in the Middle Ages.

But half a millennium of home-making had seen the number of possessions any family owned multiplied a hundredfold. 'We have become urban nomads! Just as we ourselves have become mobile, we must have movable possessions,' proclaimed the writer Alix Rohde-Liebenau in Soviet-occupied Berlin. Open-plan was in this respect the opposite of what Catharine Beecher had proposed. No longer 'A place for every thing, and every thing in its place', but now no fixed place for anything. Even some of the proponents of modernism wavered between commitment to its theory and an unrecognized adherence to older patterns of expectations of the requirements of domesticity. The German architect Alexander Klein was an early advocate of open-plan housing – his apartments featured a single area for living, cooking and eating, separated from areas for bathing, dressing and sleeping. The adoption of this style of living, he wrote in *Functional House for Frictionless Living* (1928), would avoid the problem that recurred in traditional housing, where family members constantly crossed paths as they went about their daily lives. Open-plan living created a domestic environment where individual family members' daily routines could be kept separate. Instead of seeming modern, however, his concern is curiously reminiscent of nineteenth-century practice, where separation was the overriding desire.

Henry James, hardly a proponent of modernism, did not notice Klein's attempts to separate family members in their new open-plan living arrangements. He was, instead, horrified by the style's desire to annihilate the distinction between interior and exterior, public and private. 'This diffused vagueness of separation between apartments, between hall and room, between one room and another, between the one you are in and the one you are not in, between place of passage and place of privacy is a provocation to despair.' Everything, he mourned, was 'visible, visitable, penetrable'.

Klein's mixed motivations, his uncertainties as to whether it was openness or privacy that was being sought – all make clear how revolutionary were the changes modernism had brought. In only a couple of decades, modernism tried to overturn the organic development of 500 years of the making of home. It is unsurprising, therefore, that today's homeowners tend to select a handful of design and technology elements from the twentieth century, and are otherwise content to hang on to the possessions that have come to signify 'home' over the centuries: their cushions, their upholstery, their privet hedges and picket fences. Walter Benjamin had promoted the use of glass because it was 'the enemy of secrets…the enemy of possession'. Yet secrets, or at least privacy, and possessions – the many ways of having a room of one's own, the possession of comfort, of nostalgia, of belonging, as well as the possession of possessions – are what homes are made of.

Home vs modernism was never going to be a fair fight. Benjamin's 'secret', in German, is *Geheimnis*, a word which encompasses not merely secrets, but a mystery, that which is concealed, and unknowable. *Geheimnis* derives, very obviously, from *Heim*, just as its opposite, *unheimlich*, the German for 'uncanny', is, literally, un-home-like. The weird, the unearthly, is embedded in German as being not-at-home, Dorothy once she has been swept away to Oz. Even if our own personal Kansas might be grey, dry and unlovely, at the end of half a millennium of adaptation and evolution there is still, finally, No place like home.

Notes

HOME THOUGHTS: AN INTRODUCTION

p. 1   'one wanted to be': 'There is no place like home': L. Frank Baum, *The Wizard of Oz* ([1900, as *The Wonderful Wizard of Oz*], London, Hutchinson & Co., [1926]), p. 34.

p. 3   'steady heartbeat': The notion that *Crusoe's* success is in part owing to its exploration of daily life is from Ian Watt, *The Rise of the Novel: Studies in Defoe, Richardson and Fielding* (Harmondsworth, Penguin, 1972), p. 74; a fuller discussion of this, and the idea of comfort that follows, John Crowley, *The Invention of Comfort: Sensibilities and Design in Early Modern Britain and Early America* (Baltimore, Johns Hopkins University Press, 2001), pp. 154–5. The citations are from Daniel Defoe, *Robinson Crusoe: An Authoritative Text, Contexts, Criticism*, Michael Shinagel, ed. (New York, W. W. Norton, 1994), pp. 50, 51, 139.

p. 3   '[land and his house and his home]': origins of word 'home': Carl Darling Buck, *A Dictionary of Selected Synonyms in the Principal Indo-European Languages: A Contribution to the History of Ideas* (Chicago, University of Chicago Press, facsimile of 1949 edition, 1988), pp. 458–9; 1275 poem: cited in the *OED's* definition of 'home', the verses 'The Latemest Day', B. Cotton MS Caligula A, ix, can be found in Carleton Brown, ed., *English Lyrics of the XIIIth Century* (Oxford, Clarendon, 1932), line 22, p. 50.

p. 4   'to maintain them': French: Martine Segalen, 'The House Between Public and Private: A Socio-Historical Overview', in Anton Schuurman and Pieter Spierenburg, eds, *Private Domain, Public Inquiry: Families and Lifestyles in the Netherlands and Europe, 1550 to the Present* (Hilversum, Uitgeverij Verloren, 1996), p. 240, and Sharon Marcus, *Apartment Stories: City and Home in Nineteenth-Century Paris and London* (Berkeley, University of California Press, 1999), pp. 64, 151; Russian: Martine Segalen, 'Material Conditions of Family Life', David I. Kertzer and Marzio Barbagli, eds, *The History of the European Family*, vol. 2: *Family Life in the Long Nineteenth Century, 1789–1913* (London, Yale University Press, 2002), p. 10.

p. 5   'one element among many': community or house as focus: Amos Rapoport, *House, Form and Culture* (Englewood Cliffs, Prentice-Hall, 1969), p. 70

283

p. 6   'any house they knew': 'Costly and Curious': Sir Richard Carnac Temple, ed., *The Travels of Peter Mundy in Europe and Asia, 1608–1667* (Cambridge, Hakluyt Society, 1925), vol. 4, p. 70.

p. 8   'were artists' props': John Loughman, 'Between Reality and Artful Fiction: The Representation of the Domestic Interior in Seventeenth-Century Dutch Art', in Jeremy Aynsley and Charlotte Grant, eds, *Imagined Interiors: Representing the Domestic Interior since the Renaissance* (London, V&A Publications, 2006), p. 95.

p. 8   'one from this time': the detail of the reality of furnishings in Dutch houses in these paragraphs comes from C. Willemijn Fock, 'Semblance or Reality? The Domestic Interior in Seventeenth-Century Dutch Genre Painting', Mariët Westermann, *Art and Home: Dutch Interiors in the Age of Rembrandt* (Zwolle, Waanders, 2001), pp. 83–95, unless otherwise noted.

p. 9   'therefore, is unknowable': porcelain and patterned fabrics: John Loughman and John Michael Montias, *Public and Private Spaces: Works of Art in Seventeenth-Century Dutch Houses* (Zwolle, Waanders, 2000), p. 15; 'in their stalle': Temple, *The Travels of Peter Mundy*, vol. 4, p. 70; millions of paintings: Klaske Muizelaar and Derek Phillips, *Picturing Men and Women in the Dutch Golden Age: Paintings and People in Historical Perspective* (New Haven, Yale University Press, 2003), p. 184; dollshouses: it is Muizelaar and Phillips, *Men and Women*, p. 196, who suggest relying on them. Two of the three surviving dollshouses are in the Rijksmuseum, the other is in the Centraal Museum, Utretcht.

p. 11   'God's truth is eternal': *The Procuress*: Svetlana Alpers, 'Picturing Dutch Culture', Wayne E. Franits, ed., *Looking at Seventeenth-Century Dutch Art: Realism Reconsidered* (Cambridge, Cambridge University Press, 1997), pp. 57–67; children as stand-ins for the new republic: Simon Schama, *The Embarrassment of Riches: An Interpretation of Dutch Culture in the Golden Age* (London, Collins, 1987), p. 499; the symbols of Dutch art and their meaning, apart from those noted above, are drawn from: Eddy de Jongh, 'Realism and Seeming Realism in Seventeenth-Century Dutch Painting', Franits, *Looking at Seventeenth-Century Dutch Art*, pp. 48–52, Mary Frances Durantini, *The Child in Seventeenth-Century Dutch Painting* (Ann Arbor, UMI Research Press, 1983), pp. 27–31, 87–9, 114, 183, 190, 215–17.

p. 12   'every eight Amsterdammers': Dutch maids, almanacs, plague statistics: Muizelaar and Phillips, *Men and Women*, pp. 14, 26; 'wonderful Nett and cleane': Temple, *The Travels of Peter Mundy*, vol. 4, p. 71.

p. 13   'a spitter's poor aim': 'I find very convenient': Samuel Pepys, *The Diary of Samuel Pepys*, Robert Latham and William Matthews, eds (London, Bell & Hyman, 1983), vol. 3, p. 262; spitting-sheet: the Latham and Matthews edition is the most complete, but makes no mention of the phrase in its fifteen-page glossary, nor its extensive notes. The out-of-copyright Project Gutenberg version, available online at http://www.gutenberg.org/files/4200/4200-h/4200-h.htm

NOTES TO PAGES 14–25

(accessed 11 March 2013), is edited by David Widger, the author of '??', and is based on Henry B. Wheatley's very good 1893 edition.

p. 14   'indoors as well as out': 'I was not troubled at it at all': Pepys, *Diary*, Monday, 28 January 1661, vol. 2, p. 25; 'in great discomfort': the author was Jean-Nicolas Parival, and he wrote in 1669; cited in Paul Zumthor, *Daily Life in Rembrandt's Holland*, trs. Simon Watson Taylor (London, Weidenfeld and Nicolson, 1962), pp. 137–8.

p. 15   'a matter of routine': German spittoons: Daniel L. Purdy, *The Tyranny of Elegance: Consumer Cosmopolitanism in the Era of Goethe* (Baltimore, Johns Hopkins University Press, 1998), pp. 57, 59; American mother of 1851: cited in Elisabeth Donaghy Garrett, *At Home: The American Family, 1750–1870* (New York, Abrams, 1990), p. 68. She too uses the word 'none' in reference to the lack of reproductions of spittoons in professional or amateur art.

p. 17   'behaviour commonly existed': *Punch* cartoon: Jane Hamlett, *Material Relations: Domestic Interiors and Middle-Class Families in England, 1850–1910* (Manchester, Manchester University Press, 2010), p. 44; illustrations of men: those that spring to mind are two in Richard Doyle's *Manners and Customs of ye Englishe*, Maginn's illustration to 'Story without a Tail' and Maclise's 'The Fraserians'. My thanks to Guy Woolnough, D. E. Latané and Patrick Leary for helping me gather even this small handful.

p. 18   'to be eternal truths': 1710 households: Tim Meldrum, 'Domestic Service, Privacy and the Eighteenth-Century Metropolitan Household', *Urban History*, 26, 1999, pp. 33–4.

p. 20   'the Victorian widow': 'be untaught and rude': Edmund Spenser, *A View of the Present State of Ireland*, W. L. Renwick, ed. (Oxford, Clarendon, 1970), pp. 1–3; 1865 inquest: this inquest was cited in John Ruskin, *Sesame and Lilies: Two Lectures* ([1867], Orpington, George Allen, 1882), pp. 78–9. He dated it to the year of his lecture, 1867, and named the *Daily Telegraph* as his source. While I have been unable to locate the article he cites, the inquest, which in reality was held on 10 February 1865, was widely reported, for example in the *Caledonian Mercury*, 13 February 1865, p. 3.

I. THE FAMILY WAY

p. 25   'the world combined': Max Weber, *The Protestant Ethic and the Spirit of Capitalism*, trs. Talcott Parsons, foreword by R. H. Tawney (London, G. Allen & Unwin, 1930); coal mining: E. A. Wrigley, *Continuity, Chance and Change: The Character of the Industrial Revolution in England* (Cambridge, Cambridge University Press, 1988), p. 54.

p. 25   'cumulative great effect': Samuel Johnson, *The Works of Samuel Johnson*, D. J. Greene, ed. (New Haven, Yale University Press, 1977), vol. 10, pp. 365–6, cited by Geoffrey Parker, *Global Crisis: War, Climate Change and Catastrophe in the Seventeenth Century* (London, Yale University Press), p. xxvi.

p. 25   'wreck of his ship': Christopher Hill, 'Robinson Crusoe', *History Workshop*, autumn 1980, pp. 6–24.

p. 26   'much more valuable': 'Writing upon Trade': Daniel Defoe, *A Weekly Review of the Affairs of France*, vol. 9, 11 June 1713, p. 214.

p. 27   'consumer revolution was': Neil McKendrick, John Brewer and J. H. Plumb, *The Birth of a Consumer Society: The Commercialization of Eighteenth-Century England* (London, Hutchinson, 1982), pp. 9–33, and Colin Campbell, *The Romantic Ethic and the Spirit of Modern Consumerism* (Oxford, Blackwell, 1987), pp. 17–57, passim.

p. 28   'but necessary': revolutions: Jan de Vries, *The Industrious Revolution: Consumer Behaviour and the Household Economy, 1650 to the Present* (Cambridge, Cambridge University Press, 2008), p. ix, outlines the period 1650–1850, and the American, French and British revolutions. He doesn't specifically name the Dutch Revolt, because it is the starting point of his argument; 'capitalist economy': Jan de Vries and Ad van der Woude, *The First Modern Economy: Success, Failure, and Perseverance of the Dutch Economy, 1500–1815* (Cambridge, Cambridge University Press, 1997), pp. 167, 129; land-ownership: ibid., p. 169.

p. 29   'property-enhancing purposes': Mary S. Hartman, *The Household and the Making of History: A Subversive View of the Western Past* (Cambridge, Cambridge University Press, 2004), passim.

p. 29   'reconcile your friends': Alberti cited in David Gaunt, 'Kinship: Thin Red Lines or Thick Blue Blood', David I. Kertzer and Marizio Barbagli, eds, *The History of the European Family*, vol. 1, *Family Life in Early Modern Times, 1500–1789* (London, Yale University Press, 2001), p. 259; Shakespeare, *Romeo and Juliet*, T. J. B. Spencer, ed. (Harmondsworth, Penguin, 1967), III.iv.150–52.

p. 30   'part of the family': Pepys, *Diary*, 31 December 1662, vol. 3, p. 301; eighteenth-century diarist: Gaunt, 'Kinship: Thin Red Lines or Thick Blue Blood', Kertzer and Barbagli, *The History of the European Family*, vol. 1, p. 259; *Census of Great Britain, 1851* (London, Longman Brown, 1854), p. xxxiv.

p. 30   'much of Europe': Hartman, *The Household and the Making of History*, pp. 118ff. I rely heavily on this volume for my description of the northwest European late-marriage pattern, as well as using it as a jumping-off point for my own ideas on the creation of home. Readers of Professor Hartman's revolutionary work will recognize my enormous debt to her work throughout this chapter. Her thesis, that it was the northwest European marriage pattern that precipitated the consumer revolution, is one of those radical insights that seem obvious once they are pointed out. I have merely extended her theory, to suggest that, if it was the marriage pattern that precipitated the consumer world, then it was home that acted as the reagent between the young couple with cash and the consuming world. My puzzlement at the quiet academic reception of Hartman's ground-breaking work, and my admiration for it, know no bounds.

p. 30   'non-nuclear kin resident': Rhode Island and England: Peter Laslett, *Family Life and Illicit Love in Earlier Generations: Essays in Historical Sociology* (Cambridge, Cambridge University Press, 1977), pp. 30–31; Netherlands: de Vries and van der Woude, *First Modern Economy*, p. 163.

p. 30   'calling patroness': Jane Austen, *Pride and Prejudice*, Vivien Jones, ed. ([1813], Harmondsworth, Penguin, 1996), p. 103.

p. 32   'good life companions': James Wood, 'God Talk: The Book of Common Prayer at Three Hundred and Fifty', *New Yorker*, 22 October 2012, pp. 73–6, identifies *Pride and Prejudice*'s parody of the Book of Common Prayer. Its origins in the changing role of marriage is my own.

p. 33   'communal decision': the Bible verses are, respectively, 1 Corinthians 7:9, and Genesis 2:18.

p. 34   'personal wellbeing': 'as a property arrangement': John Boswell, *Same-Sex Unions in Premodern Europe* (New York, Vintage, 1995), pp. xxi–xxii, cited in John R. Gillis, *A World of Their Own Making: Myth, Ritual and the Quest for Family Values* (New York, Basic, 1996), p. 134; domestic service: Hartman, *The Household and the Making of History*, p. 251; 40 per cent: Kertzer and Barbagli, *History of the European Family*, vol. 1, p. x; adolescents: Hartman, *The Household and the Making of History*, pp. 55ff.

p. 36   'drove capitalism's supply': Protestantism and late marriage: Hartman, *The Household and the Making of History*, pp. 210–12, 215; Black Death estimate: *Dictionary of the Middle Ages*, Joseph R. Strayer, ed. (New York, Scribner, 1983), vol. 2, pp. 257–67.

p. 38   'marriage was void': this and the previous two paragraphs based on Raffaella Sarti, *Europe at Home: Family and Material Culture, 1500–1800*, trs. Allan Cameron (London, Yale University Press, 2002), pp. 14–19, and Kertzer and Barbagli, *History of the European Family*, vol. 1, pp. xii–xiii.

p. 38   'around 50 per cent': women's longevity: Hartman, *The Household and the Making of History*, p. 96; the outline list is hers too, p. 39; interpretation of records: it is Emanuel le Roy Ladurie who suggests that women were just omitted from the records; the suggestion of infanticide is from Hartman, *The Household and the Making of History*, pp. 118, 158; population data: John R. Gillis, *For Better, for Worse: British Marriages, 1600 to the Present* (New York, Oxford University Press, 1985), p. 11.

p. 39   'at the same date': illegitimate births: Schama, *Embarrassment of Riches*, p. 522; Suffolk: Ivy Pinchbeck and Margaret Hewitt, *Children in English Society* (London, Routledge & Kegan Paul, 1969–73), vol. 2, p. 584; Austria: Hugh Cunningham, *Children and Childhood in Western Society since 1500* (London, Longman, 1995), pp. 82–3; high rates: ibid., pp. 91, 93, 94; the figures cited are from David Kertzer, *Sacrificed for Honor: Italian Infant Abandonment and the Politics of Reproductive Control* (Boston, Beacon, 1993), pp. 72–3.

p. 40   'these do not appear': bundling: Hartman, *The Household and the Making of History*, p. 62.

p. 41 'to begin withal': Lawrence Stone, *The Family, Sex and Marriage in England, 1500–1800* (London, Harper, 1977), p. 284; fiction: John Hajnal, 'European Marriage Patterns in Perspective', D. V. Glass and D. E. C. Eversley, eds, *Population in History: Essays in Historical Demography* (London, Edward Arnold, 1969), pp. 101–43. I have also drawn on John Hajnal, 'Two Kinds of Pre-Industrial Household Systems', *Population and Development Review*, 8, 3, 1982, pp. 449–94. Note that this contains sections that did not appear when the essay was republished in Richard Wall, with Jean Robin and Peter Laslett, eds, *Family Forms in Historic Europe* (Cambridge, Cambridge University Press, 1983); Hertfordshire woman: cited in Hartman, *The Household and the Making of History*, p. 27.

p. 42 'trade and colonization, slaves': Honorourable East India Company: M. W. van Boven, 'Towards a New Age of Partnership: An Ambitious World Heritage Project (UNESCO Memory of the World – reg.form, 2002)', in *VOC Archives*, accessed online, 20 January 2014, http://portal.unesco.org; footnote: de Vries and van der Woude, *First Modern Economy*, p. 400.

p. 43 '10 per cent': VOC: de Vries and van der Woude, *First Modern Economy*, pp. 359, 368, 384; 'The revolution in trade': Daniel Defoe, *A Plan of the English Commerce: Being a compleat prospect of the Trade of this Nation as well the home Trade as the Foreign* ([1728], Oxford, Blackwell, 1927), pp. 36–8; urban Netherlands: Sarti, *Europe at Home*, p. 86.

p. 44 'falling on the righteous': Reformation: these triggers for change, in slightly different form, and with different emphases, appear in André Burguière and François Lebrun, 'The One Hundred and One Families of Europe', André Burguière, Christiane Klapisch-Zuber, Martine Segalen, Françoise Zonabend, eds, *A History of the Family*, vol. 2: *The Impact of Modernity*, trs. Sarah Hanbury Tenison (Cambridge, MA, Belknap Press, 1996), pp. 21–2; conduct books: Wayne E. Franits, *Paragons of Virtue: Women and Domesticity in Seventeenth-Century Dutch Art* (Cambridge, Cambridge University Press, 1993), p. 66; footnote: John Demos, *A Little Commonwealth: Family Life in Plymouth Colony* (New York, Oxford University Press, 1970), pp. 25–33, pp. 3–4, and John Navin, '"Decrepit in Their Early Youth": English Children in Holland and Plymouth Plantation', James Marten, ed., *Children in Colonial America* (New York, New York University Press, 2007), p. 138.

p. 45 'harmony and philosophy': 'in the manner of thrifty and modest households': cited in Schama, *Embarrassment of Riches*, p. 53; Plutarch's metaphor: the interpretation of the painting is from Franits, *Paragons of Virtue*, p. 88; Sarah B. Pomeroy, ed., *Plutarch's* Advice to the Bride and Groom *and* A Consolation to His Wife, trs. Donald Russell (New York, Oxford University Press, 1999), p. 5.

p. 46 'the work repainted': Laura Lunger Knoppers, *Politicizing Domesticity: From Henrietta Maria to Milton's Eve* (Cambridge, Cambridge University Press, 2011), p. 4, highlights the portrait of the children of Charles I, p. 26, although the domestic interpretation is my own.

p. 46 'porcelain vase on display': Devis: [Anon.], *Polite Society by Arthur Devis, 1712–1787: Portraits of the English Country Gentleman and His Family* (Preston, Harris Museum and Art Gallery, 1983).

p. 47 'take on with him': Anthony Trollope, *Can You Forgive Her?*, Stephen Wall, ed. (Harmondsworth, Penguin, 1986), pp. 168, 128, cited by Deborah Cohen, *Household Gods: The British and Their Possessions* (New Haven, Yale University Press, 2006), p. 92.

p. 48 'consumption and socialization': Spenser: cited in Crowley, *Invention of Comfort*, p. 77; household and economy: Marion W. Gray, *Productive Men, Reproductive Women: The Agrarian Household and the Emergence of Separate Spheres during the German Enlightenment* (New York, Berghahn Books, 2000), pp. 51, 78–9, except for *das ganze Haus* and definition, Gaunt, 'Kinship: Thin Red Lines or Thick Blue Blood', Kertzer and Barbagli, *History of the European Family*, vol. 1, p. 280.

p. 49 'valued, and invaluable': USA: Jack Larkin, *The Reshaping of Everyday Life, 1790–1840* (New York, Harper & Row, 1988), pp. 36–7; wives' roles: Hartman, *The Household and the Making of History*, pp. 160–81; widows: ibid., p. 65–6.

p. 49 '70 per cent': New York: Diana diZerega Wall, 'Separating the Spheres in Early Nineteenth-Century New York City: Redefining Gender among the Middle Classes', James Symonds, ed., *Table Settings: The Material Culture and Social Context of Dining, AD 1700–1900* (Oxford, Oxbow Books, 2010), p. 82.

p. 51 'nature of home': children and the Industrial Revolution: de Vries and van der Woude, *First Modern Economy*, pp. 603–4, point out that in 1801, of more than 500 companies in two regions of the Netherlands in 1801, 15 per cent employed women, while 47 per cent employed children; *Familie*: Gaunt, 'Kinship: Thin Red Lines or Thick Blue Blood', in Kertzer and Barbagli, *History of the European Family*, vol. 1, p. 280.

p. 52 'emotional investment': Italian: cited in Paul Langford, *Englishness Identified: Manners and Character, 1650–1850* (Oxford, Oxford University Press, 2000), p. 44; birth announcements: Schama, *Embarrassment of Riches*, p. 521, except for the description of the favour, which is from Zumthor, *Rembrandt's Holland*, p. 96.

p. 53 'were the norm': late-marriage pattern and Industrial Revolution: Hartman, *The Household and the Making of History*, p. 11–12; James I cited in Michael McKeon, *The Secret History of Domesticity: Public, Private, and the Division of Knowledge* (Baltimore, Johns Hopkins University Press, 2005), p. 114; democracy: Hartman, *The Household and the Making of History*, p. 227.

p. 53 'new middle classes': change for the masses: this is a point made by Hartman, *The Household and the Making of History*, pp. 78ff., and also Natalie Zemon Davis, 'Ghosts, King, and Progeny: Some Features of Family Life in Early Modern France', *Daedalus*, 106, 1977, pp. 87–114. It doesn't take a particularly acute eye to note that both these historians who stress the agency of family life are women.

p. 54 'their own justification': revolts: Parker, *Global Crisis*, p. xix; 'their own justification': Hill, 'Robinson Crusoe', *History Workshop*, pp. 6–24.

2. A ROOM OF ONE'S OWN

p. 55 'a single rushlight': the information for this Siberian story comes from Vasily Peskov, *Lost in the Taiga: One Russian Family's Fifty-Year Struggle for Survival and Religious Freedom in the Siberian Wilderness*, trs. Marian Schwartz (New York, Doubleday, 1994), from *The End of the Taiga: Siberian Mysteries*, part 2, a Russian-language television documentary, http://rutube.ru/video/509db8 7f36887fd03a7ff61a0efidb2e/, accessed 20 March 2013, and translated for me by Ilona Chavasse, and from Mike Dash, 'For 40 Years, This Russian Family Was Cut Off From All Human Contact, Unaware of WWII', in Smithsonian. com, 29 January 2013, http://www.smithsonianmag.com/history-archaeology/ For-40-Years-This-Russian-Family-Was-Cut-Off-From-Human-Contact-Unaware-of-World-War-II-188843001.html, accessed 20 March 2013.

p. 57 'Latin for hearth': hearth: Crowley, *Invention of Comfort*, p. 8.

p. 57 'or for storage': there is some confusion over the word 'byre' in English. A byre was historically a place to house cows, but in the nineteenth century, the love of the archaic, and an etymological confusion between the Old English for byre and the Old Norse for farmhouse led to the application of the word 'byre' to farmhouses.

p. 58 'already proved popular': architect-designed housing: Rapoport, *House, Form and Culture*, p. 2, suggests 5 per cent, while Paul Oliver, *Dwellings: The Vernacular House Worldwide* (London, Phaidon, 2003), p. 15, thinks it is under 1 per cent; British aristocracy: Amanda Vickery, *Behind Closed Doors: At Home in Georgian England* (New Haven, Yale University Press, 2009), p. 6; speculative builders: Stefan Muthesius, *The English Terraced House* (New Haven, Yale University Press, 1982), pp. 4–5.

p. 59 'said to be original': workers' houses: Peter Ennals and Deryck W. Holdsworth, *Homeplace: The Making of the Canadian Dwelling over Three Centuries* (Toronto, University of Toronto Press, 1998), p. 52. This was said in relation to Canadian housing, but it is no less true elsewhere; Friesland: de Vries and van der Woude, *First Modern Economy*, pp. 202–3; colonial houses: James Deetz and Patricia Scott Deetz, *The Times of Their Lives: Life, Love, and Death in Plymouth Colony* (New York, W. H. Freeman and Co., 2000), p. 184.

p. 60 'two or three beds': labourers' housing: N. W. Alcock, *People at Home: Living in a Warwickshire Village, 1500–1800* (Chichester, Phillimore, 1993), pp. 121–2; sixteenth-century houses: the contents itemized in this and the next paragraph are drawn from Warwickshire inventories, ibid., pp. 49–50.

p. 61 'named "saltbox"': Plymouth colony: the thatch suggestion appears in Deetz and Deetz, *Times of Their Lives*, pp. 176–7, 183. Many historians think that thatch was banned, but I am persuaded by their suggestion that this is a misreading; house types: outlined in Demos, *A Little Commonwealth*, and

Edward A. Chappell, 'Housing a Nation: The Transformation of Living Standards in Early America', Cary Carson, Ronald Hoffman, Peter J. Albert, eds, *Of Consuming Interests: The Style of Life in the Eighteenth Century* (Charlottesville, University Press of Virginia, 1994), p. 171.

p. 62 'floors and ceilings': Tinkhams: J. B. Jackson, *Landscapes: Selected Writings of J. B. Jackson*, Ervin H. Zube, ed. ([no place of publication], University of Massachusetts Press, 1970), p. 11–15; cellars: Deetz and Deetz, *Times of Their Lives*, p. 179.

p. 62 'permanent housing': sod houses: Thomas J. Schlereth, *Victorian America: Transformations in Everyday Life, 1876–1915* (New York, HarperCollins, 1991), pp. 88–90, and Daniel E. Sutherland, *The Expansion of Everyday Life, 1860–1876* (New York, Harper and Row, 1989), p. 44.

p. 63 'two rooms above': Maryland: C. A. Weslager, *The Log Cabin in America: From Pioneer Days to the Present* (New Brunswick, NJ, Rutgers University Press, 1969), pp. 135ff.

p. 63 'purpose-built quarters': footnote: John Michael Vlach, *Back of the Big House: The Architecture of Plantation Slavery* (Chapel Hill, University of North Carolina Press, 1993), p. 2; Virginia Plantation: the complex archaeological history of this plantation is explored in James Deetz, *Flowerdew Hundred: The Archaeology of a Virginia Plantation, 1619–1864* (Charlottesville, University Press of Virginia, 1993), passim; late 1600s: Vlach, *Back of the Big House*, pp. 2–3; slaves and indentured servants: Barbara Heath, 'Space and Place within Plantation Quarters in Virginia, 1700–1825', Clifton Ellis and Rebecca Ginsburg, eds, *Cabin, Quarter, Plantation: Architecture and Landscapes of North American Slavery* (New Haven, Yale University Press, 2010), p. 162.

p. 64 'a single privy': Philadelphia: Dell Upton, *Another City: Urban Life and Urban Spaces in the New American Republic* (New Haven, Yale University Press, 2008), p. 26.

p. 64 'were behind': kitchens: Vlach, *Back of the Big House*, pp. 43.

p. 65 'dozen people per room': the suggestion of the tainting of the word 'cabin' with the reality of slavery comes from Jan Cohn, *The Palace or the Poorhouse: The American House as a Cultural Symbol* (East Lansing, Michigan State University Press, 1979), pp. 182–3; partition of slave housing: Dell Upton, 'White and Black Landscapes in Eighteenth-Century Virginia', Ellis and Ginsburg, *Cabin, Quarter, Plantation*, pp. 123–6; multiple occupancy: Vlach, *Back of the Big House*, pp. 21–2, except for the final figure, which comes from John W. Blassingame, *The Slave Community: Plantation Life in the Antebellum South* (rev. edn, New York, Oxford University Press, 1979), pp. 254–5.

p. 65 'building practices': Chesapeake: Garrett Fesler, 'Excavating the Spaces and Interpreting the Places of Enslaved Africans and Their Descendants', Ellis and Ginsburg, *Cabin, Quarter, Plantation*, pp. 33–43.

p. 66 'the entire population': northern colonies: the figure of six or seven people is for Massachusetts Bay and Rhode Island, Edward Shorter, *The Making of the*

Modern Family (London, Collins, 1976), p. 30; Henri IV's architect: Witold Rybczynski, *Home: A Short History of an Idea* (London, Heinemann, 1988), p. 39; British room occupancy: Lorna Weatherill, *Consumer Behaviour and Material Culture in Britain, 1660–1760* (2nd edn, London, Routledge, 1996), p. 94, based on inventories, which by definition leave out the great mass of the labouring poor. The suggested revision is my own; demolition: John Burnett, *A Social History of Housing, 1815–1985* (London, Methuen, 1978), pp. 36–7, 46.

p. 67 'with strangers': 1801: Larkin, *Reshaping of Everyday Life*, p. 11; 2012: 'Families and Households, 2012', Office for National Statistics, Statistical Bulletin, released 1 November 2012, http://www.ons.gov.uk/ons/rel/family-demography/families-and-households/2012/index.html, accessed 2 October 2013; taverns: Larkin, *Reshaping of Everyday Life*, p. 125.

p. 67 'was a home-advisor': I am grateful to Dr Hanna Weibye for her help with the German, and with this idea.

p. 68 'not to want them': courtesy books: Marjorie Morgan, *Manners, Morals and Class in England, 1774–1858* (Basingstoke, Macmillan, 1994), p. 10; updated editions: Norbert Elias, *The Civilizing Process: The History of Manners and State Formation and Civilization*, trs., Edmund Jephcott (Oxford, Blackwell, 1994), pp. 61ff., 134–5.

p. 69 'they did in England': 'Worthless idea': Joan DeJean, *The Age of Comfort: When Paris Discovered Casual and the Modern Home Began* (New York, Bloomsbury, 2009), p. 81; the indoor privy: Muizelaar and Phillips, *Men and Women*, p. 26; the close-stools: a sketch by Gesina Terborch, in the Rijksprentenkabinett, reproduced in Peter Thornton, *Authentic Decor: The Domestic Interior, 1620–1929* (London, Seven Dials, 2000), p. 61.

p. 69 'aristocracy had done': Pepys, *Diary*, 12 April 1665, vol. 6, p. 78; public display of Dutch beds: Thera Wijsenbeek-Olthuis, 'The Social History of the Curtain', Huub de Jonge, ed., *Ons sort mensen: Levensstijlen in Nederland* (Nijmegen, SUN, 1997), pp. 76–91; all translations from this book are by Gerard van Vuuren.

p. 70 'visitors were received': Duc de Luynes: DeJean, *The Age of Comfort*, p. 167; Ham House: Crowley, *Invention of Comfort*, pp. 74–5; *ruelle*: Sarti, 'The Material Conditions of Family Life', Kertzer and Barbagli, *History of the European Family*, vol. 1, p. 122.

p. 71 'with him to Virginia': Renaissance Italy: Sarti, *Europe at Home*, pp. 129, 132; Jefferson: DeJean, *The Age of Comfort*, p. 172.

p. 71 'receive her visitors': watercolour: Duchesse de Montebello: Mario Praz, *An Illustrated History of Interior Decoration from Pompeii to Art Nouveau* (London, Thames and Hudson, 1964), p. 192, although he does not discuss the nature of the visit; Austrian interior: Charlotte Gere, *Nineteenth Century Interiors: An Album of Watercolours*, Joseph Focarino, ed. (London, Thames and Hudson, 1992), pp. 82–3.

p. 72   'buffer-zone of privacy': the visiting Frenchman, Henri Meister, is found in Langford, *Englishness Identified*, p. 166; Horace Walpole, 28 October 1752, the electronic version of *The Yale Edition of Horace Walpole's Correspondence* (New Haven, Yale University Press, 1937–83), vol. 20, pp. 339–40, http://images.library.yale.edu/hwcorrespondence/page.asp?vol=20&seq=364&type=b, accessed 11 March 2013.

p. 72   'Convenience of the Inhabitant': Adams brothers: Meredith Martin, 'The Ascendancy of the Interior in Eighteenth-Century French Architectural Theory', Denise Amy Baxter and Meredith Martin, eds, *Architectural Space in Eighteenth-Century Europe: Constructing Identities and Interiors* (Farnham, Ashgate, 2010), p. 26; Norwich stonemason's handbook: cited in John Archer, *Architecture and Suburbia: From English Villa to American Dream House, 1690–2000* (Minneapolis, University of Minnesota Press, 2005), pp. 22–3.

p. 73   'until the nineteenth century': Château de Chambord: Sherban Cantacuzino, *European Domestic Architecture: Its Development from Early Times* (London, Studio Vista, 1969), pp. 73–4.

p. 74   'the rooms' inhabitants'': Martello: cited in Sarti, *Europe at Home*, p. 141.

p. 75   'structural upheaval': Dutch privacy: Schama, *Embarrassment of Riches*, p. 389; Thornbury Castle: Maurice Howard, *The Early Tudor Country House* (London, George Philip, 1987), pp. 55, 57, 85–7.

p. 76   'from each other': 'a long entrance': cited in Sarti, 'The Material Conditions of Family Life', Kertzer and Barbagli: *History of the European Family*, vol. 1, p. 12; 'an intollerable servitude': *The Elements of Architecture, Collected by Henry Wotton, Knight* (London, John Bull, 1624), pp. 72–3, cited in Lawrence Wright, *Warm and Snug: The History of the Bed* (London, Routledge & Kegan Paul, 1962), pp. 79–80; Sir Roger Pratt: Sarti, *Europe at Home*, p. 141.

p. 77   'their residents' minds'': William Morris: Robin Evans, 'Figures, Doors and Passages', *Architectural Design*, 4, 1978, pp. 275.

p. 78   'none at all': DeJean, *The Age of Comfort*, pp. 173–4.

p. 78   'to entertain visitors': Viennese newspaper: cited in Donald J. Olsen, *The City as a Work of Art, London, Paris, Vienna* (New Haven, Yale University Press, 1986), pp. 115–9, 125–31; Edmond de Goncourt, *La Maison d'un artiste*, 1881, cited in Elizabeth Emery, *Photojournalism and the Origins of the French Writer House Museum (1881–1914): Privacy, Publicity, and Personality* (Farnham, Ashgate, 2012), p. 11; German resident: Hermann Muthesius, *The English House*, trs. Janet Seligman and Stewart Spencer (1st complete English edn, London, Frances Lincoln, 2007), vol. 2, pp. 27–8.

p. 79   'in the Chesapeake': west African origins of shotgun houses: the suggestion is John Vlach's, cited in James Deetz, *In Small Things Forgotten: The Archaeology of Early American Life* (Garden City, New York, Anchor Books, 1977), pp. 214–16. More precisely, Vlach thinks that the style took root in New Orleans, with its large free black community, and was reinforced with immigration from Haiti early in the nineteenth century, where houses on this plan were common. The

New Orleans style used the Yoruba floorplan, French building techniques and the porch and front entrance style from the Arawak vernacular, to create an entirely creole house; porch: ibid., pp. 216, 228–9, 231; spread of verandas: ibid., pp. 228–9.

p. 79 'the main room': Leiden: Loughman and Montias, *Public and Private Spaces*, p. 26; nomenclature: ibid., p. 26.

p. 80 'an impressive dresser': yeomen farmers' houses: Crowley, *Invention of Comfort*, p. 82; *but* and *ben*: Weatherill, *Consumer Behaviour*, pp. 10–11.

p. 81 'cheese-making equipment': Leiden: Loughman and Montias, *Public and Private Spaces*, p. 26; Britain: Alcock, *People at Home*, p. 94.

p. 82 'had for centuries': Germany: Robert Lee, 'Family and "Modernisation": The Peasant Family and Social Change in Nineteenth-Century Bavaria', Richard J. Evans and W. R. Lee, eds, *The German Family: Essays on the Social History of the Family in Nineteenth- and Twentieth-Century Germany* (London, Croom Helm, 1981), pp. 85ff.; Sweden: Jonas Frykman and Orvar Löfgren, *Culture Builders: A Historical Anthropology of Middle-Class Life*, trs. Alan Crozier (New Brunswick, NJ, Rutgers University Press, 1987), p. 130.

p. 83 'replaced by mahogany': 1825 magazine: [Catherine Hutton], in *La Belle Assemblée*, 1825; Margaret Ponsonby, *Stories from Home: English Domestic Interiors, 1750–1850* (Aldershot, Ashgate, 2007), pp. 46–7, doubts that this is in reality the story of Hutton's own family.

p. 84 'household manuals suggest': Sir John Soane: these images are owned by Sir John Soane's Museum, as Soane's house now is; 1790s painting: this, by an unknown artist, is in the Museum of London.

p. 84 'the house's best room': Birmingham widow: David Hussey and Margaret Ponsonby, *The Single Homemaker and Material Culture in the Long Eighteenth Century* (Aldershot, Ashgate, 2012), p. 85; 90 per cent: Crowley, *Invention of Comfort*, p. 102; Barre Four Corners: David Jaffee, *A New Nation of Goods: The Material Culture of Early America* (Philadelphia, University of Pennsylvania Press, 2010), pp. 314–16.

p. 85 'twice a year': Swedish cooper's house: Frykman and Löfgren, *Culture Builders*, p. 135.

p. 86 'redecorated in 1697': pre-1650 inventories: C. Willemijn Fock, 'Semblance or Reality? The Domestic Interior in Seventeenth-Century Dutch Genre Painting', Westermann, *Art and Home*, pp. 97ff.; post-1650 inventories, Wijsenbeek-Olthuis, 'The Social History of the Curtain', de Jonge, *Ons sort mensen*; ground floor: ibid.; Wijsenbeek-Olthuis is the historian referred to in the footnote; I owe the 'good Calvinists have nothing to hide' to Ravi Mirchandani, who adds that, while the cultural distrust of curtains may or may not come from Calvinism, many Dutch today believe that it does; single curtains: Westermann, *Art and Home*, pp. 98, 100.

p. 86 'had none': UK statistics: Weatherill, *Consumer Behaviour*, pp. 6–8; Theophilus Eaton: Edgar de N. Mayhew, and Minor Myers, Jr, *A Documentary History of*

American Interiors: From the Colonial Era to 1915 (New York, Charles Scribner's Sons, 1980), pp. 7, 3–4; Delaware landowner: Richard L. Bushman, *The Refinement of America: Persons, Houses, Cities* (New York, Alfred A. Knopf, 1992), pp. 17.

p. 87 'earlier window-boards': window-board: David Dewing, ed., *Home and Garden, Paintings and Drawings of English, Middle-Class, Urban Domestic Spaces, 1675 to 1914* (London, Geffrye Museum, 2003), p. 40; York: Caroline Davidson, *The World of Mary Ellen Best* (London, Chatto & Windus, 1985), p. 27.

p. 88 'across the home countries': Dr Johnson cited in Hentie Louw, '"The Advantage of a Clearer Light": The Sash-window as a Harbinger of an Age of Progress and Enlightenment', Hentie Louw and Ben Farmer, eds *Companion to Contemporary Architectural Thought* (London, Routledge, 1993), p. 304; 'hard, sharp sunlight' and 'glaring mass of light': Stefan Muthesius, *The Poetic Home: Designing the 19th-Century Domestic Interior* (London, Thames and Hudson, 2009), p. 194.

p. 89 'with indoor life': 'those who love shadow': A. J. Downing, *The Architecture of Country Houses...* (New York, D. Appleton, 1852), p. 368; 'No one could possibly': Mrs [Lucy] Orrinsmith, *The Drawing-room, its Decoration and Furniture* (London, Art at Home Series, 1876), pp. 64–5.

p. 89 'household virtue': 'show order to the outside': cited in S. Muthesius, *Poetic Home*, p. 175; German colonist: Nancy R. Reagin, *Sweeping the Nation: Domesticity and National Identity in Germany, 1870–1945* (Cambridge, Cambridge University Press, 2007), p. 65.

p. 90 'new technologies': Falke: cited in S. Muthesius, *Poetic Home*, p. 184; advertisement of Schäffer and Walcker, Berlin: ibid., p. 195.

p. 90 'we are indoors': the gardening writer is John Worlidge: cited in Louw, 'The Advantage of a Clearer Light', Louw and Farmer, *Companion to Contemporary Architectural Thought*, p. 306; Falke, Wilde and Morris: cited in S. Muthesius, *Poetic Home*, p. 175–6; Gurlitt: cited in Wolfgang Schivelbusch, *Disenchanted Night: The Industrialization of Light in the Nineteenth Century*, trs. Angela Davies (Berkeley, University of California Press, 1995), p. 183.

p. 91 'an outdoor activity': footnote: London housing: S. Muthesius, *English Terraced House*, pp. 1–3; Parisian benches: Marcus, *Apartment Stories*, pp. 24–8.

p. 91 'a period of time': boarding house: Shirley Teresa Wajda, '"A Pretty Custom" Updated: From "Going to Housekeeping" to Bridal Showers in the United States, 1850s–1930s', David Hussey and Margaret Ponsonby, eds, *Buying for the Home: Shopping for the Domestic from the Seventeenth Century to the Present* (Aldershot, Ashgate, 2008), pp. 140–414.

p. 92 'became more exposed': Leeds: Burnett, *Social History of Housing*, pp. 62–3.

p. 93 'century and more': Houghton Hall: Earl of Ilchester, ed., *Lord Hervey and His Friends, 1726–38: Based on Letters from Holland House, Melbury, and Ickworth* (London, John Murray, 1950), p. 71, cited by Stephen Taylor, 'Walpole, Robert, first earl of Orford (1676–1745)', *Oxford Dictionary of National Biography*,

Oxford University Press, 2004; online edn, January 2008 [http://www.oxforddnb.com.ezproxy.londonlibrary.co.uk/view/article/28601, accessed 14 March 2013].

3. HOME AND THE WORLD

p. 95 'primary unit in society': precedence to family: John Demos, *Past, Present, and Personal: The Family and the Life Course in American History* (New York, Oxford University Press, 1986), p. 29.

p. 96 'the public sphere': Pitt's speech: *Anecdotes of the Life of the Rt Hon William Pitt...* (1792), vol. 1, pp. 250–51, cited in George K. Behlmer, *Friends of the Family: The English Home and its Guardians, 1850–1940* (Stanford, Stanford University Press, 1998), pp. 8–9, where he also traces the evolution of the phrase.

p. 96 'in a family setting': Fabre d'Eglantine cited in Lynn Hunt, 'The Unstable Boundaries of the French Revolution', Philippe Ariès and Georges Duby, eds, *A History of Private Life*, trs. Arthur Goldhammer (Cambridge, MA, Belknap Press, 1987–91), vol. 4: *From the Fires of Revolution to the Great War*, Michelle Perrot, ed., p. 18; I am grateful to Hilary Mantel for adding nuance to this too-brief look at women and the Revolutionary clubs; her essay, 'Rescued by Marat', in the *London Review of Books*, 28 May 1992, pp. 15–16, gave me further enlightenment.

p. 97 'tainted by society': 'hereditary depravity': John Calvin, *The Institutes of Christian Religion*, II.1.8; John Locke, *Some Thoughts Concerning Education* (London, A. & J. Churchill, 1693), p. 2.

p. 98 'agreeable and sweet': Jean-Jacques Rousseau, *Émile, or Treatise on Education*, trs. William H. Payne (Amherst, NY, Prometheus, 2003), pp. 161–2, 263; Gisborne, *Enquiry into the Duties of the Female Sex*, cited in Robert Shoemaker, *Gender in English Society, 1650–1850: The Emergence of Separate Spheres?* (London, Longman, 1998), p. 32.

p. 101 'hotel lobbies': 1854 journalist: cited in Katherine C. Grier, *Culture and Comfort: Parlor Making and Middle-Class Identity, 1850–1930* (Washington, DC, Smithsonian, 1988), pp. 22–3.

p. 102 'even-more-private areas above': American yards: Larkin, *Reshaping of Everyday Life*, p. 129–30; I-house: Henry Glassie, 'Artifact and Culture, Architecture and Society', S. J. Bronner, ed., *American Material Culture and Folklife: A Prologue and Dialogue* (Ann Arbor, University of Michigan Research Press, 1985), pp. 53–5.

p. 103 'the following day': hours spent on chores: Sarti, 'Material Conditions of Everyday Life', Kertzer and Barbagli, *History of the European Family*, vol. 1, p. 19, although I have omitted the time she allocates for brewing and baking, as this was outsourced in much of Britain by the eighteenth century. I have also increased the hours she gives to laundry. Her four hours a week seems to me a substantial underestimate.

p. 104   'ironmongery, needles': American rural women's activities: Ruth Schwartz Cowan, *A Social History of American Technology* (New York, Oxford University Press, 1997), pp. 29–30.

p. 105   'whittled clothes-pegs': footnote: Cowan, *Social History of American Technology*, pp. 20, 39; division of labour: Ruth Schwartz Cowan, *More Work for Mother: The Ironies of Household Technology from the Open Hearth to the Microwave* (New York, Basic, 1983), pp. 23–5; laundry chores: Jane C. Nylander, *Our Own Snug Fireside: Images of the New England Home, 1760–1860* (New Haven, Yale University Press, 1994), pp. 131–7.

p. 105   'to both arenas': John Pintard: Jeanne Boydston, *Home and Work: Housework, Wages, and the Ideology of Labor in the Early Republic* (New York, Oxford University Press, 1990), p. 43; Esther Burr: Boydston, *Home and Work*, pp. 15–16; accounts: Geoffrey Crossick and Heinz-Gerhard Haupt, *The Petite Bourgeoisie in Europe, 1780–1914* (London, Routledge, 1995), p. 92.

p. 106   'from their husbands': English vocabulary of roles: Boydston, *Home and Work*, pp. 8–9; German vocabulary: Gray, *Productive Men, Reproductive Women*, p. 105; women 'supplementing' income: Joel Mokyr, 'Why "More Work for Mother"? Knowledge and Household Behavior, 1870–1945', *Journal of Economic History*, March 2000, 6/1, p. 3; *The Mothering Heart*: Kathleen Anne McHugh, *American Domesticity: From How-to Manual to Hollywood Melodrama* (New York, Oxford University Press, 1999), pp. 93–6. The film can be viewed in full at http://www.youtube.com/watch?v=7B-SpMqlfrg, accessed 18 December 2013.

p. 107   'her sailor husband': Salem housewife: Boydston, *Home and Work*, pp. 18–19, 51.

p. 108   'no longer work': 'tranquil pastime': [Edward Bulwer-Lytton], *A Strange Story* (London, Sampson Low, Son, & Co., 1862), vol. II, p. 73; *New York Mercury*: cited in Boydston, *Home and Work*, p. 10; 1881 census: McKeon, *Secret History of Domesticity*, p. 179.

p. 109   'as its housewife': Henriette Davidis's cookbook: Reagin, *Sweeping the Nation*, p. 23; *Book of Household Management*: Susan Zlotnick, 'On the Publication of Isabella Beeton's *Book of Household Management*, 1861', *Branch: Britain, Representation, and Nineteenth-Century History*, ed. Dino Franco Felluga, extension of *Romanticism and Victorianism on the Net*, http://www.branchcollective.org/?ps_articles=susan-zlotnick-on-the-publication-of-isabella-beetons-book-of-household-management-1861, accessed 25 August 2013.

p. 110   'effort it took': 'not half as cheap': McHugh, *American Domesticity*, p. 29; oilcloth: Reagin, *Sweeping the Nation*, pp. 36–42.

p. 111   'value of labour': sock darning: Reagin, *Sweeping the Nation*, pp. 58, 60, 17; American manual advice: McHugh, *American Domesticity*, p. 29.

p. 112   'produced by one': I am grateful to Laura Mason, who patiently instructed me in the varieties and survival rates of yeast, both by email and in her essay,

'Barms and Leavens – Medieval to Modern', in Ivan Day, ed., *Over a Red Hot Stove: Essays in Early Cooking Technology* (London, Prospect, 2009), pp. 125–48.

p. 113   'by the women': stoves: Leonore Davidoff and Ruth Hawthorn, *A Day in the Life of the Victorian Servant* (London, Allen & Unwin, 1976), p. 78.

'six and a half hours': Susan Strasser, *Never Done: A History of American Housework* (New York, Pantheon, 1982), p. 41.

p. 114   'more washing of towels': Harriet Beecher Stowe: cited in Nylander, *Our Own Snug Fireside*, p. 109; the ideas and information in this and the previous two paragraphs come from Cowan, *More Work for Mother*, pp. 45, 48, 50–1, 61–6, apart from the citation from Laura Ingalls Wilder, *The Little House Books*, ed. Caroline Fraser, vol. 1: *Little House in the Big Woods, Farmer Boy, Little House on the Prairie, On the Banks of Plum Creek* (New York, Library of America, 2012), p. 280. The quote is found in *Little House on the Prairie*.

p. 115   'had to be cleaned': 'Glass windows must have curtains': Wilder, *The Little House Books*, vol. 1, pp. 471, 473, *On the Banks of Plum Creek*.

p. 115   'we prefer to live': 'a set of attitudes': Christine Frederick, *The Ignoramus Book of Housekeeping*, cited in Phyllis Palmer, *Domesticity and Dirt: Housewives and Domestic Servants in the United States, 1920–45* (Philadelphia, Temple University Press, 1989), p. 26.

p. 116   'the outside world': tinned pineapple: Christina Hardyment, *From Mangle to Microwave: The Mechanization of Household Work* (Cambridge, Polity, 1988), pp. 145–6; ice-chests: ibid., pp. 139–40.

p. 117   'being sold annually': washing-machine dealers: Hardyment, *From Mangle to Microwave*, p. 59; washing-machine sales: ibid., p. 62.

p. 118   'the same function': 'get a bigger bell': Pepys, *Diary*, 6 October 1663, vol. 4, p. 325; footnote: advertisement cited in David E. Nye, *Electrifying America: Social Meanings of a New Technology, 1880–1940* (Cambridge, MA, MIT Press, 1990), pp. 258–9.

p. 118   'little extra expense': central heating and lighting: Candace M. Volz, 'The Modern Look of the Early-Twentieth-Century House: A Mirror of Changing Lifestyles', Jessica H. Foy and Thomas J. Schlereth, eds, *American Home Life, 1880–1930: A Social History of Spaces and Services* (Knoxville, University of Tennessee Press, 1992), pp. 36–7.

p. 119   'entirely private one': migration of radio: Thomas Berker, Maren Hartmann, Yves Punie and Katie Ward, *Domestication of Media and Technology* (Maidenhead, Open University, 2006), p. 29, and Denise Lawrence-Zúñiga, 'Material Conditions of Family Life', Kertzer and Barbagli, *History of the European Family*, vol. 3, p. 38.

p. 119   'turned in on itself': Muncie: Robert S. Lynd and Helen Merrell Lynd, *Middletown: A Study in Modern American Culture* (London, Constable, 1929), pp. 95–6; porches: Clifford Edward Clark, Jr, *The American Family Home, 1800–1960* (Chapel Hill, University of North Carolina Press, 1986), p. 228.

p. 120 'decidedly odd': hedges: Andrew Ballantyne and Andrew Law, *Tudoresque: In Pursuit of the Ideal Home* (London, Reaktion, 2011), p. 117; 'if people sat in their front gardens': I use the conditional, as, after thirty-four years in England, I have never seen anyone do it.

p. 122 'downplays her achievement': Mrs Beeton, *Mrs Beeton's Book of Household Management*, abridged edn, Nicola Humble, ed. ([1861], Harmondsworth, Penguin, 2000), p. 7; Mary Pattison's frontispiece: McHugh, *American Domesticity*, p. 72.

p. 122 'in public as in private': *gezellig*: Henk Driessen, 'About the Borders of "Gezelligheid"', de Jonge, *Ons sort mensen*; the 1938 etiquette book is E. Knuvelder-Ariëns and I. Cammaert, *Gezelligheid in huis en hoe onthaal ik mijn gasten goed* (4th edn, 's-Hertogenbosch, 1938), pp. 6–8.

p. 123 'supermarket food and more': 'family' and 'home' used in industry: Gillis, *A World of Their Own Making*, p. 324.

4. HOME FURNISHINGS

p. 125 'implicitly tea': William Cowper, *The Task, and Other Poems* (Philadelphia, Carey and Hart, 1849), Book IV, 'The Winter Evening', p. 94; footnote: Siris, ¶217, *Notes and Queries*, 2nd ser., no. 25, 21 June 1856, p. 490.

p. 125 'not of utility': furniture as display: I owe this idea to Lewis Mumford, *The Culture of Cities* (London, Secker and Warburg, 1997), p. 115.

p. 127 'things forgot': labourer's inventory: Alcock, *People at Home*, pp. 121–2.

p. 128 'bed and bedding': lack of beds in American colonies: Sarti, *Europe at Home*, p. 103; slaves' sleeping quarters: Crowley, *Invention of Comfort*, p. 89; cost of beds in Netherlands: Sarti, 'The Material Conditions of Family Life', Kertzer and Barbagli, *History of the European Family*, vol. 1, p. 119; cost of beds in Italy: Sarti, *Europe at Home*, p. 101.

p. 128 'braid and fringe': beds given pride of place: Muizelaar and Phillips, *Picturing Men and Women*, p. 30.

p. 129 'their wealth publicly': window curtains as wealth display: Wijsenbeek-Olthuis, 'The Social History of the Curtain', de Jonge, *Ons sort mensen*.

p. 129 'Dublin Castle': 1653 painting: I am grateful to Peter Kristiansen, the curator at Rosenborg Castle, who has patiently answered questions, and who re-looked at the original and noticed the curtain rod; Ham House: Peter Thornton, *Seventeenth-Century Interior Decoration in England, France, and Holland* (New Haven, Yale University Press, 1978), pp. 137–8. Thornton is one of the experts on period decoration, but I have approached his work with some caution; he dates the symmetrical curtains in Ham House to both the 1640s and 1670s, and, more worryingly, in his *Authentic Decor: The Domestic Interior, 1620–1929*, p. 8, he argues strongly for the verisimilitude of Dutch Golden Age art: the departure from reality for artists 'is never all that large', he writes, rebutting the work of Dutch academics who have studied the inventories, p. 6, and questioning how, if there were no carpets in houses, artists could then 'find carpets on floors to depict so accurately', apparently taking for granted that artists paint only what they habitually see, that they do not own props, nor create staged settings to paint, nor even paint from the imagination. Thornton's store of knowledge was formidable, but I must question how some of it was applied.

p. 130 'paired curtains appear': 'a blind in Italian taffeta': DeJean, *The Age of Comfort*, p. 158; Friderich Lütken's study: the images appear in Tove Clemmensen, *Skaebner og Interiører: Danske Tegninger fra Barok til Klunketid* (Skive, Nationalmuseet, 1984), pp. 24, 37.

p. 130 'of it at night': *Romeo and Juliet*, I.v.6–7.

p. 131 'stools beside them': Plymouth household: Deetz and Deetz, *Times of Their Lives*, p. 198; *A Peasant Family at Meal-time*: Bushman, *Refinement of America*, pp. 74–5, 77.

p. 132 'without surprise': Bologna theft: Sarti, *Europe at Home*, pp. 128–9.

p. 134 'fatal excesses': cost of cupboards: Schama, *Embarrassment of Riches*, pp. 316, 318; cupboard-top displays: Hester C. Dibbits, 'Between Society and Family Values: The Linen Cupboard in Early-Modern Households', Schuurman and Spierenburg, *Private Domain*, pp. 126–7, 133; Daniel Defoe, *A Tour Through the Island of Great Britain*, G. D. H. Cole and D. C. Browning, eds ([1792], London, Dent, Everyman, 1962), vol. 1, p. 166.

p. 134 'everything in its place': *commode*: DeJean, *The Age of Comfort*, pp. 131–2; *Stollenschränke*: H. Muthesius, *The English House*, vol. 3, p. 21; Brunswick: Michael North, *'Material Delight and the Joy of Living': Cultural Consumption in the Age of Enlightenment in Germany*, trs. Pamela Selwyn (Aldershot, Ashgate, 2008), p. 65; Parisian workmen: Sarti, *Europe at Home*, pp. 128–9; Dutch poem: the quote is famous beyond measure, but the poet remains anonymous; cited by Dibbits in Schuurman and Spierenburg, *Private Domain*, pp. 125–6.

p. 135 'fashion items': Whitehall Palace: these armchairs together with the bed that forms the suite are National Trust Inventory No. 129448.1 and 129448I.2. I am grateful to Emily Watts, house steward at Knole, for her help in identifying these pieces; information on Thomas Roberts: Adam Bowett, 'The English "Horsebone" Chair, 1685–1710', *The Burlington Magazine*, May 1999, vol. 141, p. 263; information on Poitevin: Tessa Murdoch, 'Worthy of the Monarch: Immigrant Craftsmen and the Production of State Beds, 1660–1714', *From Strangers to Citizens: The Integration of Immigrant Communities in Britain, Ireland, and Colonial America, 1550–1750*, Randolph Vigne and Charles Littleton, eds (London, Huguenot Society of Great Britain and Ireland, Sussex Academic Press, 2001), pp. 153–4; chairs as fashion items: DeJean, *The Age of Comfort*, pp. 121–2.

p. 136 'designed for display': chairs for comfort: Rybczynski, *Home*, pp. 81ff.

p. 137 'the middling classes': Horace Walpole, 3 October 1743, the electronic version of *The Yale Edition of Horace Walpole's Correspondence*, vol. 18, p. 315, http://

images.library.yale.edu/hwcorrespondence/page.asp?vol=18&page=315&s rch=mortel, accessed 18 December 2013; Battersea barber-surgeon: Frank E. Brown, 'Continuity and Change in the Urban House: Developments in Domestic Space Organization in Seventeenth-Century London', *Comparative Studies in Society and History*, 28, 1986, p. 583; Hamburg merchant: North, *Material Delight*, pp. 66–7; Linley Sambourne: Shirley Nicholson, *A Victorian Household* (rev. edn, Stroud, Sutton, 1994), pp. 21–2; matching chairs: Alcock, *People at Home*, pp. 54, 63.

p. 137 'lack of sociability': rooms like furniture shops: Louis Simond, *Journal of a Tour and Residence in Great Britain During the Years 1810 and 1811*, 'by a French traveller' (Edinburgh, Constable, 1815), vol. 2, p. 219; 'At first sight': Langford, *Englishness Identified*, pp. 188, 190–91.

p. 138 'back to the wall': 1861 woman: cited in Hamlett, *Material Relations*, p. 85; footnote: the idea is my own, and it must be said that many disagree strongly.

p. 139 'Industrial Revolution': 'little skuttling' things: John Byng, 5th Viscount Torrington, *The Torrington Diaries: A Selection from the Tours of the Hon. John Byng...*, C. Buryn Andrews, ed. (London, Eyre and Spottiswood, 1934–8), vol. 3, pp. 156–7; William Cobbett, *Rural Rides in the Southern, Western and Eastern Counties of England...*, G. D. H. and Margaret Cole, eds (London, Peter Davies, 1930), vol. 1, pp. 276–8.

p. 139 'coufey pot': difference in quality: Crowley, *Invention of Comfort*, p. 6.; aristocratic Englishwoman: Marcia Pointon, *Strategies for Showing: Women, Possession and Representation in English Visual Culture, 1665–1800* (Oxford, Oxford University Press, 1997), p. 28.

p. 140 'another novelty': Denis Diderot, 'Regrets sur ma vieille robe de chambre, ou, Avis à ceux qui ont plus de gout que de fortune' (1772). The translation is my own, with assistance from Frank Wynne, to whom I am grateful.

p. 141 'replaced coarse canvas': value of Dutch bedding: Schama, *Embarrassment of Riches*, p. 319; expenditure on marriage: Sarti, *Europe at Home*, p. 101; mattresses: Praz, *An Illustrated History of Interior Decoration*, p. 105, points to an engraving after Jan van der Straet's *Women Embroidering*, p. 105.

p. 141 'three hundred napkins': Dutch linens: Zumthor, *Rembrandt's Holland*, pp. 38–9.

p. 142 'nine in ten did': proliferation of household items: Muizelaar and Phillips, *Men and Women*, pp. 37, 44, 46–50; copies of imports: Westermann, *Art and Home*, p. 36; lower income homes: Muizelaar and Phillips, *Men and Women*, p. 30; 'in generall strives': *The Travels of Peter Mundy*, vol. 4, pp. 70–71; pendulum clocks: de Vries, *Industrious Revolution*, p. 1; the measure of prosperity is those with more than ten cows.

p. 143 'crossed the Atlantic': 'the Linnen for the Table': John Wood, *A Description of Bath*, cited in James Ayres, *Domestic Interiors: The British Tradition, 1500–1850* (New Haven, Yale University Press, 2003), p. 9; increase in house contents: these are averages from across all of England, from Weatherill, *Consumer*

Behaviour, p. 26 and Mark Overton, et al., *Production and Consumption in English Households, 1600–1750* (London, Routledge, 2004), pp. 91, 99.

p. 143 'Pudding Dishes': Virginia planter: Kevin M. Sweeney, 'High Style Vernacular: Lifestyles of the Colonial Elite', Carson, et al., *Of Consuming Interests*, pp. 3–4; footnote: mid-Atlantic states: Joan M. Jensen, *Loosening the Bonds: Mid-Atlantic Farm Women, 1750–1850* (New Haven, Yale University Press, 1986), pp. 217–20; militiamen: T. H. Breen, *The Marketplace of Revolution: How Consumer Politics Shaped American Independence* (New York, Oxford University Press, 2004), pp. 49–50; Virginia: Breen, *Marketplace of Revolution*, pp. 34–5; northern working class: Cary Carson, 'The Consumer Revolution in Colonial British America: Why Demand?', Carson, et al., *Of Consuming Interests*, p. 505; New York merchant: T. H. Breen, 'The Meaning of Things: Interpreting the Consumer Economy in the Eighteenth Century', John Brewer and Roy Porter, eds, *Consumption and the World of Goods* (London, Routledge, 1993), p. 253.

p. 145 'and reasonable': 1714 magazine: [Joseph Addison], *The Lover*, 18 March 1714, cited in Beverly Lemire, *The Business of Everyday Life: Gender, Practice and Social Politics in England, c.1600–1900* (Manchester, Manchester University Press, 2005), p. 93.

p. 146 'consumption as patriotism': list of proscribed items: cited in Breen, *Marketplace of Revolution*, p. 236.

p. 147 'fable had foretold': US cupboards: ibid., p. 46.

p. 147 'saucers, and more': historic sugar consumption: Carole Shammas, 'Changes in English and Anglo-American Consumption from 1550–1800', Brewer and Porter, *Consumption and the World of Goods*, pp. 181–2; current sugar consumption: Food and Agriculture Organization of the United Nations, website, http://faostat3.fao.org/faostat-gateway/go/to/download/FB/*/E, accessed 5 September 2013. My thanks to Alex Tomlinson for guiding me to these figures; affordability of tea: John E. Wills, Jr, 'European Consumption and Asian Production in the Seventeenth and Eighteenth Centuries', in Brewer and Porter, *Consumption and the World of Goods*, pp. 141–3.

p. 148 'not be maintained': 'you should have a home': Marlene Elizabeth Heck, '"Appearance and Effect is Everything": The James River Houses of Samuel, Joseph, and George Cabell', Eleanor Thompson, ed., *The American Home: Material Culture, Domestic Space, and Family Life* (Hanover, NH, University Press of New England, 1998), p. 11; 'custom demands many luxuries': Prince Pückler-Muskau, in the mid-1820s, cited in Dana Arnold, *The Georgian Country House: Architecture, Landscape and Society* (Stroud, Sutton, 1998), pp. 24–5; Kant: cited in North, *Material Delight*, p. 2.

p. 149 'contemporary idiom': owners' identification: Carson, 'The Consumer Revolution in Colonial British America', Carson, et al., *Of Consuming Interests*, pp. 553–4; decoration of possessions: Gwendolyn Wright, *Building the Dream: A Social History of Housing in America* (New York, Pantheon, 1981), pp. 16–17.

p. 150 'better people': Adam Smith, *The Theory of Moral Sentiments*, D. D. Raphael and A. L. Macfie, eds (Oxford, Oxford University Press, 1976), p. 180; Daniel Defoe cited in Charles Saumarez-Smith, *The Rise of Design: Design and the Domestic Interior in Eighteenth-Century England* (London, Pimlico, 2000), pp. 46–8; *Niles' Weekly Register*: cited in Grier, *Culture and Comfort*, p. 20.

p. 151 'technological comfort': labour-saving devices: Bee Wilson, *Consider the Fork: A History of Invention in the Kitchen* (London, Particular Books, 2012), p. 218.

p. 151 'the French courts': Anthony Trollope, *Barchester Towers*, Robin Gilmour, ed. ([1857], Harmondsworth, Penguin, 1994), p. 78.

p. 152 '"suites" of furniture': model rooms: Grier, *Culture and Comfort*, pp. 22–3, 30, 55; 'Celebrities at Home': D. Cohen, *Household Gods*, p. 122–3.

p. 153 'become all-important': buffet: Garrett, *At Home*, pp. 40ff.; 1897 three-piece suite: Grier, *Culture and Comfort*, p. 147.

p. 153 'civilized folks again': Wilder, *The Little House Books*, vol. 1, pp. 317, 323.

p. 154 'three serving spoons': increase in earthenware: Sarti, *Europe at Home*, p. 127; German inventories: North, *Material Delight*, pp. 68–9.

p. 154 'and fork too': Italian and German: Sarti, *Europe at Home*, pp. 150–51.

p. 155 'simply "non-existent"': forks for pasta: Wilson, *Consider the Fork*, p. 255; Plymouth colony: Demos, *A Little Commonwealth*, p. 42.

p. 156 'new fashions': Dutch merchant: cited in Lisa Jardine, *Going Dutch: How England Plundered Holland's Glory* (London, HarperCollins, 2008), p. 243; London: Weatherill, *Consumer Behaviour*, p. 26; New York: Bushman, *Refinement of America*, pp. 76–7; Massachusetts: Laurel Thatcher Ulrich, *Good Wives: Image and Reality in the Lives of Women in Northern New England, 1650–1750* (New York, Alfred A. Knopf, 1982), p. 69; Greifswald: North, *Material Culture*, pp. 69–70, notes their arrival, but the suggestion about location is my own.

p. 156 'forks until 1897': flat plates: Wilson, *Consider the Fork*, pp. 257–8; footnote: Deetz, *In Small Things Forgotten*, p. 123; British Navy: Wilson, *Consider the Fork*, p. 257.

p. 157 'mug between them': Maryland couple: Bushman, *Refinement of America*, pp. 75–6; Wilder, *The Little House Books*, vol. 1, p. 281.

p. 158 'life was very short': Delft tiles: Westermann, *Art and Home*, p. 68. The tiles are in the Philadelphia Museum of Art; Warwickshire child: Linda Pollock, *A Lasting Relationship: Parents and Children over Three Centuries* (London, Fourth Estate, 1987), p. 143.

p. 159 'playing-toys': Shakespeare, *The Taming of the Shrew*, IV.iii.67, *A Midsummer Night's Dream*, V.i.3, *A Winter's Tale*, IV.iv.317.

p. 159 'and so ungodly': Locke, *Some Thoughts Concerning Education* (1693), cited in Karin Calvert, *Children in the House: The Material Culture of Early Childhood, 1600–1900* (Boston, Northeastern University Press, 1992), p. 80; colonial attitudes to play: Calvert, *Children in the House*, pp. 48–51.

p. 160 'her own doll': Calvert, *Children in the House*, pp. 110–17; Rousseau, *Émile*, p. 265.

p. 160 'patient perseverance': board games: Colin Heywood, *A History of Childhood: Children and Childhood in the West from Medieval to Modern Times* (Cambridge, Polity, 2001), p. 93; Maria Edgeworth: Paula S. Fass and Mary Ann Mason, *Childhood in America* (New York, New York University Press, 2000), pp. 49–50.

p. 161 'family members worked': miniature chairs and stools: both can be seen in Jan van der Straet's *Women Embroidering*, illustrated in Praz, *An Illustrated History of Interior Decoration*, p. 105.

p. 162 'with their fathers': colonial babies' dress: Calvert, *Children in the House*, pp. 41–2.

p. 163 'whalebone bodices': boys' dress: Calvert, *Children in the House*, pp. 79–83; upper-class children: *The Diary of Anne Clifford*, April and May 1617, cited in Pollock, *A Lasting Relationship*, p. 81.

p. 163 'especially for them': American children: Calvert, *Children in the House*, pp. 27, 33, 38; footnote: Sally Kevill-Davies, *Yesterday's Children: The Antiques and History of Childcare* (Woodbridge, Antique Collectors' Club, 1991), pp. 78–82, 89, 97, 110.

p. 164 'first and foremost': 'an abomination unto the Lord': *Godey's Lady's Magazine*, cited in Calvert, *Children in the House*, p. 100.

p. 164 'contaminations of the world.': 'of their innocence and happy ignorance': Dr Struve, *Domestic Education of Children*, cited in Calvert, *Children in the House*, p. 103.

5. BUILDING MYTHS

p. 165 'thoughts of the dying': north London house: Ayres, *Domestic Interiors*, pp. 2–4; souls of houses: Vickery, *Behind Closed Doors*, p. 29; brides: Segalen, 'The House Between Public and Private', Schuurman and Spierenburg, *Private Domain*, p. 247; 'Don't you sometimes': [Andrew K. H. Boyd], *The Recreations of a Country Parson* (Boston, Fields, Osgood and Co., 1870), vol. 2, p. 390.

p. 166 'gods of home': Lupino: cited in Hamlett, *Material Relations*, p. 180; F. Scott Fitzgerald, *The Bodley Head Scott Fitzgerald*, vol. 1, *The Great Gatsby* (London, The Bodley Head, 1958), p. 213.

p. 167 'peace and contentment': 'The Englishman sees': H. Muthesius, *The English House*, vol. 1, p. 1; footnote: Henrik Ibsen, *Ghosts*, trs. Peter Watts (Harmondsworth, Penguin, 1964), pp. 42–3; Newton: cited in Gavin Stamp and André Goulancourt, *The English House 1860–1914: The Flowering of English Domestic Architecture* (London, Faber, 1986), p. 14.

p. 167 'cold world outside': Renan: cited in Walter Benjamin, *The Arcades Project*, trs. Howard Eiland and Kevin McLaughlin (Cambridge, MA, Belknap Press, 1999), p. 554.

p. 168 'generous and ceremonial': Chicago: Mihaly Csikszentmihalyi and Eugene Rochberg-Halton, *The Meaning of Things: Domestic Symbols and the*

Self (Cambridge, Cambridge University Press, 1981), p. 127; *gemütlich*: S. Muthesius, *Poetic Home*, p. 28; 'incidents and situations from common life': Preface to the Second Edition of *Lyrical Ballads*, in *The Poetical Works of William Wordsworth* (London, E. Moxon, 1870), vol. 6, p. 826; *gezellig*: Henk Driessen, 'About the Borders of *Gezelligheid*', de Jonge, *Ons sort mensen*.

p. 169   'Philadelphia in the 1860s': journal editor: cited in Clark, *American Family Home*, p. 23.

p. 169   'capturing the city': Greek Revival for residential architecture: Burnett, *A Social History of Housing*, p. 104.

p. 170   'flat Greek roof': *The Pioneers*: cited in Cohn, *Palace or Poorhouse*, pp. 30, 35–7.

p. 171   'for his workers': workers' housing: Ballantyne and Law, *Tudoresque*, pp. 90–91, 97–9.

p. 172   'they were "restored"': nineteenth-century 'restoration': Ballantyne and Law, *Tudoresque*, pp. 36, 41, 44.

p. 174   'saying "America"': colonial houses: Larkin, *Reshaping of Everyday Life*, pp. 128–31; New York and the Hudson: Garrett, *At Home*, pp. 17–20.

p. 175   'Golden Age art': *Kamer van Jan Steen*: S. Muthesius, *Poetic Home*, pp. 235–7, 290.

p. 176   'peasant connotations': development of Altdeutsch: S. Muthesius, *Poetic Home*, p. 227.

p. 176   'a physical sense': Old Alpine: S. Muthesius, *Poetic Home*, pp. 264–5.

p. 177   'the ideal home': north London: Alan A. Jackson, *Semi-Detached London: Suburban Development, Life and Transport, 1900–39* (London, George Allen & Unwin, 1973), p. 37; 2013 advertisement for Vincent Timber UK: email of 7 March 2013, received by the author.

p. 178   'out of reach': 'A farmer's house' and 'the hardest': Lewis F. Allen, *Rural Architecture: Being a Complete Description of Farm Houses, Cottages, and Out Buildings…* (New York, C. M. Saxton, 1852), and Henry W. Cleaveland, William Backus and Samuel D. Backus, *Village and Farm Cottages: The Requirements of American Village Homes Considered…* (New York, D. Appleton, 1856), cited in Grier, *Culture and Comfort*, pp. 103. The interpretation is my own.

p. 179   'happy olden days': Franklin house: Nylander, *Our Own Snug Fireside*, pp. 15–16; Colonial kitchen: Grier, *Culture and Comfort*, p. 54; footnote: Nylander, *Our Own Snug Fireside*, p. 16; old forms of lighting: Andreas Blühm and Louise Lippincott, *Light: The Industrial Age, 1750–1900: Art and Science, Technology and Society* (London, Thames and Hudson, 2000), p. 234.

p. 180   'were abominations': William Morris, 'Manifesto of The Society for the Protection of Ancient Buildings (S.P.A.B.)', *Art and Architecture: Essays 1870–1884* (Holicong, PA, Wildside Press, 2003) p. 14, accessed online, http://bit.ly/10bSG2I, 28 March 2013.

p. 182 'of an emotion': early Heimat museum: Alon Confino, *Nation as a Local Metaphor: Württemberg, Imperial Germany, and National Memory, 1871–1918* (Chapel Hill, University of North Carolina Press, 1997), pp. 137, 144.

p. 183 'historical inaccuracy': success of country-house style: Ponsonby, *Stories from Home*, pp. 159ff.

p. 183 'authentic either': authenticity of Frankfurt kitchen: Jeremy Aynsley, 'The Modern Period Room – A Contradiction in Terms?', Penny Sparke, Brenda Martin and Trevor Keeble, eds, *The Modern Period Room: The Construction of the Exhibited Interior, 1870 to 1950* (London, Routledge, 2006), p. 17.

p. 184 '99 per cent': elegance of Colonial Williamsburg: Eric Gable and Richard Handler, 'In Colonial Williamsburg, the New History Meets the Old', *Chronicle of Higher Education*, 30 October 1998, 45, pp. B10–11.

p. 184 'an imaginary past': my reading of nostalgia has been informed by Svetlana Boym, *The Future of Nostalgia* (New York, Basic, 2001), especially pp. xiv–xv, 6, 11–15.

p. 185 'past or present': Cape Cod's emotional resonance: Clark, *American Family Home*, pp. 201–3.

p. 185 'only to 1750': log cabin term: Weslager, *The Log Cabin*, pp. 99ff., p. 54.

p. 186 'Swedish settlers': footnote: Weslager, *The Log Cabin*, makes the distinctions as clear as possible, pp. 56–7; Swedish-settled areas: ibid., pp. 140–2, 155.

p. 187 'the basic formula': immigration waves: Weslager, *The Log Cabin*, pp. 199–200, 209, 212, 226.

p. 188 'indigenous and simple': Harrison's supporters: Weslager, *The Log Cabin*, pp. 265–7; Harrison's 'log cabin': Cohn, *Palace or Poorhouse*, pp. 177, 183–4; [James Fenimore Cooper], *The Pioneers, or, The Sources of the Susquehanna, A Descriptive Tale* (London, T. Allman and C. Daly, [n.d.]), p. 223.

p. 189 'shape of logs': Lincoln's Birthplace: Weslager, *The Log Cabin*, p. 289–90, 305–6; footnote: http://www.abrahamlincolnonline.org/lincoln/sites/birth.htm, accessed 25 April 2013; Lincoln logs: http://www.knex.com/Lincoln-Logs/history.php, accessed 9 October 2013; Log Cabin syrup: Deetz and Deetz, *Times of Their Lives*, pp. 174–5, says the tins in the 1940s in the USA were shaped like a log cabin, with the spout where the chimney should be. In my Canadian childhood in the 1960s, they were just square tins printed with a picture of the cabin. I assume the American ones were the same. For current packaging, http://www.logcabinsyrups.com/products/, accessed 9 October 2013.

p. 190 'in the 1850s': Henry Wadsworth Longfellow, *The Courtship of Miles Standish* (Boston, Ticknor and Fields, 1858), p. 31; the New England inventories pre-1650: cited by Laurel Thatcher Ulrich, *The Age of Homespun: Objects and Stories in the Creation of an American Myth* (New York, Alfred A. Knopf, 2001), p. 84; limited yarn production: Nylander, *Our Own Snug Fireside*, p. 169; Mary Cooper: Boydston, *Home and Work*, p. 13; Olmsted: cited in Elizabeth

Fox-Genovese, *Within the Plantation Household: Black and White Women of the Old South* (Chapel Hill, University of North Carolina Press, 1988), p. 121.

p. 191 'to the cash-rich': 'tear… into bits': cited in McHugh, *American Domesticity*, p. 25.

p. 192 'dancing take place?': apart from the citation from McHugh, above, this paragraph and the previous one derive from Nylander, *Our Own Snug Fireside*, pp. 228–9, and Susan Strasser, *Waste and Want: A Social History of Trash* (New York, Metropolitan, 1999), pp. 53–9.

p. 192 'new one each year': Northamptonshire: Laslett, *Family Life*, p. 71; servant turnover: ibid., p. 72.

p. 194 'age of twenty-one': '40 per cent': Laslett, *Family Life*, pp. 3–4, 162, 164, 166; modern figures for divorce: Michael Anderson, 'What is new about the modern family: an historical perspective', OPCS Occasional Paper 21, *The Family*, p. 5. Laslett's figure of 40 per cent is estimated, based on the 32 per cent of children in the census figures, and extrapolating to include the parents of servants, who were not enumerated; Netherlands: Rudolf Dekker, 'Children on their Own: Changing Relations in the Family. The Experiences of Dutch Autobiographers, Seventeenth to Nineteenth Centuries', Schuurman and Spierenburg, *Private Domain*, p. 65; American south: Jane Turner Censer, *North Carolina Planters and Their Children 1800–1860* (Baton Rouge, Louisiana State University Press, 1984), pp. 20–21.

p. 194 'otherwise occupied': *Morning Chronicle*: cited in Gillis, 'Making Time for Family', *Journal of Family History*, p. 13; census Sunday church attendance: Ashton, *Victorian Bloomsbury* (London, Yale University Press, 2012), p. 159.

p. 195 'or enough chairs': survey: John R. Gillis, 'Making Time for Family: The Invention of Family Time(s) and the Reinvention of Family History', *Journal of Family History*, 21, 1996, pp. 4–5, finds this gem of a report in the *New York Times*, where it appeared as Daniel Goleman, 'Family Rituals May Promote Better Emotional Adjustment', 11 March 1992, http://www.nytimes.com/1992/03/11/news/family-rituals-may-promote-better-emotional-adjustment.html?pagewanted=all&src=pm, accessed 23 October 2013.

6. HEARTH AND HOME

p. 199 'walloped, or boiled': focus: Arien Mack, ed., 'Home: A Place in the World', *Social Research*, 58, 1, 1991, p. 42; footnote: cited in Crowley, *Invention of Comfort*, p. 57; church statute: McKeon, *Secret History of Domesticity*, p. 143; 'camino': Sarti, *Europe at Home*, p. 118; 'potwalloper' boroughs: Vickery, *Behind Closed Doors*, p. 8.

p. 200 'married to its hearth': 'a hearth of one's own is worth gold': this proverb is found in Germany, the Netherlands and Scandinavia; the German cited in Reagin, *Sweeping the Nation*, p. 44; Cobbett: cited in Langford, *Englishness Identified*, pp. 115–16.

p. 201 'remained standard': first fireplace: Sarti, 'The Material Conditions of Family Life', Kertzer and Barbagli, *History of the European Family*, vol. 1, p. 3, suggests Venice, but Crowley, *Invention of Comfort*, p. 23, cites the much older St Gall appearance.

p. 201 'the brick chimney': position of hearth: Shammas, 'The Domestic Environment in Early Modern England and America', Peter Charles Hoffer, ed., *Colonial Women and Domesticity: Selected Articles on Gender in Early America* (New York, Garland, 1988), p. 198; footnote: central hearths in Scotland and Ireland, Ayres, *Domestic Interiors*, p. 20.

p. 202 'comfortable living': 'old men': William Harrison, *The Description of England*, George Edelen, ed. (Ithaca, for the Folger Shakespeare Library by Cornell University Press, 1968), pp. 200–1. The date of the observation is open to question: Harrison wrote the work in 1560 and revised it twice, in 1577 and 1587.

p. 202 'hole in the roof': American colony chimneys: Demos, *A Little Commonwealth*, pp. 25–6; frontier houses: Cowan, *Social History of American Technology*, pp. 29–30.

p. 203 'way with braziers': heating preferences: Sarti, 'The Material Conditions of Family Life', Kertzer and Barbagli, *History of the European Family*, vol. 1, p. 3.

p. 203 'a welcome addition': *Stube*: Sarti, 'The Material Conditions of Family Life', Kertzer and Barbagli, *History of the European Family*, vol. 1, pp. 4–6.

p. 204 'little insulating space': Dutch hood dimensions: Muizelaar and Phillips, *Men and Women*, p. 57; Dutch firepots: Zumthor, *Rembrandt's Holland*, pp. 45–6; footwarmers: Franits, *Paragons of Virtue*, p. 50; *zoldertje*: Loughman, 'Between Reality and Artful Fiction', Aynsley and Grant, *Imagined Interiors*, pp. 82–3.

p. 205 'might have one': repeal of coal tax: Ayres, *Domestic Interiors*, p. 16; Cambridgeshire and Norwich: Crowley, *Invention of Comfort*, pp. 56–8; numbers of fireplaces: Sarti, 'The Material Conditions of Family Life', Kertzer and Barbagli, *History of the European Family*, vol. 1, p. 8.

p. 206 'of the population': Biographical information on Muthesius is drawn from the introduction to H. Muthesius, *The English House*, pp. xiv, xix, xx, while the sentence quoted in the footnote is from vol. 2, p. 68. The footnote's gas take-up statistics are from Caroline Davidson, *A Woman's Work is Never Done: A History of Housework in the British Isles, 1650–1950* (London, Chatto & Windus, 1982), pp. 67, 112; acceptance of draughts: H. Muthesius, *The English House*, vol. 2, pp. 1–3, 30; ubiquity of coal fires: Davidson, *A Woman's Work is Never Done*, p. 100; 'Keep the Home-Fires Burning', originally entitled "Till the Boys Come Home', 1914, by Ivor Novello and Lena Gilbert Ford.

p. 206 'impossible to say': watercolour: 'Dining Room of Dr Whitridge's, Tiverton, Rhode Island' is owned by the Old Dartmouth Historical Society, New Bedford, Massachusetts, and is reproduced in Garrett, *At Home*, p. 79.

p. 207 'rooms of the house': spread of family through house: this very interesting idea is presented by Candace M. Volz, 'The Modern Look of the

Early-Twentieth-Century House: A Mirror of Changing Lifestyles', Foy and Schlereth, *American Home Life*, p. 37.

p. 208   'value of the heat': American fiancé: cited in Gillis, *A World of Their Own Making*, p. 144; Pugin houses: Stamp and Goulancourt, *The English House*, p. 33.

p. 209   'reality of home-making': it is Gavin Stamp who points out this paradox of visual vs practical, Stamp and Goulancourt, *The English House*, pp. 32–4.

p. 210   'door or a window': 1790 house: Vickery, *Behind Closed Doors*, p. 29; unspoken rule: Crowley, *Invention of Comfort*, pp. 36–7.

p. 211   'wooden shutters, or both': Jarrow church: Crowley, *Invention of Comfort*, p. 39.

p. 211   'part of the window': 'no perfect house': Crowley, *Invention of Comfort*, p. 65.

p. 212   'room became typical': Oxfordshire inventories: Shammas, 'The Domestic Environment in Early Modern England and America', Hoffer, *Colonial Women and Domesticity*, p. 198; three glazed windows: Crowley, *Invention of Comfort*, p. 67.

p. 212   'shipped to the colonies': colonists' fear of windows: G. Wright, *Building the Dream*, p. 12; advice to settlers: Demos, *A Little Commonwealth*, p. 28; Flowerdew Hundred: Deetz, *Flowerdew Hundred*, p. 108.

p. 213   'wish'd they were less': windows as furniture: Crowley, *Invention of Comfort*, p. 67; 'For windowes': cited in Demos, *A Little Commonwealth*, p. 28; New England minister: cited in David H. Flaherty, *Privacy in Colonial New England* (Charlottesville, University Press of Virginia, 1972), p. 41.

p. 213   'anywhere on the property': lack of windows in USA: Crowley, *Invention of Comfort*, p. 105; slatted shutters: Garrett, *At Home*, p. 24; Olmsted: cited in Vlach, *Back of the Big House*, pp. 9–10.

p. 214   'the wealthiest few': Tessin and French windows: DeJean, *The Age of Comfort*, p. 155; luxury of French windows: ibid., p. 155.

p. 215   'were easily felt': I am indebted, in the discussion of the history of the sash window that follows, to H. J. Louw, 'The Origin of the Sash Window', *Architectural History*, 26, 1983, pp. 49–72. Not only was this essay groundbreaking in its analysis of the history of the sash window, but it also repatriated its invention to England from the Netherlands.

p. 216   'at that date': Boston merchant: Hentie Louw and Robert Crayford, 'A Constructional History of the Sash-Window c. 1670–c.1725' (Parts 1 and 2), *Architectural History*, 41, 1998, pp. 82–130, and 42, 1999, pp. 173–239; part 1, p. 95.

p. 217   'and maintained': Dutch street patrol: Zumthor, *Rembrandt's Holland*, pp. 19–20; Amsterdam brighter than Paris: de Vries, *Industrious Revolution*, pp. 128–9, and Sarti, 'The Material Conditions of Family Life', in Kertzer and Barbagli, *History of the European Family*, vol. 1, p. 8; London parishes: Schivelbusch, *Disenchanted Night*, pp. 85–6, 89.

p. 218 'of their possessions': breaking street lamps: Schivelbusch, *Disenchanted Night*, pp. 97; footnote: ibid., pp. 99–100; link-bearers in London and Paris: ibid., p. 89.

p. 219 'on moonlit nights': Jane Austen, *Sense and Sensibility*, Ros Ballaster, ed. ([1811], Harmondsworth, Penguin, 1995), p. 35; Lancashire minister: Brian Bowers, *Lengthening the Day: A History of Lighting Technology* (Oxford, Oxford University Press, 1998), p. 2.

p. 220 'domesticated stars': spread of gas street lighting: Rybczynski, *Home*, p. 140; civic obligation: de Vries, *Industrious Revolution*, pp. 128–9; Pall Mall experiment: Hugh Barty-King, *New Flame: How Gas Changed the Commercial, Domestic and Industrial Life of Britain...* (Tavistock, Graphmitre, 1984), p. 28; the rest of the information is from Schivelbusch, *Disenchanted Night*, p. 32, although he does not give population figures. He, or his translator, refers to 'Germany' in this pre-unification period. If Prussia is included with the German Confederation, the population was 52 million; without Prussia it was 47 million. I have compromised, therefore, on a round figure of 50 million; mid-1860s: the date is Rybczynski's, *Home*, p. 140; [Anon.], review of 'An Historical Sketch of the Origin, Progress and Present State of Gas-Lighting' by William Matthews, *Westminster Review*, October 1829, p. 302; Robert Louis Stevenson, 'A Plea for Gas-lamps', *Virginibus Puerisque and Other Essays* (Newcastle-upon-Tyne, Cambridge Scholars, 2009), pp. 90–91; footnote: trials have occurred for a range of reasons, in a range of cities and towns, from Highland Park, Detroit (money-saving), to entire areas of Buckinghamshire (eco-friendly), and Toulouse (eco-friendly, with the addition that they are using heat-sensitive lights that switch on when a pedestrian walks past). Highland Park, http://www.nytimes.com/2011/12/30/us/cities-cost-cuttings-leave-residents-in-the-dark.html?pagewanted=all&_r=0; Buckinghamshire, http://www.buckscc.gov.uk/bcc/transport/Streetlights_useful_documents. page, Toulouse, http://www.guardian.co.uk/world/2009/oct/26/toulouse-heat-sensitive-lampposts, all accessed 23 January 2013.

p. 221 'few alternatives': technology of burning candles: Jonathan Bourne and Vanessa Brett, *Lighting in the Domestic Interior: Renaissance to Art Nouveau* (London, Sotheby's, 1991), p. 59; resinous wood: John Caspall, *Making Fire and Light in the Home pre-1820* (Woodbridge, Antique Collectors' Club), p. 262.

p. 222 'relumed without danger': wick technology: Bowers, *Lengthening the Day*, p. 20; tallow: Muizelaar and Phillips, *Men and Women*, p. 58; percentage of light loss: calculated by Count Rumford, cited in Schivelbusch, *Disenchanted Night*, p. 43; footnote: Bourne and Brett, *Lighting in the Domestic Interior*, p. 59; James Boswell, *Boswell's London Journal, 1762–1763*, Frederick A. Pottle, ed. (London, Heinemann, 1950), 21 March 1762/3, p. 224; the modern historian in the footnote is Davidson, *A Woman's Work is Never Done*, p. 96.

p. 222 'them as "numerous"': Ham House: Crowley, *Invention of Comfort*, p. 120.

p. 223 'varying heights': cost of rushlight vs candlelight: this was the calculation made by the naturalist Gilbert White, cited in Bowers, *Lengthening the Day*, pp. 18–19.

p. 224 'heaped upon profligacy': I am referring here to the Hogarth engravings; the original paintings, in Sir John Soane's Museum, show slightly different numbers and combinations, although the increase is similar. I am indebted to Crowley, *Invention of Comfort*, pp. 133ff., for the reading. He, however, uses the paintings.

p. 224 'and 31 snuffers': Crowley, *Invention of Comfort*, pp. 113, 137. Crowley thinks that 'there is virtually no evidence' for the use of rushlights in seventeenth- and eighteenth-century North America. He acknowledges that others, including Monta Lee Dakin, 'Brilliant with Lighting' (Ph.D. thesis, George Washington University, 1983), think otherwise. With the reservation that candlewood and other woods were used to supplement candles, I agree with Crowley; candlestick statistics: Crowley, *Invention of Comfort*, p. 137; Lord Botetourt's household: ibid., p. 138.

p. 225 'could see every body': 'splendid' party: Crowley, *Invention of Comfort*, p. 138; 'was so well lighted': Garrett, *At Home*, p. 160.

p. 226 'outweigh this liability': manufacture of paraffin: Bowers, *Lengthening the Day*, pp. 27, 30, 33.

p. 227 'protect their furniture': drawbacks of oil lamps: Alice Taylor, *Quench the Lamp* (Dingle, Brandon, 1990), pp. 180ff.; 'They went out': cited in Nylander, *Our Own Snug Fireside*, pp. 112–13; lamp rugs: ibid., pp. 112–13.

p. 228 'a similar rate': access to gas in Britain: Davidson, *A Woman's Work is Never Done*, p. 112.

p. 229 'late as the 1960s': outdoor electric lighting: Bowers, *Lengthening the Day*, pp. 18–80, 130; Hilaire Belloc, 'The Benefits which the Electric Light Confers on us, especially at night', cited in ibid., pp. 160–61; coverage of the electric grid: ibid., p. 162.

p. 230 'brighter lighting': footnote: Garrett, *At Home*, p. 39–40; 'dancing a jig': Catharine Beecher, *A Treatise on Domestic Economy, for the Use of Young Ladies at Home, and at School* (Boston: Marsh, Capen, Lyon & Webb, 1841), cited in ibid., p. 39.

p. 230 'fabric of the house': electric light switches: Schivelbusch, *Disenchanted Night*, pp. 67–8.

p. 231 'represented were not': *Amerika zu Haus*: Greg Castillo, 'The American "Fat Kitchen" in Europe: Postwar Domestic Modernity and Marshall Plan Strategies of Enchantment', Ruth Oldenziel and Karin Zachmann, eds, *Cold War Kitchen: Americanization, Technology, and European Users* (Cambridge, MA, MIT Press, 2009), pp. 33–57.

7. THE HOME NETWORK

p. 235 '30–45 minutes': bakehouses: Nancy Cox, '"A Flesh pott, or a Brasse pott or a pott to boile in": Changes in Metal and Fuel Technology in the Early Modern Period and the Implications for Cooking', Moira Donald and Linda Hurcombe, eds, *Gender and Material Culture in Historical Perspective* (Basingstoke, Macmillan, 2000), pp. 145ff.

p. 236 'a small fireplace': open-fire cooking: Susan Strasser: 'Enlarged Human Existence?', Sarah Fenstermaker Berk, ed., *Women and Household Labor* (Beverly Hills, Sage, 1980), p. 36.

p. 237 'twentieth century': Catharine Beecher and Harriet Beecher Stowe, *The American Woman's Home, or, Principles of Domestic Science* (New York, J. B. Ford & Co., 1869), p. 34.

p. 237 'anything like it': Wilder, *The Little House Books*, vol. 2, p. 278.

p. 238 'heard of Mrs Beecher': limitations of Hoosier Kitchen: Wilson, *Consider the Fork*, p. 349.

p. 239 'dining room and kitchen': spread of American efficiency experts to Europe: Lawrence-Zúñiga, 'Material Conditions of Family Life', Kertzer and Barbagli, *History of the European Family*, vol. 3, pp. 16–17.

p. 239 'cooking and storage': politics: Reagin, *Sweeping the Nation*, pp. 80, 84, 86; Bauhaus: Siegfried Giedion, *Mechanization Takes Command: A Contribution to Anonymous History* (New York, Oxford University Press), 1948, pp. 522–3.

p. 241 'the near dark': this and the previous paragraph on the Frankfurt kitchen are drawn from Martina Hessler, 'The Frankfurt Kitchen: The Model of Modernity and the "Madness" of Traditional Users, 1926 to 1933', Oldenziel and Zachmann, *Cold War Kitchen*, pp. 163–77; Lawrence-Zúñiga, 'Material Conditions of Family Life', Kertzer and Barbagli, *History of the European Family*, vol. 3, pp. 16–17, 19; Reagin, *Sweeping the Nation*, pp. 80, 86.

p. 242 'cold running water': lack of equipment: Strasser, 'Englarged Human Existence?', Berk, *Women and Household Labor*, p. 41; reduction in cooking and cleaning time: Gary Cross, *An All-Consuming Century: Why Commercialism Won in Modern America* (New York, Columbia University Press, 2000), pp. 18, 27; running water: Ruth Schwartz Cowan, 'Coal Stoves and Clean Sinks: Housework between 1890 and 1930', Foy and Schlereth, *American Home Life*, pp. 211ff., 220.

p. 243 'but unhygienic': floor sand: Garrett, *At Home*, p. 75; 'boughten' broom: Wilder, *The Little House Books*, vol. 1, p. 476; dust becomes dirt: Bushman, *Refinement of America*, p. 265; insects: Suellen Hoy, *Chasing Dirt: The American Pursuit of Cleanliness* (New York, Oxford University Press, 1995), pp. 10–11.

p. 243 'applied in the past': footnote: *Brewer's Dictionary of Phrase and Fable*, and cited by James Crail, 'Body and Soil', *Artnet*, http://www.artnet.com/magazineus/books/croak/summer-reading-6-18-12.asp, accessed 1 April 2013.

p. 244 'out of windows': Charles II: Sophie Gee, *Making Waste: Leftovers and the Eighteenth-Century Imagination* (Princeton, Princeton University Press, 2010), pp. 6–7; Dutch legislation: Schama, *Embarrassment of Riches*, p. 378.

p. 245 'the animal warmth': chamber-pots: Davidson, *A Woman's Work is Never Done*, p. 115; city dwellers' shock: ibid., p. 117; courtyard farms in Skåne, spinning groups in Dalarna: Frykman and Löfgren, *Culture Builders*, pp. 158, 179–80. I am grateful to Frank Wynne for the information on the different acidities of male and female urine.

p. 246 'and quality': La Rochefoucauld: cited in Davidson, *A Woman's Work is Never Done*, p. 115.

p. 246 'was very different': architectural treatises: DeJean, *The Age of Comfort*, pp. 73, 71 cites these examples, but she has more faith in their existence than I do.

p. 247 'wait at street pumps': water pipes: Davidson, *A Woman's Work is Never Done*, p. 28.

p. 248 'even more, at 8d': Manchester: ibid., pp. 28–31; water prices: ibid., p. 18.

p. 248 'after World War II': Philadelphia: Thomas J. Schlereth, 'Conduits and conduct: Home Utilities in Victorian America, 1876–1915', Foy and Schlereth, *American Home Life*, pp. 226–7; rural supply: Hoy, *Chasing Dirt*, p. 15.

p. 249 'remove the dirt': lack of sewage systems: Larkin, *Reshaping of Everyday Life*, pp. 159, 161; Muncie: Lynd and Lynd, *Middletown*, p. 27. This famous sociological study looked at the town of Muncie, Indiana, in 1925, using data for comparison from 1890. In 1885, the town had been an agricultural county seat with 6,000 people; by 1920 it had grown to 35,000. There were several industries, including glass, metal and automotive. The nearest big city was nearly 100 kilometres away, with a train link but no 'hard-surface roads for motoring' when the study was undertaken. A weakness of the study is that although 2 per cent of the population was 'foreign-born', and 6 per cent black, it nevertheless focused on white, native-born residents.

p. 249 'on their shoulders': North Carolina: Strasser, 'Enlarged Human Existence?', Berk, *Women and Household Labor*, p. 43.

p. 250 'be disposed of': pump queues: Davidson, *A Woman's Work is Never Done*, p. 12, mentions Gateshead, where lines averaged three hours; estimate of rainwater butt capacity: ibid., p. 8; historic data: ibid., p. 14; contemporary water usage rates for 2006/7 in England and Wales: 'Water and the Environment: International Comparisons of Domestic Per Capita Consumption', Reference: L219/B5/6000/025b (Bristol, Environment Agency, 2008), http://a0768b4a8a31e106d8b0-50dc802554eb38a24458b98ff72d550b.r19.cf3.rackcdn.com/geh00809bqtd-e-e.pdf, accessed online 7 November 2013. I have omitted North American contemporary usage, where more extreme climate, and therefore air-conditioning, frequently doubles UK figures, and makes it a less useful comparator for historic data.

p. 251 'the 1950s began': Muncie: Lynd and Lynd, *Middletown*, p. 97; Scotland: Sarti, *Europe at Home*, p. 114; Ireland: Davidson, *A Woman's Work is Never Done*,

p. 32. She adds that while 70 per cent (England and Wales) and 67 per cent (Scotland) were said to have access to piped water by 1944, even then it may be that street standpipes were the 'pipes' many of these people were using.

p. 251 'had no bathroom': Muncie: Lynd and Lynd, *Middletown*, p. 256.

p. 252 'American Standard company': washing becoming private: Larkin, *Reshaping of Everyday Life*, pp. 163–4; bathroom suite: Schlereth, *Victorian America*, pp. 128–9.

p. 252 'dangerous wiring': British guide: S. Stephens Hellyer, *The Plumber and Sanitary Houses: A Practical Treatise on the Principles of Internal Plumbing Work...* (London, B. T. Batsford, 1877), p. v.

p. 254 'put in prison': John Ratcliffe: Cohn, *Palace or Poorhouse*, pp. 6, 7–8; German child: cited in Reagin, *Sweeping the Nation*, p. 38.

p. 255 'super-consumption of restraint': *banketjestukken*: Schama, *Embarrassment of Riches*, p. 160.

p. 255 'living with it': moral dimension of consumer goods: Gwendolyn Wright, *Moralism and the Model Home: Domestic Architecture and Cultural Conflict in Chicago* (Chicago, University of Chicago Press, 1980), p. 19.

p. 255 'hygiene and thrift': respectable and not-respectable households: this point is made by Leonore Davidoff, 'The Rationalization of Housework', Diana Leonard Barker and Sheila Allen, eds, *Dependence and Exploitation in Work and Marriage* (London, Longman, 1976), p. 140. The judgement is passed, almost unconsciously, in James Littlejohn, *Westrigg: The Sociology of a Cheviot Parish* (London, Routledge & Kegan Paul, 1963), p. 123.

p. 256 'two in battle': life expectancy figures: Bruce Haley, *The Healthy Body and Victorian Culture* (Cambridge, MA, Harvard University Press, 1978), p. 8; US soldiers' deaths by disease: Hoy, *Chasing Dirt*, p. 58.

p. 257 'domestically produced health': housewives' responsibility for health: Mokyr, 'Why "More Work for Mother"?', p.22.

p. 258 'fruit and vegetables': Lynd and Lynd, *Middletown*, pp. 156–7 cite the advertisement that promised to cure 'spring sickness' and 'sluggishness', and they list the Midwestern winter diet, which I have supplemented with the diet of the rest of the USA, as well as northern Europe. The remaining diseases come from late-nineteenth-century advertisements for Pabst Malt Beef Extract, Clarke's Blood Mixture and, of course, Morison's Pills.

p. 258 'the finished product': 'patriotic duty': Charles Lathrop Pack, *The War Garden Victorious* (Philadelphia, J. B. Lippincott, 1919), Appendix II, p. 3; 'We Can' poster in National Agricultural Library, USDA poster collection, https://archive.org/details/CAT31123264, accessed online 5 November 2013; food preservation: Strasser, *Never Done*, pp. 22–3.

p. 260 'days a week': 'the business of cleanliness': Hoy, *Chasing Dirt*, pp. 140–48.

p. 260 'to be American': Booker T. Washington: Hoy, *Chasing Dirt*, p. 89; Christine Frederick, *The New Housekeeping: Efficiency Studies in Home Management*

(Garden City, NY, Doubleday, Page & Co., 1913), p. 11, cited in McHugh, *American Domesticity*, p. 64.

p. 261 'form of citizenship': superiority of German housekeeping: Reagin, *Sweeping the Nation*, pp. 49, 53–5; girls' domestic education: ibid., pp. 46–7; 'service to the country': Käthe Schirmacher, cited in ibid., pp. 74–5, 78.

p. 261 '"respectable" household': good housekeeping connected to good citizenship: Reagin, *Sweeping the Nation*, pp. 9, 110–11, 118.

p. 264 'promoted this equation': 'for public use': [no author], *Yosemite: The National Parks: Shaping the System* (Washington, DC, Harper's Ferry Center, US Department of the Interior, 2004), p. 12, http://www.nps.gov/history/history/ online_books/shaping/part2.pdf, accessed 25 October 2013.

p. 264 'unspoiled land': Ebenezer Howard, *To-morrow: A Peaceful Path to Real Reform*, which was reissued and retitled as *Garden Cities of To-morrow* (London, Swan Sonnenschein, 1902).

p. 266 'private spaces': William Morris, *Collected Letters of William Morris*, Norman Kelvin, ed. (Princeton, Princeton University Press, 1984), vol. 3, p. 164.

p. 267 'at no cost': UK government involvement: Lawrence-Zúñiga, 'Material Conditions of Family Life', Kertzer and Barbagli, *History of the European Family*, vol. 3, p. 12; US government involvement: Stephanie Coontz, *The Way We Never Were: American Families and the Nostalgia Trap* (New York, Basic, 1992), pp. 76–7; Clark, *American Family Home*, p. 219.

p. 268 'ultimately more expensive': William Levitt: Clark, *American Family Home*, pp. 218–22.

p. 269 'and for everyone': flight to suburbia: Dolores Hayden, *Building Suburbia: Green Fields and Urban Growth, 1820–2000* (New York, Pantheon, 2003), p. 10.

p. 271 'produce no smoke': Santa Fe: Nezar AlSayyad, *Consuming Tradition, Manufacturing Heritage: Global Norms and Urban Forms in the Age of Tourism* (London, Routledge, 2001), p. 12.

p. 271 'their suburban dreams': heritage as fear of future: my starting point for this idea is AlSayyad, *Consuming Tradition*, p. 14: 'If tradition is about the absence of choice…heritage then is the deliberate embrace of a single choice as a means of defining the past in relationship to the future.'

CODA: NOT AT HOME

p. 274 'followed naturally': Catharine Beecher's innovations: Rybczynski, *Home*, p. 164.

p. 275 'The house is past': Loos: cited in Christopher Reed, ed., *Not at Home: The Suppression of Domesticity in Modern Art and Architecture* (London, Thames and Hudson, 1996), p. 9, from whom I have also borrowed the title of this chapter; Adorno: Hilde Heynen, 'Modernity and Domesticity: Tensions and Contradictions', Hilde Heynen and Güslüm Baydar, eds, *Negotiating Domesticity: Spatial Productions of Gender in Modern Architecture* (London, Routledge, 2005), p. 2.

p. 276 'does humanity begin': Charles Baudelaire, 'The Painter of Modern Life', in *Selected Writings on Art and Literature*, trs. P. E. Charvet (Harmondsworth, Penguin, 2006), pp. 399–400; Benjamin, *The Arcades Project*, pp. 216, 220; Adolf Behne, *Die Wiederkehr der Kunst* (Nedeln, Kurt Wolff, 1973), pp. 67–8, cited in Karina van Herck, '"Only Where Comfort Ends, Does Humanity Begin": On the Coldness of Avant-Garde Architecture in the Weimar Period', Heynen and Baydar, *Negotiating Domesticity*, p. 123; I have amended the translation slightly.

p. 278 'just looked good': Gropius: cited in Lawrence-Zúñiga, 'Material Conditions of Family Life', Kertzer and Barbagli, *History of the European Family*, vol. 3, p. 17.

p. 278 'ways of living': modernists and utility: this idea is argued with great cogency in Rybczynski, *Home*, pp. 188–91.

p. 280 'the overriding desire': Alix Rohde-Liebenau: Castillo, 'The American "Fat Kitchen" in Europe', Oldenziel and Zachmann, *Cold War Kitchen*, pp. 37, 36; open-plan living: Evans, 'Figures, Doors and Passages', p. 276

p. 280 'visible, visitable, penetrable': Henry James, *The American Scene* (London, Granville, 1987), p. 119.

p. 280 'are made of': the citations from Benjamin and Behne, and the ideas in these paragraphs: Heynen, 'Modernity and Domesticity', Heynen and Baydar, *Negotiating Domesticity*, pp. 1–29. I am grateful to Dr Hanna Weibye, who returned to the original German for me, and discussed the various '*heim*'s embedded in secrets and the supernatural.

Bibliography

Anon., *The Absent Presence: The Uninhabited Interior in 19th and 20th Century British Art* (Sheffield, Sheffield City Art Galleries, 1991)

Anon., *Polite Society by Arthur Devis, 1712–1787: Portraits of the English Country Gentleman and His Family* (Preston, Harris Museum and Art Gallery, 1983)

Anon., *Richard Hamilton, Interiors, 1964–79* (London, Waddington, 1979)

Anon., *Social Change and Taste in Mid-Victorian England: Report of a Conference at the Victoria and Albert Museum* ([London, Victorian Society, 1963?])

Abbott, Mary, *Family Ties: English Families, 1540–1920* (London, Routledge, 1993)

Alcock, N. W., *People at Home: Living in a Warwickshire Village, 1500–1800* (Chichester, Phillimore, 1993)

Alofsin, Anthony, *When Buildings Speak: Architecture as Language in the Habsburg Empire and its Aftermath, 1867–1933* (Chicago, University of Chicago Press, 2006)

AlSayyad, Nezar, ed., *Consuming Tradition, Manufacturing Heritage: Global Norms and Urban Forms in the Age of Tourism* (London, Routledge, 2001)

—, and J. P. Bourdier, eds, *Dwellings, Settlements and Tradition: Cross-Cultural Perspectives* (Lanham, University Press of America, 1989)

Alter, George, 'New Perspectives on European Marriage in the 19th Century', *Journal of Family History*, 16, 1991

Ames, Kenneth L., *Death in the Dining Room, and Other Tales of Victorian Culture* (Philadelphia, Temple University Press, 1992)

Amussen, Susan Dwyer, *An Ordered Society: Gender and Class in Early Modern England* (Oxford, Blackwell, 1988)

—, and Adele Seeff, eds, *Attending to Early Modern Women* (Newark, University of Delaware Press, 1998)

Anderson, Michael, *Approaches to the History of the Western Family, 1500–1914* (London, Macmillan, 1980)

Archer, John, *Architecture and Suburbia: From English Villa to American Dream House, 1690–2000* (Minneapolis, University of Minnesota Press, 2005)

Ariès, Philippe, and Georges Duby, eds, *A History of Private Life*, trs. Arthur Goldhammer (Cambridge, MA, Belknap Press, 1987–1991), vol. 4: *From the Fires of Revolution to the Great War*, ed. Michelle Perrot

Arnold, Dana, *The Georgian Country House: Architecture, Landscape and Society* (Stroud, Sutton, 1998)

—, ed., *The Georgian Villa* (Stroud, Alan Sutton, 1996)

317

Asendorf, Christoph, *Batteries of Life: On the History of Things and Their Perception in Modernity*, trs. Don Reneau (Berkeley, University of California Press, 1993)

Aynsley, Jeremy, and Charlotte Grant, eds, *Imagined Interiors: Representing the Domestic Interior since the Renaissance* (London, V&A Publications, 2006)

Ayres, James, *Building the Georgian City* (New Haven, Yale University Press, 1998)

—, *Domestic Interiors: The British Tradition, 1500–1850* (New Haven, Yale University Press, 2003)

Bachelard, Gaston, *La Poétique de l'espace* (Paris, Presses universitaires de France, 1970)

Ballantyne, Andrew, and Andrew Law, *Tudoresque: In Pursuit of the Ideal Home* (London, Reaktion, 2011)

Barker, Diana Leonard, and Sheila Allen, eds, *Dependence and Exploitation in Work and Marriage* (London, Longman, 1976)

Barns, Cass G., *The Sod House* (Lincoln, University of Nebraska Press, 1970)

Baxter, Denise Amy, and Meredith Martin, eds, *Architectural Space in Eighteenth-Century Europe: Constructing Identities and Interiors* (Farnham, Ashgate, 2010)

Beard, Geoffrey, *Upholsterers and Interior Furnishing in England: 1530–1840* (London, Yale University Press, 1997)

Beecher, Catharine, *A Treatise on Domestic Economy, for the Use of Young Ladies at Home, and at School* (Boston, Marsh, Capen, Lyon & Webb, 1841); revised and expanded, as Catharine Beecher and Harriet Beecher Stowe, *The American Woman's Home, or, Principles of Domestic Science* (New York, J. B. Ford & Co., 1869)

Behlmer, George K., *Friends of the Family: The English Home and its Guardians, 1850–1940* (Stanford, Stanford University Press, 1998)

Berg, Maxine, *Luxury and Pleasure in Eighteenth-Century Britain* (Oxford, Oxford University Press, 2005)

—, and Helen Clifford, eds, *Consumers and Luxury: Consumer Culture in Europe, 1650–1850* (Manchester, Manchester University Press, 1999)

Berk, Sarah Fenstermaker, ed., *Women and Household Labor* (Beverly Hills, Sage, 1980)

Berker, Thomas, Maren Hartmann, Yves Punie and Katie Ward, *Domestication of Media and Technology* (Maidenhead, Open University, 2006)

Bermingham, Ann, and John Brewer, eds, *The Consumption of Culture, 1600–1800: Image, Object, Text* (London, Routledge, 1995)

Betts, Paul, *The Authority of Everyday Objects: A Cultural History of West German Industrial Design* (Berkeley, University of California Press, 2004)

Black, Lawrence, and Nicole Robertson, eds, *Consumerism and the Co-operative Movement in Modern British History: Taking Stock* (Manchester, Manchester University Press, 2009)

Blackwell, Mark, ed., *The Secret Life of Things: Animals, Objects, and It-Narratives in Eighteenth-Century England* (Lewisburg, Bucknell University Press, 2007)

Blassingame, John W., *The Slave Community: Plantation Life in the Antebellum South* (rev. edn, New York, Oxford University Press, 1979)

Blühm, Andreas, and Louise Lippincott, *Light: The Industrial Age, 1750–1900: Art and Science, Technology and Society* (London, Thames and Hudson, 2000)

Borsay, Peter, *The English Urban Renaissance: Culture and Society in the Provincial Town, 1660–1700* (Oxford, Clarendon, 1989)

Bourne, Jonathan, and Vanessa Brett, *Lighting in the Domestic Interior: Renaissance to Art Nouveau* (London, Sotheby's, 1991)

Borzello, Frances, *At Home: The Domestic Interior in Art* (London, Thames and Hudson, 2006)

Boswell, James, *Boswell's London Journal, 1762–1763*, ed. Frederick A. Pottle (London, Heinemann, 1950)

Bowers, Brian, *Lengthening the Day: A History of Lighting Technology* (Oxford, Oxford University Press, 1998)

Boyd, Diane E., and Marta Kvande, eds, *Everyday Revolutions: Eighteenth-Century Women Transforming Public and Private* (Newark, University of Delaware Press, 2008)

Boydston, Jeanne, *Home and Work: Housework, Wages, and the Ideology of Labor in the Early Republic* (New York, Oxford University Press, 1990)

Boym, Svetlana, *The Future of Nostalgia* (New York, Basic, 2001)

Braudel, Fernand, *Capitalism and Material Life, 1400–1800*, trs. Miriam Kochan (London, Weidenfeld and Nicolson, 1973)

Breen, T. H., *The Marketplace of Revolution: How Consumer Politics Shaped American Independence* (New York, Oxford University Press, 2004)

Brewer, John, 'Childhood Revisited: The Genesis of the Modern Toy', *History Today*, 30, 1980, pp. 32–9

—, and Roy Porter, eds, *Consumption and the World of Goods* (London, Routledge, 1993)

Bronner, S. J., ed., *American Material Culture and Folklife: A Prologue and Dialogue* (Ann Arbor, University of Michigan Research Press, 1985)

Brown, Frank E., 'Continuity and Change in the Urban House: Developments in Domestic Space Organization in Seventeenth-Century London', *Comparative Studies in Society and History*, 28, 1986

Brunskill, R. W., *Houses* (London, Collins, 1982)

Bryden, Inga, and Janet Floyd, eds, *Domestic Space: Reading the Nineteenth-Century Interior* (Manchester, Manchester University Press, 1999)

Buck, Carl Darling, *A Dictionary of Selected Synonyms in the Principal Indo-European Languages: A Contribution to the History of Ideas* (facsimile of 1949 edition, Chicago, University of Chicago Press, 1988)

Burguière, André, Christiane Klapisch-Zuber, Martine Segalen and Françoise Zonabend, eds, *A History of the Family*, vol. 2: *The Impact of Modernity*, trs. Sarah Hanbury Tenison (Cambridge, MA, Belknap Press, 1996)

Burnett, John, ed., *Destiny Obscure: Autobiographies of Childhood, Education and Family from the 1820s to the 1920s* (London, Allen Lane, 1982)

—, *A Social History of Housing, 1815–1985* (London, Methuen, 1978)

Buruma, Ian, 'Artist of the Floating World', *New York Review of Books*, 44, 9 January 1997, pp. 8–11

Bushman, Richard L., *The Refinement of America: Persons, Houses, Cities* (New York, Alfred A. Knopf, 1992)

Calder, Lendol, *Financing the American Dream: A Cultural History of Consumer Credit* (Princeton, Princeton University Press, 1999)

Calvert, Karin, *Children in the House: The Material Culture of Early Childhood, 1600–1900* (Boston, Northeastern University Press, 1992)

Campbell, Colin, *The Romantic Ethic and the Spirit of Modern Consumerism* (Oxford, Blackwell, 1987)

Cantacuzino, Sherban, *European Domestic Architecture: Its Development from Early Times* (London, Studio Vista, 1969)

Carr, Lois Green, Philip D. Morgan and Jean B. Russo, eds, *Colonial Chesapeake Society* (Chapel Hill, University of North Carolina Press, 1988)

Carson, Cary, Ronald Hoffman and Peter J. Albert, eds, *Of Consuming Interests: The Style of Life in the Eighteenth Century* (Charlottesville, University Press of Virginia, 1994)

Casey, James, *The History of the Family* (Oxford, Basil Blackwell, 1989)

Caspall, John, *Making Fire and Light in the Home pre-1820* (Woodbridge, Antique Collectors' Club, 1987)

Castiglione, Dario, and Lesley Sharpe, *Shifting the Boundaries: Transforming the Languages of Public and Private in the Eighteenth Century* (Exeter, University of Exeter Press, 1995)

Censer, Jane Turner, *North Carolina Planters and Their Children 1800–1860* (Baton Rouge, Louisiana State University Press, 1984)

Chase, Karen, and Michael Levenson, *The Spectacle of Intimacy: A Public Life for the Victorian Family* (Princeton, Princeton University Press, 2000)

Cieraad, Irene, ed., *At Home: An Anthropology of Domestic Space* (Syracuse, Syracuse University Press, 1999)

Clark, Jr, Clifford Edward, 'Domestic Architecture as an Index to Social History: The Romantic Revival and the Cult of Domesticity in America, 1840–1870', *Journal of Interdisciplinary History*, Summer 1976, pp. 33–56

—, *The American Family Home, 1800–1960* (Chapel Hill, University of North Carolina Press, 1986)

Clemmensen, Tove, *Skaebner og Interiører: Danske Tegninger fra Barok til Klunketid* (Skive, Nationalmuseet, 1984)

Cohen, Deborah, *Household Gods: The British and Their Possessions* (New Haven, Yale University Press, 2006)

Cohen, Lizabeth, *A Consumers' Republic: The Politics of Mass Consumption in Postwar America* (New York, Vintage, 2004)

Cohen, Monica F., *Professional Domesticity in the Victorian Novel: Women, Work and Home* (Cambridge, Cambridge University Press, 1998)

Cohn, Jan, *The Palace or the Poorhouse: The American House as a Cultural Symbol* (East Lansing, Michigan State University Press, 1979)

Confino, Alon, *Nation as a Local Metaphor: Württemberg, Imperial Germany, and National Memory, 1871–1918* (Chapel Hill, University of North Carolina Press, 1997)

Coontz, Stephanie, *The Social Origins of Private Life: A History of American Families, 1600–1900* (London, Verso, 1988)

—, *The Way We Never Were: American Families and the Nostalgia Trap* (New York, Basic, 1992)

Cowan, Ruth Schwartz, *More Work for Mother: The Ironies of Household Technology from the Open Hearth to the Microwave* (New York, Basic, 1983)

—, *A Social History of American Technology* (New York, Oxford University Press, 1997)

Cramer, Richard D., 'Images of Home', *AIA Journal*, 34, 3, 1960, pp. 40–49

Cross, Gary, *An All-Consuming Century: Why Commercialism Won in Modern America* (New York, Columbia University Press, 2000)

Crossick, Geoffrey, and Heinz-Gerhard Haupt, *The Petite Bourgeoisie in Europe, 1780–1914* (London, Routledge, 1995)

Crowley, John, *The Invention of Comfort: Sensibilities and Design in Early Modern Britain and Early America* (Baltimore, Johns Hopkins University Press, 2001)

Csikszentmihalyi, Mihaly and Eugene Rochberg-Halton, *The Meaning of Things: Domestic Symbols and the Self* (Cambridge, Cambridge University Press, 1981)

Cummings, Abbott Lowell, ed., *Rural Household Inventories: Establishing the Names, Uses and Furnishings of Rooms in the Colonial New England Home, 1675–1775* (Boston, Society for the Preservation of New England Antiquities, 1964)

Cunningham, Hugh, *Children and Childhood in Western Society since 1500* (London, Longman, 1995)

Darling, E., and L. Whitworth, eds, *Women and the Making of Built Space in England, 1870–1950* (Aldershot, Ashgate, 2007)

Daunton, M. J., *House and Home in the Victorian City: Working-Class Housing, 1850–1914* (London, Edward Arnold, 1983)

Davidoff, Leonore, and Catherine Hall, *Family Fortunes: Men and Women of the English Middle Class, 1780–1850* (rev. edn, London, Routledge, 1987)

—, and Ruth Hawthorn, *A Day in the Life of the Victorian Servant* (London, Allen & Unwin, 1976)

Davidson, Caroline, *A Woman's Work is Never Done: A History of Housework in the British Isles, 1650–1950* (London, Chatto & Windus, 1982)

—, *The World of Mary Ellen Best* (London, Chatto & Windus, 1985)

Day, Ivan, ed., *Eat, Drink & be Merry: The British at Table, 1600–2000* (London, Philip Wilson, 2000)

—, ed., *Over a Red Hot Stove: Essays in Early Cooking Technology* (London, Prospect, 2009)

Deetz, James, *Flowerdew Hundred: The Archaeology of a Virginia Plantation, 1619–1864* (Charlottesville, University Press of Virginia, 1993)

—, *In Small Things Forgotten: The Archaeology of Early American Life* (Garden City, New York, Anchor Books, 1977)

—, and Patricia Scott Deetz, *The Times of Their Lives: Life, Love, and Death in Plymouth Colony* (New York, W. H. Freeman and Co., 2000)

Defoe, Daniel, *Robinson Crusoe: An Authoritative Text, Contexts, Criticism*, ed. Michael Shinagel (New York, W. W. Norton, 1994)

DeJean, Joan, *The Age of Comfort: When Paris Discovered Casual and the Modern Home Began* (New York, Bloomsbury, 2009)

Delap, Lucy, Ben Griffin and Abigail Wills, eds, *The Politics of Domestic Authority in Britain since 1800* (Basingstoke, Palgrave Macmillan, 2009)

Demos, John, *A Little Commonwealth: Family Life in Plymouth Colony* (New York, Oxford University Press, 1970)

—, *Past, Present, and Personal: The Family and the Life Course in American History* (New York, Oxford University Press, 1986)

Dewing, David, ed., *Home and Garden, Paintings and Drawings of English, Middle-Class, Urban Domestic Spaces, 1675 to 1914* (London, Geffrye Museum, 2003)

D'Oench, Ellen, *The Conversation Piece: Arthur Devis and His Contemporaries* (New Haven, Yale University Press, 1980)

Donald, Moira, and Linda Hurcombe, eds, *Gender and Material Culture in Historical Perspective* (Basingstoke, Macmillan, 2000)

Donzelot, Jacques, *The Policing of Families*, trs. Robert Hurley (London, Hutchinson, 1980)

Douglas, Ann, *The Feminization of American Culture* (London, Macmillan, 1977)

Durantini, Mary Frances, *The Child in Seventeenth-Century Dutch Painting* (Ann Arbor, University of Michigan Research Press, 1983)

Earle, Peter, *The Making of the English Middle Class: Business, Society and Family Life in London, 1660–1730* (London, Methuen, 1989)

Edwards, Clive, *Turning Houses into Homes: A History of the Retailing and Consumption of Domestic Furnishings* (Aldershot, Ashgate, 2005)

Eleb-Vidal, Monique, avec Anne Debarre-Blanchard, *Architectures de la vie privée: maisons et modernités, XVIIe-XIXe siècles* (Bruxelles, Éditions des Archives d'architecture moderne, 1989)

Elias, Norbert, *The Civilizing Process: The History of Manners and State Formation and Civilization*, trs. Edmund Jephcott (Oxford, Blackwell, 1994)

Ellis, Clifton, and Rebecca Ginsburg, eds, *Cabin, Quarter, Plantation: Architecture and Landscapes of North American Slavery* (New Haven, Yale University Press, 2010)

Emery, Elizabeth, *Photojournalism and the Origins of the French Writer House Museum (1881–1914): Privacy, Publicity, and Personality* (Farnham, Ashgate, 2012)

Ennals, Peter, and Deryck W. Holdsworth, *Homeplace: The Making of the Canadian Dwelling over Three Centuries* (Toronto, University of Toronto Press, 1998)

Etlin, Richard, '"Les Dedans", Jacques-François Blondel and the System of the Home, c.1740', *Gazette des Beaux-Arts*, April 1978, XCI

Evans, Richard J., and W. R. Lee, eds, *The German Family: Essays on the Social History of the Family in Nineteenth- and Twentieth-Century Germany* (London, Croom Helm, 1981)

Evans, Robin, 'Figures, Doors and Passages', *Architectural Design*, 4, 1978, pp. 267–78

Fass, Paula S., and Mary Ann Mason, eds, *Childhood in America* (New York, New York University Press, 2000)

Feild, Rachael, *Irons in the Fire: A History of Cooking Equipment* (Marlborough, Crowood Press, 1984)

Fielding, Thomas, *Select Proverbs of all Nations* (London, Longman, Hurst, Rees, Orme, Brown and Green, 1824)

Finn, Margot, 'Men's Things: Masculine Possession in the Consumer Revolution', *Social History*, 25, 2000, pp. 133–55

Flaherty, David H., *Privacy in Colonial New England* (Charlottesville, University Press of Virginia, 1972)

Flandrin, Jean-Louis, *Families in Former Times: Kinship, Household and Sexuality*, trs. Richard Southern (Cambridge University Press, 1979)

Formanek-Brunell, Miriam, *Made to Play House: Dolls and the Commercialization of American Girlhood, 1830–1930* (New Haven, Yale University Press, 1993)

Fox-Genovese, Elizabeth, *Within the Plantation Household: Black and White Women of the Old South* (Chapel Hill, University of North Carolina Press, 1988)

Foy, Jessica H., and Thomas J. Schlereth, eds, *American Home Life, 1880–1930: A Social History of Spaces and Services* (Knoxville, University of Tennessee Press, 1992)

Franits, Wayne E., ed., *Looking at Seventeenth-Century Dutch Art: Realism Reconsidered* (Cambridge, Cambridge University Press, 1997)

—, *Paragons of Virtue: Women and Domesticity in Seventeenth-Century Dutch Art* (Cambridge, Cambridge University Press, 1993)

Fraser, W. Hamish, *The Coming of the Mass Market, 1850–1914* (London, Macmillan, 1981)

Frederick, Christine, *Household Engineering* (Chicago, American School of Home Economics, 1919)

—, *The New Housekeeping: Efficiency Studies in Home Management* (Garden City, Doubleday, Page & Co., 1913)

Frykman, Jonas, and Orvar Löfgren, *Culture Builders: A Historical Anthropology of Middle-Class Life*, trs. Alan Crozier (New Brunswick, NJ, Rutgers University Press, 1987)

Gable, Eric, and Richard Handler, 'In Colonial Williamsburg, the New History Meets the Old', *Chronicle of Higher Education*, 30 October 1998, 45, pp. B10–11

Garrett, Elisabeth Donaghy, *At Home: The American Family, 1750–1870* (New York, Abrams, 1990)

Gee, Sophie, *Making Waste: Leftovers and the Eighteenth-Century Imagination* (Princeton, Princeton University Press, 2010)

Gere, Charlotte, *Nineteenth-Century Decoration: The Art of the Interior* (London, Abrams, 1989)

—, *Nineteenth Century Interiors: An Album of Watercolours*, ed. Joseph Focarino (London, Thames and Hudson, 1992)

Giedion, Siegfried, *Mechanization Takes Command: A Contribution to Anonymous History* (New York, Oxford University Press), 1948

Giles, Judy, *The Parlour and the Suburb: Domestic Identities, Class, Femininity and Modernity* (Oxford, Berg, 2004)

Gillis, John R., *For Better, for Worse: British Marriages, 1600 to the Present* (New York, Oxford University Press, 1985)

—, 'Making Time for Family: The Invention of Family Time(s) and the Reinvention of Family History', *Journal of Family History*, 21, 1996, pp. 4–21

—, *A World of Their Own Making: Myth, Ritual and the Quest for Family Values* (New York, Basic, 1996)

—, *Youth and History: Tradition and Change in European Age Relations, 1770–Present* (New York, Academic Press, 1974)

Giltaij, Jeroen, ed., *Senses and Sins: Dutch Painters of Daily Life in the Seventeenth Century* (Ostfildern-Ruit, Germany, Hatje Cantz Verlag, 2004)

Glassie, Henry, *Folk Housing in Middle Virginia: Structural Analysis of Historic Artifacts* (Knoxville, University of Tennessee Press, 1975)

Goody, Jack, *The Development of the Family and Marriage in Europe* (Cambridge, Cambridge University Press, 1983)

Gottlieb, Beatrice, *The Family in the Western World from the Black Death to the Industrial Age* (New York, Oxford University Press, 1993)

Gray, Marion W., *Productive Men, Reproductive Women: The Agrarian Household and the Emergence of Separate Spheres during the German Enlightenment* (New York, Berghahn Books, 2000)

Grazia, Victoria de, and Ellen Furlough, eds, *The Sex of Things: Gender and Consumption in Historical Perspective* (Berkeley, University of California Press, 1996)

Greven, Jr, Philip J., *The Protestant Temperament: Patterns of Child-Rearing, Religious Experience, and the Self in Early America* (New York, Alfred A. Knopf, 1977)

Grier, Katherine C., *Culture and Comfort: Parlor Making and Middle-Class Identity, 1850–1930* (Washington, DC, Smithsonian, 1988)

Guillery, Peter, *The Small House in Eighteenth-Century London: A Social and Architectural History* (London, Yale University Press, 2004)

Habermas, Jürgen, *The Structural Transformation of the Public Sphere: An Inquiry into a Category of Bourgeois Society*, trs. Thomas Burger and Frederick Lawrence (Cambridge, MA, MIT Press, 1989)

Hajnal, John, 'European Marriage Patterns in Perspective', *Population in History: Essays in Historical Demography*, eds D. V. Glass and D. E. C. Eversley (London, Edward Arnold, 1969)

—, 'Two Kinds of Pre-Industrial Household Systems', *Population and Development Review*, 8, 3, 1982, pp. 449–94

Hall, Catherine, *White, Male and Middle-Class: Explorations in Feminism and History* (Cambridge, Polity Press, 1992)

Hall, Edward T., *The Hidden Dimension: Man's Use of Space in Public and Private* (London, Bodley Head, 1966)

Hamilton, Richard, *Painting by Numbers* (London, Editions Hansjörg Mayer, 2006)

Hamlett, Jane, *Material Relations: Domestic Interiors and Middle-Class Families in England, 1850–1910* (Manchester, Manchester University Press, 2010)

Hammond, Robert, *The Electric Light in Our Homes* (London, Frederick Warne, [1884])

Handlin, David P., *The American Home, Architecture and Society, 1815–1915* (Boston, Little, Brown and Co., 1979)

Hardyment, Christina, *Behind the Scenes: Domestic Arrangements in Historic Houses* (London, National Trust, 1997)

—, *From Mangle to Microwave: The Mechanization of Household Work* (Cambridge, Polity, 1988)

Hartman, Mary S., *The Household and the Making of History: A Subversive View of the Western Past* (Cambridge, Cambridge University Press, 2004)

Hawes, J. M., and N. R. Hiner, eds, *Children in Historical and Comparative Perspective: An International Handbook and Research Guide* (New York, Greenwood, 1991)

Hayden, Dolores, *Building Suburbia: Green Fields and Urban Growth, 1820–2000* (New York, Pantheon, 2003)

—, *Redesigning the American Dream: The Future of Housing, Work, and Family Life* (rev. edn, New York, W. W. Norton, 2002)

Hellman, Caroline Chamberlin, *Domesticity and Design in American Women's Lives and Literature: Stowe, Alcott, Cather, and Wharton Writing at Home* (New York, Routledge, 2011)

Hellman, Mimi, 'Furniture, Sociability, and the Works of Leisure in Eighteenth-Century France', *Eighteenth-Century Studies*, 32, 4, 1999

Herman, Bernard L., *Town House: Architecture and Material Life in the Early American City, 1780–1830* (Chapel Hill, University of North Carolina Press, 2005)

Heynen, Hilde, and Güslüm Baydar, eds, *Negotiating Domesticity: Spatial Productions of Gender in Modern Architecture* (London, Routledge, 2005)

Heywood, Colin, *A History of Childhood: Children and Childhood in the West from Medieval to Modern Times* (Cambridge, Polity, 2001)

Hoffer, Peter Charles, ed., *Colonial Women and Domesticity: Selected Articles on Gender in Early America* (New York, Garland, 1988)

Houlbrooke, Ralph A., *The English Family 1450–1700* (London, Longman, 1984)

Howard, Maurice, *The Early Tudor Country House* (London, George Philip, 1987)

Hoy, Suellen, *Chasing Dirt: The American Pursuit of Cleanliness* (New York, Oxford University Press, 1995)

Huizinga, Johan, *Dutch Civilization in the Seventeenth Century, and Other Essays*, Pieter Geyl and F. W. N. Hugenholts, eds, trs. Arnold J. Pomerans (London, Collins, 1968)

Hussey, David, and Margaret Ponsonby, eds, *Buying for the Home: Shopping for the Domestic from the Seventeenth Century to the Present* (Aldershot, Ashgate, 2008)

—, *The Single Homemaker and Material Culture in the Long Eighteenth Century* (Aldershot, Ashgate, 2012)

Jackson, Alan A., *Semi-Detached London: Suburban Development, Life and Transport, 1900–39* (London, George Allen & Unwin, 1973)

Jackson, J. B., *Landscapes: Selected Writings of J. B. Jackson*, ed. Ervin H. Zube ([no place of publication], University of Massachusetts Press, 1970)

Jaffee, David, *A New Nation of Goods: The Material Culture of Early America* (Philadelphia, University of Pennsylvania Press, 2010)

James, Henry, *The American Scene* (London, Granville, 1987)

Jardine, Lisa, *Going Dutch: How England Plundered Holland's Glory* (London, HarperCollins, 2008)

Jensen, Joan M., *Calling This Place Home: Women on the Wisconsin Frontier, 1850–1925* (St Paul, Minnesota Historical Society Press, 2006)

—, *Loosening the Bonds: Mid-Atlantic Farm Women, 1750–1850* (New Haven, Yale University Press, 1986)

Jonge, Huub de, ed., *Ons sort mensen: Levensstijlen in Nederland* (Nijmegen, SUN, 1997)

Kasson, John F., *Civilizing the Machine: Technology and Republican Values in America, 1776–1900* (New York, Grossman, 1976)

Kertzer, David I., and Marzio Barbagli, eds, *The History of the European Family*, vol. 1: *Family Life in Early Modern Times, 1500–1789*; vol. 2: *Family Life in the Long Nineteenth Century, 1789–1913*; vol. 3: *Family Life in the Twentieth Century* (London, Yale University Press, 2001–2003)

Kevill-Davies, Sally, *Yesterday's Children: The Antiques and History of Childcare* (Woodbridge, Antique Collectors' Club, 1991)

Knoppers, Laura Lunger, *Politicizing Domesticity: From Henrietta Maria to Milton's Eve* (Cambridge, Cambridge University Press, 2011)

Konner, Melvin, *The Evolution of Childhood: Relationships, Emotion, Mind* (Cambridge, MA, Belknap Press, 2010)

Kornwolf, James D., *Architecture and Town Planning in Colonial North America* (Baltimore, Johns Hopkins University Press, 2002)

Kowaleski-Wallace, Elizabeth, *Consuming Subjects: Women, Shopping, and Business in the Eighteenth Century* (New York, Columbia University Press, 1997)

Langford, Paul, *Englishness Identified: Manners and Character, 1650–1850* (Oxford, Oxford University Press, 2000)

Larkin, Jack, *The Reshaping of Everyday Life, 1790–1840* (New York, Harper & Row, 1988)

Lasch, Christopher, *Haven in a Heartless World: The Family Besieged* (New York, W. W. Norton, 1995)

Laslett, Peter, *Family Life and Illicit Love in Earlier Generations: Essays in Historical Sociology* (Cambridge, Cambridge University Press, 1977)

—, *The World We Have Lost* (2nd edn, London, Methuen, 1971)

—, and Richard Wall, eds, *Household and Family in Past Time: Comparative studies in the size and structure of the domestic group over the last three centuries in England, France, Serbia, Japan and colonial North America, with further materials from Western Europe* (Cambridge, Cambridge University Press, 1972)

Laver, James, *The Age of Illusion: Manners and Morals, 1750–1848* (London, Weidenfeld and Nicolson, 1972)

Lemire, Beverly, *The Business of Everyday Life: Gender, Practice and Social Politics in England, c.1600–1900* (Manchester, Manchester University Press, 2005)

—, *Fashion's Favourite: The Cotton Trade and the Consumer in Britain, 1660–1800* (Oxford, Oxford University Press, 1991)

Logan, Thad, *The Victorian Parlour* (Cambridge, Cambridge University Press, 2001)

Loughman, John, and John Michael Montias, *Public and Private Spaces: Works of Art in Seventeenth-Century Dutch Houses* (Zwolle, Waanders, 2000)

Louw, H. J., 'The Origin of the Sash-Window', *Architectural History*, 26, 1983, pp. 49–72

Louw, Hentie, and Robert Crayford, 'A Constructional History of the Sash-Window c.1670–c.1725 (Parts 1 and 2)', *Architectural History*, 41, 1998, pp. 82–130, and 42, 1999, pp. 173–239

Louw, Hentie, and Ben Farmer, eds, *Companion to Contemporary Architectural Thought* (London, Routledge, 1993)

Lukecs, John, 'The Bourgeois Interior', *American Scholar*, 39, 1970

Lyall, Sutherland, *Dream Cottages: From Cottage Orné to Stockbroker Tudor: 200 Years of the Cult of the Vernacular* (London, Robert Hale, 1988)

Lynd, Robert S., and Helen Merrell Lynd, *Middletown: A Study in Modern American Culture* (London, Constable, 1929)

—, *Middletown in Transition: A Study in Cultural Conflicts* (London, Constable, 1937)

McBride, Theresa, *The Domestic Revolution: The Modernization of Household Service in England and France, 1820–1920* (London, Croom Helm, 1976)

Macfarlane, Alan, *The Family Life of Ralph Josselin, a Seventeenth-Century Clergyman; An Essay in Historical Anthropology* (Cambridge, Cambridge University Press, 1970)

—, *Marriage and Love in England: Modes of Reproduction, 1300–1840* (Oxford, Blackwell, 1986)

McHugh, Kathleen Anne, *American Domesticity: From How-to Manual to Hollywood Melodrama* (New York, Oxford University Press, 1999)

Mack, Arien, ed., 'Home: A Place in the World', *Social Research*, 58, 1, 1991 [entire issue]

McKendrick, Neil, ed., *Historical Perspectives: Studies in English Thought and Society in Honour of J. H. Plumb* (London, Europa, 1974)

—, John Brewer and J. H. Plumb, *The Birth of a Consumer Society: The Commercialization of Eighteenth-Century England* (London, Hutchinson, 1982)

McKeon, Michael, *The Secret History of Domesticity: Public, Private, and the Division of Knowledge* (Baltimore, Johns Hopkins University Press, 2005)

McMurry, Sally, *Families and Farmhouses in Nineteenth-Century America: Vernacular Design and Social Change* (New York, Oxford University Press, 1988)

—, and Nancy van Dolsen, eds, *Architecture and Landscape of the Pennsylvania Germans, 1720–1920* (Philadelphia, University of Pennsylvania Press, 2011)

Marcus, Sharon, *Apartment Stories: City and Home in Nineteenth-Century Paris and London* (Berkeley, University of California Press, 1999)

Marten, James, ed., *Children in Colonial America* (New York, New York University Press, 2007)

Matthews, Glenna, *Just a Housewife: The Rise and Fall of Domesticity in America* (New York, Oxford University Press, 1987)

Mayhew, Edgar de N., and Minor Myers, Jr, *A Documentary History of American Interiors: From the Colonial Era to 1915* (New York, Charles Scribner's Sons, 1980)

Meldrum, Tim, 'Domestic Service, Privacy and the Eighteenth-Century Metropolitan Household', *Urban History*, 26, 1999, pp. 27–39

Mitterauer, Michael, and Reinhard Sieder, *The European Family: Patriarchy to Partnership from the Middle Ages to the Present*, trs. Karla Oosterveen and Manfred Hörzinger (Oxford, Basil Blackwell, 1982)

Mohney, David, and Keller Easterling, eds, *Seaside: Making a Town in America* (London, Phaidon, 1991)

Mokyr, Joel, 'Why "More Work for Mother"? Knowledge and Household Behavior, 1870–1945', *Journal of Economic History*, March 2000, 6/1, pp. 1–41

Morgan, Marjorie, *Manners, Morals and Class in England, 1774–1858* (Basingstoke, Macmillan, 1994)

Muizelaar, Klaske, and Derek Phillips, *Picturing Men and Women in the Dutch Golden Age: Paintings and People in Historical Perspective* (New Haven, Yale University Press, 2003)

Mundy, Peter, *The Travels of Peter Mundy in Europe and Asia, 1608–1667*, ed. Sir Richard Carnac Temple; vol. 4, *Travels in Europe, 1639–1647* (London, Hakluyt Society, 1925)

Muthesius, Hermann, *The English House*, trs. Janet Seligman and Stewart Spencer (1st complete English edn, London, Frances Lincoln, 2007)

Muthesius, Stefan, *The English Terraced House* (New Haven, Yale University Press, 1982)

—, *The Poetic Home: Designing the 19th-Century Domestic Interior* (London, Thames and Hudson, 2009)

Nora, Pierre, *Rethinking France, Les Lieux de Mémoire*, trs. Mary Trouille, under the direction of David P. Jordan (4 vols., Chicago, University of Chicago Press, 2001–10)

North, Michael, '*Material Delight and the Joy of Living*': Cultural Consumption in the Age of Enlightenment in Germany, trs. Pamela Selwyn (Aldershot, Ashgate, 2008)

Nye, David E., *Electrifying America: Social Meanings of a New Technology, 1880–1940* (Cambridge, MA, MIT Press, 1990)

Nylander, Jane C., *Our Own Snug Fireside: Images of the New England Home, 1760–1860* (New Haven, Yale University Press, 1994)

O'Day, Rosemary, *The Family and Family Relationships, 1500–1900, England, France and the USA* (Basingstoke, Macmillan, 1994)

Oldenziel, Ruth, and Karin Zachmann, eds, *Cold War Kitchen: Americanization, Technology, and European Users* (Cambridge, MA, MIT Press, 2009)

Oliver, Paul, *Dwellings: The Vernacular House Worldwide* (London, Phaidon, 2003)

Olsen, Donald J., *The City as a Work of Art, London, Paris, Vienna* (New Haven, Yale University Press, 1986)

Overton, Mark, et al., *Production and Consumption in English Households, 1600–1750* (London, Routledge, 2004)

Ozment, Steven, *Flesh and Spirit: Private Life in Early Modern Germany* (Harmondsworth, Penguin, 2001)

Palmer, Phyllis, *Domesticity and Dirt: Housewives and Domestic Servants in the United States, 1920–45* (Philadelphia, Temple University Press, 1989)

Parissien, Steven, *Interiors: The Home Since 1700* (London, Laurence King, 2009)

Pattison, Mary, *Principles of Domestic Engineering; or, The what, why and how of a home; an attempt to evolve a solution of the domestic 'labor and capital' problem – to standardize and professionalize housework – to reorganize the home upon 'scientific management' principles – and to point out the importance of the public and personal element therein as well as the practical* (New York, Trow, 1915)

Pepys, Samuel, *The Diary of Samuel Pepys*, Robert Latham and William Matthews, eds (London, Bell & Hyman, 1983)

Perry, Ruth, *Novel Relations: The Transformation of Kinship in English Literature and Culture, 1748–1818* (Cambridge, Cambridge University Press, 2004)

Peskov, Vasily, *Lost in the Taiga: One Russian Family's Fifty-Year Struggle for Survival and Religious Freedom in the Siberian Wilderness*, trs. Marian Schwartz (New York, Doubleday, 1994)

Pick, Frederick, *Inside Out: Historic Watercolour Drawings, Oil-sketches and Paintings of Exteriors and Interiors, 1770–1870* (London, Stair, 2000)

Pinchbeck, Ivy, and Margaret Hewitt, *Children in English Society* (London, Routledge & Kegan Paul, 1969–73), 2 vols.

Plumb, J. H., intro to Edward J. Nygren, Nancy L. Pressly, *The Pursuit of Happiness: A View of Life in Georgian England* (New Haven, Yale Center for British Art, 1977)

Pointon, Marcia, *Strategies for Showing: Women, Possession and Representation in English Visual Culture, 1665–1800* (Oxford, Oxford University Press, 1997)

Pollock, Linda, *A Lasting Relationship: Parents and Children over Three Centuries* (London, Fourth Estate, 1987)

Ponsonby, Margaret, *Stories from Home: English Domestic Interiors, 1750–1850* (Aldershot, Ashgate, 2007)

Pounds, Norman J. G., *Hearth and Home: A History of Material Culture* (Bloomington, Indiana University Press, 1989)

Praz, Mario, *Conversation Pieces: A Survey of the Informal Group Portrait in Europe and America* (London, Methuen, 1971)

—, *An Illustrated History of Interior Decoration from Pompeii to Art Nouveau* (London, Thames and Hudson, 1964)

Priestley, Ursula, and P. J. Corfield, 'Rooms and room use in Norwich housing, 1580–1730', *Post-Medieval Archaeology*, 16, 1982, pp. 93–123

Purdy, Daniel L., *The Tyranny of Elegance: Consumer Cosmopolitanism in the Era of Goethe* (Baltimore, Johns Hopkins University Press, 1998)

Quiney, Anthony, *House and Home: A History of the Small English House* (London, BBC, 1986)

Rapoport, Amos, *Culture, Architecture, and Design* (Chicago, Locke Science, 2005)

—, *House, Form and Culture* (Englewood Cliffs, Prentice-Hall, 1969)

Razi, Zvi, 'The Myth of the Immutable English Family', *Past & Present*, 140, 1993

Reagin, Nancy R., *Sweeping the Nation: Domesticity and National Identity in Germany, 1870–1945* (Cambridge, Cambridge University Press, 2007)

Reed, Christopher, *Bloomsbury Rooms: Modernism, Subculture, and Domesticity* (New Haven, Yale University Press, 2004)

—, ed., *Not at Home: The Suppression of Domesticity in Modern Art and Architecture* (London, Thames and Hudson, 1996)

Reiff, Daniel D., *Small Georgian Houses in England and Virginia: Origins and Development through the 1750s* (Cranbury, University of Delaware Press, 1986)

Reiter, Rayna R., ed., *Toward an Anthropology of Women* (New York, Monthly Review Press, 1975)

Retford, Kate, *The Art of Domestic Life: Family Portraiture in Eighteenth-Century England* (New Haven, Yale University Press, 2006)

Rice, Charles, *The Emergence of the Interior: Architecture, Modernity, Domesticity* (Abingdon, Routledge, 2007)

Rich, Rachel, *Bourgeois Consumption: Food, Space and Identity in London and Paris, 1850–1914* (Manchester, Manchester University Press, 2011)

Rosenau, Helen, *Social Purpose in Architecture: Paris and London Compared, 1760–1800* (London, Studio Vista, 1970)

Rosner, Victoria, *Modernism and the Architecture of Private Life* (New York, Columbia University Press, 2005)

Rousseau, Jean-Jacques, *Émile, or, Treatise on Education*, trs. William H. Payne (Amherst, NY, Prometheus, 2009)

Ruskin, John, *Sesame and Lilies: Two Lectures* ([1867], Orpington, George Allen, 1882)

Ryan, Mary P., *Cradle of the Middle Class: The Family in Oneida County, New York, 1790–1865* (Cambridge, Cambridge University Press, 1981)

Rybczynski, Witold, *Home: A Short History of an Idea* (London, Heinemann, 1988)

Rykwert, Joseph, 'House and Home', *Social Research*, 58, 1991

Sabean, David Warren, *Property, Production, and Family in Neckarhausen, 1700–1870* (Cambridge, Cambridge University Press, 1990)

Sarti, Raffaella, *Europe at Home: Family and Material Culture, 1500–1800*, trs. Allan Cameron (London, Yale University Press, 2002)

Saumarez Smith, Charles, *Eighteenth-Century Decoration: Design and the Domestic Interior in England* (London, Weidenfeld and Nicolson, 1993)

—, *The Rise of Design: Design and the Domestic Interior in Eighteenth-Century England* (London, Pimlico, 2000)

Sayer, Karen, *Country Cottages: A Cultural History* (Manchester, Manchester University Press, 2000)

Schama, Simon, *The Embarrassment of Riches: An Interpretation of Dutch Culture in the Golden Age* (London, Collins, 1987)

Schivelbusch, Wolfgang, *Disenchanted Night: The Industrialization of Light in the Nineteenth Century*, trs. Angela Davies (Berkeley, University of California Press, 1995)

Schlereth, Thomas J., *Victorian America: Transformations in Everyday Life, 1876–1915* (New York, HarperCollins, 1991)

Schucking, Levin L., *The Puritan Family: A Social Study from the Literary Sources*, trs. Brian Battershaw (London, Routledge & Kegan Paul, 1969)

Schuurman, Anton, and Pieter Spierenburg, eds, *Private Domain, Public Inquiry: Families and Lifestyles in the Netherlands and Europe, 1550 to the Present* (Hilversum, Uitgeverij Verloren, 1996)

Schuurman, Anton J., and Lorena Walsh, eds, *Material Culture: Consumption, Life-Style, Standard of Living, 1500–1900*, in *Proceedings of the 11th International Economic History Congress, Milan, September 1994* (Milan, Università Bocconi, 1994)

Seccombe, Wally, *A Millennium of Family Change: Feudalism to Capitalism in Northwestern Europe* (London, Verso, 1992)

Sennett, Richard, *The Conscience of the Eye: The Design and Social Life of Cities* (London, Faber, 1991)

Shammas, Carole, 'The Domestic Environment in Early Modern England and America', *Journal of Social History*, 14, 1980, pp. 3–24

—, 'Explaining Past Changes in Consumption and Consumer Behaviour', *Historical Methods*, 22, 1989, pp. 69–75

Shoemaker, Robert, *Gender in English Society, 1650–1850: The Emergence of Separate Spheres?* (London, Longman, 1998)

Shorter, Edward, *The Making of the Modern Family* (London, Collins, 1976)

Sirjamaki, John, *The American Family in the Twentieth Century* (Cambridge, MA, Harvard University Press, 1953)

Sitwell, Sacheverell, *Conversation Pieces: A Survey of English Domestic Portraits and their Painters* (London, Batsford, 1936)

Smith, Adam, *The Theory of Moral Sentiments*, D. D. Raphael and A. L. Macfie, eds, ([1759] Oxford, Clarendon, 1976)

Smyth, Gerry, and Jo Croft, eds, *Our House: The Representation of Domestic Space in Modern Culture* (Amsterdam, Rodopi, 2006)

Sparke, Penny, Brenda Martin and Trevor Keeble, eds, *The Modern Period Room: The Construction of the Exhibited Interior, 1870 to 1950* (London, Routledge, 2006)

Stamp, Gavin, and André Goulancourt, *The English House 1860–1914: The Flowering of English Domestic Architecture* (London, Faber, 1986)

Starobinski, Jean, 'The Idea of Nostalgia', *Diogenes*, 54, 1966

Steedman, Carolyn, *Labours Lost: Domestic Service and the Making of Modern England* (Cambridge, Cambridge University Press, 2009)

Stevenson, Robert Louis, *Virginibus Puerisque and Other Essays* (Newcastle-upon-Tyne, Cambridge Scholars, 2009)

Stewart, Rachel, *The Town House in Georgian London* (New Haven, Yale University Press, 2009)

Stone, Lawrence, *The Family, Sex and Marriage in England, 1500–1800* (London, Harper, 1977)

Strasser, Susan, *Never Done: A History of American Housework* (New York, Pantheon, 1982)

—, *Satisfaction Guaranteed: The Making of the American Mass Market* (Washington, DC, Smithsonian Institution Press, 1989)

—, *Waste and Want: A Social History of Trash* (New York, Metropolitan, 1999)

—, Charles McGovern and Matthias Judt, eds, *Getting and Spending: European and American Consumer Societies in the Twentieth Century* (Cambridge, Cambridge University Press, 1998)

Sutherland, Daniel E., *The Expansion of Everyday Life, 1860–1876* (New York, Harper and Row, 1989)

Symonds, James, ed., *Table Settings: The Material Culture and Social Context of Dining, AD 1700–1900* (Oxford, Oxbow Books, 2010)

Tadmor, Naomi, 'The Concept of the Household-Family in 18th-Century England', *Past & Present*, 151, 1996, pp. 111–40

—, *Family and Friends in Eighteenth-Century England: Household, Kinship, and Patronage* (Cambridge, Cambridge University Press, [2001])

Tange, Andrea Kaston, *Architectural Identities: Domesticity, Literature, and the Victorian Middle Classes* (Toronto, University of Toronto Press, 2010)

Thiel, Elizabeth, *The Fantasy of Family: Nineteenth-Century Children's Literature and the Myth of the Domestic Ideal* (London, Routledge, 2008)

Thompson. E. P., *Customs in Common* (London, Merlin Press, 1991)

Thompson, Eleanor, ed., *The American Home: Material Culture, Domestic Space, and Family Life* (Hanover, NH, University Press of New England, 1998)

Thornton, Peter, *Authentic Decor: The Domestic Interior, 1620–1929* (London, Seven Dials, 2000)

—, *Seventeenth-Century Interior Decoration in England, France, and Holland* (New Haven, Yale University Press, 1978)

Tilley, Morris Palmer, *A Dictionary of the Proverbs in England in the Sixteenth and Seventeenth Centuries: A Collection of the Proverbs Found in English Literature and the Dictionaries of the Period* (Ann Arbor, University of Michigan Press, 1950)

Tinniswood, Adrian, *Life in the English Country Cottage* (London, Weidenfeld and Nicolson, 1995)

Tosh, John, *A Man's Place: Masculinity and the Middle-Class Home in Victorian England* (New Haven, Yale University Press, 2007)

Trumbach, Randolph, *The Rise of the Egalitarian Family: Aristocratic Kinship and Domestic Relations in Eighteenth-Century England* (New York, Academic Press, 1978)

Ulrich, Laurel Thatcher, *The Age of Homespun: Objects and Stories in the Creation of an American Myth* (New York, Alfred A. Knopf, 2001)

—, *Good Wives: Image and Reality in the Lives of Women in Northern New England, 1650–1750* (New York, Alfred A. Knopf, 1982)

Upton, Dell, *Another City: Urban Life and Urban Spaces in the New American Republic* (New Haven, Yale University Press, 2008)

—, and John Michael Vlach, *Common Places: Readings in American Vernacular Architecture* (Athens, GA, University of Georgia Press, 1986)

Vickery, Amanda, *Behind Closed Doors: At Home in Georgian England* (New Haven, Yale University Press, 2009)

—, 'An Englishman's Home Is His Castle? Thresholds, Boundaries and Privacies in the Eighteenth-Century London House', *Past & Present*, 199, May 2008, pp. 147–73

—, *The Gentleman's Daughter: Women's Lives in Georgian England* (London, Yale University Press, 1998)

Vlach, John Michael, *Back of the Big House: The Architecture of Plantation Slavery* (Chapel Hill, University of North Carolina Press, 1993)

Vries, Jan de, *The Dutch Rural Economy in the Golden Age, 1500–1700* (New Haven, Yale University Press, 1974)

—, *European Urbanization, 1500–1800* (London, Methuen, 1984)

—, 'The Industrial Revolution and the Industrious Revolution', *Journal of Economic History*, 54, 1994, pp. 249–70

—, *The Industrious Revolution: Consumer Behaviour and the Household Economy, 1650 to the Present* (Cambridge, Cambridge University Press, 2008)

—, and Ad van der Woude, *The First Modern Economy: Success, Failure, and Perseverance of the Dutch Economy, 1500–1815* (Cambridge, Cambridge University Press, 1997)

Wall, Richard, Jean Robin and Peter Laslett, eds, *Family Forms in Historical Europe* (Cambridge, Cambridge University Press, 1983)

Walker, Mack, *German Home Towns, Community, State, and General Estates, 1650–1871* (Ithaca, NY Cornell University Press, 1971)

Warren, Samuel D., and Louis D. Brandeis, 'The Right to Privacy', *Harvard Law Review*, vol. 4, no. 5, 15 December 1890, pp. 193–220

Watkins, Susan C., 'If All We Knew About Women was What We Read in *Demography*, What Would We Know?', *Demography*, 30/4, 1993, pp. 551–78

Weatherill, Lorna, *Consumer Behaviour and Material Culture in Britain, 1660–1760* (2nd edn, London, Routledge, 1996)

—, 'A Possession of One's Own: Women and Consumer Behaviour in England, 1660–1740', *Journal of British Studies*, 23, 1986, pp. 131–56

Weber, Max, *The Protestant Ethic and the Spirit of Capitalism*, trs. Talcott Parsons, foreword by R. H. Tawney (London, G. Allen & Unwin, 1930)

Weinberg, H. Barbara, and Carrie Rebora Barratt, eds, *American Stories: Paintings of Everyday Life, 1765–1915* (New York, Metropolitan Museum of Art, 2009)

Weslager, C. A., *The Log Cabin in America: From Pioneer Days to the Present* (New Brunswick, NJ, Rutgers University Press, 1969)

West, Patricia, *Domesticating History: The Political Origins of America's House Museums* (Washington, DC, Smithsonian Institution Press, 1999)

Westermann, Mariët, *Art and Home: Dutch Interiors in the Age of Rembrandt* (Zwolle, Waanders, 2001)

Wilder, Laura Ingalls, *The Little House Books*, Caroline Fraser, ed., vol. 1: *Little House in the Big Woods, Farmer Boy, Little House on the Prairie, On the Banks of Plum Creek*; vol. 2: *By the Shores of Silver Lake, The Long Winter, Little Town on the Prairie, These Happy Golden Years, The First Four Years* (New York, Library of America, 2012)

Williams, Michael Ann, *Homeplace: The Social Use and Meaning of Folk Dwellings in Southwestern North Carolina* (Athens, GA, University of Georgia Press, 1993)

Williams, Raymond, *Keywords: A Vocabulary of Culture and Society* (London, Fontana, 1976)

Wilson, Bee, *Consider the Fork: A History of Invention in the Kitchen* (London, Particular Books, 2012)

Worsley, Giles, *Classical Architecture in Britain: The Heroic Age* (New Haven, Yale University Press, 1995)

—, *Inigo Jones and the European Classicist Tradition* (New Haven, Yale University Press, 2007)

Wright, Gwendolyn, *Building the Dream: A Social History of Housing in America* (New York, Pantheon, 1981)

—, *Moralism and the Model Home: Domestic Architecture and Cultural Conflict in Chicago* (Chicago, University of Chicago Press, 1980)

Wright, Lawrence, *Warm and Snug: The History of the Bed* (London, Routledge & Kegan Paul, 1962)

Wrigley, E. A., *Continuity, Chance and Change: The Character of the Industrial Revolution in England* (Cambridge, Cambridge University Press, 1988)

Woolgar, C. M., *The Great Household in Late Medieval England* (New Haven, Yale University Press, 1999)

Zaretsky, Eli, *Capitalism, the Family, and Personal Life* (2nd edn, New York, Perennial, 1986)

Zumthor, Paul, *Daily Life in Rembrandt's Holland*, trs. Simon Watson Taylor (London, Weidenfeld and Nicolson, 1962)

Index

INDEX

shotgun houses, 78

Shrewsbury, Elizabeth Talbot, Countess of ('Bess of Hardwick'), 211

sideboards *see* dressers

silk, 150 & n

slavery, slaves, 42; quarters, 64–5, 78, 127

Smith, Adam: on non-utility goods, 149; *The Wealth of Nations*, 26

Snow, Dr John, 256

Soane, Sir John, 83

Society for the Protection of Ancient Buildings (Britain), 179

sod-houses, 62

sofas, 125, 136

Sorgh, Henrick: *Portrait of Jacob Bierens and His Family* (painting), 45

Spain: nuclear family, 31

Spenser, Edmund, 19–20, 41, 47

spermaceti oil, 222

spinning-wheel: mythology of, 189

spitting, 13–16

spitting-sheets, 13

spittoons, 13–16

spoons, 154

spring sickness, 257

status (social), 254

stearine oil, 222

Steen, Jan, 7, 158, 174; *A Peasant Family at Meal-time* (painting), 131

Stevenson, Robert Louis, 220

Stockholm: Skansen (open-air museum), 180

Stone, Lawrence, 41

stoves: close ranges (cooking), 112–13, 236; porcelain (heating), 117; Rumford, 151; heating, 203

Stowe, Harriet Beecher, 114, 274

suburbs, 262–8

sugar, 147

supply and demand, 26

Sweden: house design and occupation, 81–2; and Skansen (open-air

museum), 180; origins of log cabin, 185–7; animal manure, 244–5

tablecloths, 153

tables, 130

tableware, 154, 156

tallow *see* candles

Tawney, R.H., 35

Taylor, Frederick W., 121, 238–9

tea, 125, 147

technology: effect on work and activities, 114–17, 118, 151, 230, 242, 277–8; increases privacy, 119

Tennyson, Alfred, 1st Baron, 152

ter Borch, Gerard, the younger, 5

Tessin, Nicodemus, 214–15

textiles: increased availability, 128–9

Thornbury Castle, near Bristol, 75

Thorpe, John, 75

thrift, 254–5

Tiffany, Louis Comfort, 89

tinder-boxes, 221 & n

Tinkham, Nehemiah and Submit, 61–2

tinned foods, 116

Toulouse: abandoned babies, 39

toys, 158–9

trade: Defoe on, 25–6; with East, 42; and availability of goods, 140

transport: development, 262

trenchers, 154, 156

Tring Park, Hertfordshire, 170

Trollope, Anthony, 151; *Can You Forgive Her?*, 47

Trollope, Frances (Fanny), 48n

Truman Show, The (film), 271n

Tudor style (architectural), 170–72, 176, 269

Tussaud, Madame: waxworks, 152n

United States of America: suburban housing projects, 26, 265, 268, 269; illegitimate births, 40; Great Rebuilding (18th century), 59;

A Note on the Author

Judith Flanders, a Senior Research Fellow at the University of Buckingham, is the author of the bestselling *The Victorian House: Domestic Life from Childbirth to Deathbed* (2003); the critically acclaimed *Consuming Passions: Leisure and Pleasure in Victorian Britain* (2006); *The Invention of Murder* (2011), which was shortlisted for the Crime Writers' Association Non-Fiction Dagger; *A Circle of Sisters* (2001), which was nominated for the Guardian First Book Award; and, most recently, *The Victorian City: Everyday Life in Dickens' London* (2012).